Spring Boot & Data Persistence

For Beginners

Spring Boot & Data Persistence

For Beginners

Sharanam Shah
Vaishali Shah

THE X TEAM

SHROFF PUBLISHERS & DISTRIBUTORS PVT. LTD.
Navi Mumbai

Spring Boot & Data Persistence for Beginners
by Sharanam Shah and Vaishali Shah

Series Editor: Ivan Bayross

First Edition: August 2025

ISBN : 978-93-6808-172-2

Printed at Gapmeta Ventures Pvt. Ltd., Navi Mumbai • Published by Shroff Publishers and Distributors Pvt. Ltd. B-103, Railway Commercial Complex, Sector 3, Sanpada (E), Navi Mumbai 400705 • Tel: (91 22) 4158 4158 WhatsApp +91 7304487700 4158 4141 • E-mail: spdorders@shroffpublishers.com • URL: www.shroffpublishers.com

Kick off your Spring Boot journey

Welcome to Spring Boot & Data Persistence for Beginners! This book is your comprehensive guide to mastering modern Java web development using the powerful Spring Boot framework and advanced data persistence techniques. Starting with the fundamentals and progressing to building sophisticated, real-world applications, this book is designed to transform you from a beginner into a confident Spring Boot developer. Critically, in today's tech landscape, we dive deep into integrating Artificial Intelligence (AI) with modern APIs like Cohere and Gemini, ensuring you're equipped not just with robust web development skills, but also with the ability to build intelligent, AI-enhanced applications. Culminating in not one, but TWO major finale projects—an AI-powered TaskManager and a complete AI-enhanced E-commerce website—where you'll learn to translate requirements into working systems, this book takes you on the ultimate development journey. If you're ready to build scalable, feature-rich, and AI-powered Spring Boot solutions that employers are desperately seeking, your transformation starts here.

This book is dedicated to our kids. Thank you for coming to this world as our kids. You both are the most precious we could ever ask for. We love you both more than our life.

About this book

This book serves as your complete roadmap to the powerful world of Spring Boot, data persistence, and AI integration. We guide you through the essential frameworks and concepts, ensuring you build a solid foundation in modern web development while embracing cutting-edge AI capabilities. From understanding dependency injection to deploying full-stack, intelligent applications, including TWO comprehensive finale projects, each chapter is crafted with practical examples and hands-on projects to accelerate your learning. We aim to make sure that by the end of this book, you can confidently self-code not only standard Spring Boot applications but also those enhanced with powerful AI features that give you a competitive edge in today's job market.

What you'll learn?

Our book is thoughtfully structured into logical sections that build upon each other:

- **Foundation - Launching your Spring journey:** We start with the essentials: Modern Java fundamentals, Spring Boot setup, and your first application. Master dependency injection and Inversion of Control—the core principles that make Spring so powerful. Build your first command-line quote generator to solidify these concepts.

- **Data mastery - Persistence with Hibernate and Spring Data JPA:** Dive deep into the world of data persistence. Learn JPA entity mapping, harness the power of Spring Data JPA repositories to eliminate boilerplate code, and master database transactions. Build a complete contact manager to demonstrate real-world data handling.
- **Web development excellence - Building web applications:** Explore Spring MVC architecture, create dynamic web pages with Thymeleaf templates, handle complex web forms with validation, and build professional REST APIs. Develop a fully functional URL shortener web application.
- **AI revolution - Integrating AI with Spring applications:** A dedicated section that sets this book apart! Understand why AI integration is crucial for modern developers, implement AI-powered content generation with Cohere, and supercharge web applications with Google's Gemini API. These skills are what employers are looking for RIGHT NOW.
- **Grand culminations - Two major finale projects:** The crescendo of your learning journey features not one, but TWO comprehensive finale projects:
    - **AI-powered TaskManager application:** Build an intelligent task management system that leverages AI to create sub-tasks and generate summaries
    - **AI-enhanced E-commerce website:** Develop a complete e-commerce platform with product discovery, shopping cart management, checkout processing, and AI-powered features
- **Advanced learning path:** An appendix with detailed project challenges and next steps to continue your growth beyond this book.

<u>Special focus: AI-powered Spring Boot applications</u>

In today's competitive tech landscape, AI integration separates good developers from great ones. This book emphasizes getting you ahead of the curve with AI within Spring Boot:

- **Why AI matters:** Understand the critical use cases for AI in modern web applications and why companies are prioritizing developers with these skills.
- **Getting started:** Learn to explore AI API providers (focus on Cohere and Gemini), securely manage API keys, and architect AI-enabled applications.
- **Direct API integration:** Master calling external AI services using Spring's WebClient and RestTemplate.
- **Practical AI projects:** Build functional AI-powered applications step-by-step, from content generators to intelligent assistants.

This ensures you're learning Spring Boot in the context of modern, AI-driven development—exactly what the industry demands.

Learning reinforcement structure

We believe in learning by doing and explicitly connecting theory to practice through our proven methodology:

- **What you'll learn -** Each chapter starts with clear, actionable goals.

- **Examples -** Chapters are packed with practical, production-ready code.
- **Hands-on project -** Most chapters include a comprehensive project to apply concepts immediately. Crucially, these project sections feature dedicated topics:
  - **Bridging the gap: Learned concepts and application implementation -** Explicitly shows how the concepts taught in the chapter are mapped and used within the project code.
  - **Exploring application behaviour: A practical run-through -** Demonstrates how the application works in real-time, reinforcing the practical impact of the learned features.
  - **Harnessing Spring Boot features in real-world contexts -** Discusses the relevance and application of the features in broader, real-world scenarios. This structure ensures you not only learn what a feature does, but how and where to apply it effectively in your career.
- **Wrapping up:** Each chapter concludes with a comprehensive summary.
- **Culmination projects:** Major sections end with larger projects integrating section learnings.
- **Finale section:** TWO major finale projects reinforce book-wide knowledge, starting from requirements and building complete, deployable applications.

Hands-on projects

Theory meets practice! You'll gain invaluable experience by building:

- **Core Spring Boot projects:** Your first Spring Boot application, dependency injection examples, command-line quote generator with AI integration.
- **Data Persistence projects:** H2 and MySQL database setup, JPA entity creation with Lombok integration, Spring Data JPA repository implementation, transaction management with rollback scenarios, comprehensive contact management system.
- **Web Development projects:** Spring MVC controllers with request mapping, dynamic Thymeleaf templates, complex web forms with Jakarta Bean Validation, professional REST API endpoints with proper HTTP status codes, URL shortener web application.
- **AI Integration projects:**
  - AI-powered content generator with Cohere
  - Dynamic quote system with AI enhancement
  - Intelligent email assistant with Gemini
  - Web application AI supercharging
- **Grand Finale projects:**
  - **AI-powered TaskManager application:** Complete task management system with AI-generated sub-tasks and intelligent summaries.
  - **AI-enhanced E-commerce website:** Full-featured online store with product catalog, shopping cart, checkout system, order management, and AI-powered features.

Each project is designed to simulate real-world development scenarios you'll encounter in your career.

Who should dive in?

This book is ideal for:
This book is perfect for:

- **Java developers** wanting to master Spring Boot with modern AI capabilities and stand out in the job market.
- **Students and beginners** seeking a structured, comprehensive path to Spring Boot mastery with cutting-edge AI integration.
- **Developers transitioning** from other frameworks who want to leverage Spring Boot's power and ecosystem.
- **Career changers** looking to enter the high-demand field of Spring Boot development with AI skills.
- **Anyone aiming** to build robust, modern, intelligent web applications that employers are actively seeking, including complete e-commerce systems from the ground up.

Our story

Based in Mumbai, India, my journey into technical writing has been anything but conventional. With experience in application development and tech project management, I discovered a passion for simplifying complex concepts through clear, engaging documentation at a leading technology firm. Today, I blend my love for technology and writing to create accessible developer materials. Together with my wife, Vaishali, we have co-authored over 30 technical books. We both relish exploring emerging technologies and, once we master them, sharing our insights with the world through our books. For more about us, please visit www.sharanamshah.com.

Downloadable resources

All examples and projects, including AI integrations and both finale (TaskManager and E-Commerce), are available for download.

Visit: https://www.sharanamshah.com/books/springbootdatapersistenceforbeginners/bookcodes.zip
Password: **codesbysharanamvaishali**

Gratitude and acknowledgments

This book is the result of passion, persistence, and the unwavering support of our families, peers, and the vibrant Spring Boot community. We are especially grateful to our publisher, Mr. Aziz Shroff, whose support and vision were instrumental in bringing this book to life. Your encouragement and feedback have been invaluable in shaping this book into a resource we hope will inspire and empower you.

If you have any questions, comments or just feel like communicating, please contact us at **enquiries@sharanamshah.com**.

Dive in and enjoy your journey into Spring Boot, data persistence, and AI integration—each line of code brings you closer to building powerful, intelligent solutions, culminating in your own TaskManager and E-commerce applications built from requirements to reality. The future of web development is here, and it's AI-powered. Happy coding!

Sharanam & Vaishali Shah

Table Of Contents

Chapter 1

Section 01: Launching your Spring journey - Initial setup and first steps

Modern Java essentials: Setting the stage for Spring Boot

What you'll learn

- Java ecosystem basics
- Spring Boot introduction
- Build tool fundamentals
- Spring Framework introduction
- IoC/DI overview
- Environment setup

Welcome to the beginning of your journey into the powerful world of Spring Boot! In today's fast-paced software development landscape, Java remains a dominant force, powering everything from large-scale enterprise systems to nimble microservices and Android applications. Frameworks like Spring Boot and JPA have become essential tools for modern Java developers, dramatically simplifying the process of building robust, scalable, and maintainable applications. This chapter lays the groundwork, ensuring you have a solid understanding of the core Java ecosystem and the tools needed before we dive into the specifics of Spring Boot.

The Java ecosystem: JDK, JVM, Jakarta EE overview

Before we jump into Spring, let's quickly review the fundamental components of the Java world you'll encounter:

- **Java Development Kit (JDK):** This is the core toolkit you need to write and run Java applications. It includes the compiler (javac), which turns your human-readable Java code into bytecode, and the Java Runtime Environment (JRE). You'll need at least JDK 17+ installed for this book, though JDK 24 is the target version for the latest features discussed later.
- **Java Virtual Machine (JVM):** Part of the JRE, the JVM is the engine that actually executes your compiled Java bytecode. It's the key to Java's "write once, run anywhere" philosophy, as JVMs are available for many different operating systems.
- **Jakarta EE (formerly Java EE):** This is a set of specifications that extend standard Java with capabilities needed for enterprise-level applications. Think web applications, web services, persistence, messaging, and more. While Spring Boot often provides its own solutions or integrations, it heavily leverages Jakarta EE standards like the Servlet API for web applications and the Persistence API (JPA 3.1) for database interaction.

Understanding these pieces helps contextualize where Spring and JPA fit - they build upon the foundation provided by the JDK and often implement or integrate with Jakarta EE specifications.

What is the Spring Framework?

The Spring Framework emerged years ago with a core philosophy: to make Java development easier, more flexible, and more productive, especially for complex enterprise applications. Before Spring, building robust Java applications often involved cumbersome APIs and a lot of boilerplate code.

Spring tackled this by introducing key principles and providing modules for almost every aspect of application development:

- **Core container:** Manages the lifecycle of application components (called beans) using Inversion of Control (IoC) and Dependency Injection (DI).
- **Web:** Support for building web applications (Spring MVC).
- **Data access:** Simplified integration with data technologies like JDBC and Object-Relational Mapping (ORM) tools like Hibernate.
- **And much more:** Integration with messaging systems, testing support, security, etc.

The goal was (and still is) to allow developers to focus on business logic rather than wrestling with low-level infrastructure concerns.

Introducing Spring Boot: Simplifying Spring development

While the Spring Framework was a massive improvement, setting up a new Spring project still required significant configuration (often involving XML files). Spring Boot is an evolution built ***on top*** of the Spring Framework, designed to radically simplify this setup process.

Spring Boot's key goals

- **Rapid application development:** Get applications up and running very quickly.
- **Convention over configuration:** Provide sensible defaults based on the libraries you include, reducing the need for explicit configuration.
- **Opinionated defaults:** Offer pre-packaged "Starters" that bring in common sets of dependencies for specific tasks (like building web apps or connecting to databases).
- **Embedded servers:** Easily run web applications without needing to deploy them to a separate web server.
- **Production-ready features:** Include features like metrics, health checks, and externalized configuration out-of-the-box.

Essentially, Spring Boot takes the power of the Spring Framework and makes it incredibly easy to get started and build applications efficiently. This book focuses primarily on Spring Boot, leveraging its simplicity.

Core principles: Inversion of Control (IoC) and Dependency Injection (DI) - A first look

Two fundamental concepts underpin the Spring Framework (and therefore Spring Boot) are Inversion of Control (IoC) and Dependency Injection (DI).

- **Inversion of Control (IoC):** Traditionally, your code creates and manages the objects it needs. If ClassA needs an instance of ClassB, ClassA explicitly creates it (new ClassB()). With IoC, this control is inverted. Instead of your objects controlling their dependencies, an external container (the Spring IoC Container) is responsible for creating and managing the objects (called "beans") and their lifecycles.

- **Dependency Injection (DI):** DI is the *mechanism* by which IoC is achieved. Instead of an object creating its own dependencies, the container ***injects*** those dependencies into the object when it's created. This "injection" can happen through constructors, setter methods, or directly into fields.

Why is this important? IoC and DI lead to **loosely coupled** applications. Components don't need to know how to create each other; they just declare what they need. This makes the code:

- **More modular:** Components are self-contained units.
- **Easier to test:** You can easily provide mock or test versions of dependencies.
- **More maintainable:** Changes in one component are less likely to break others.

We'll dive much deeper into IoC and DI in ***Chapter 3 - Wiring up your application: Dependency Injection with Spring***, but it's crucial to grasp the basic idea now as it's central to how Spring works.

Setting up your development environment

Before you can write any code, you need the essential tools installed.

Installing JDK 17+

As mentioned, you need a Java Development Kit. Spring Boot 4.0.0 requires at least JDK 17. We recommend installing the latest Long-Term Support (LTS) version available (like JDK 17 or 21) or JDK 24 if you want the newest features.

1. Visit the **Oracle Java SE Downloads** page or the OpenJDK project page to find the latest version of JDK.
2. Select the JDK version that matches your operating system (Windows, macOS, or Linux).
3. Download the latest version. This book uses the latest version ***jdk-24_windows-x64_bin.exe*** for a Windows based OS.
4. Run the installer and follow the on-screen instructions to complete the installation.

The applications demonstrated in this book are **developed under Microsoft Windows**. The process on other operating systems should be similar.

To check if Java is installed and to see the version, open a command prompt and type:

```
java -version
```

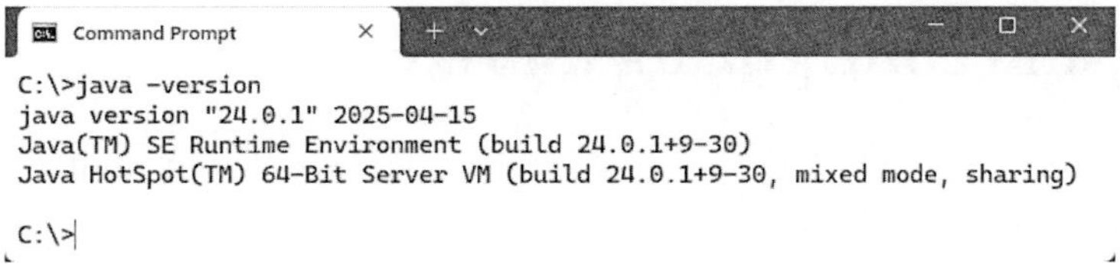

If this command doesn't show the correct output, make sure the bin directory (e.g., C:\Program Files\Java\jdk-24\bin) is included in the PATH environment variable.

Setting the path environment variable

After installing JDK, you need to set the PATH environment variable so your system can find the Java tools. Here's how to do it:
Windows:

1. Select **Start → Control Panel → System**.
2. In the **System** window, select the **Advanced system settings** link to view the **System Properties**.
3. In the **System Properties** dialog box, select the **Advanced** tab to view the **Advanced settings**.
4. In the **Advanced settings**, click **Environment Variables...**.
5. In the **Environment Variables** dialog box, go to **System Variables** list, select **Path** and click **Edit...**.
6. **Edit System Variable** dialog box appears, which allows editing the **Path** variable.
7. Click **New** and add the path to the JDK's bin directory.
8. Click **OK** to save your changes.

The exact name of the bin directory varies according to the installation made in the machine. For example,
C:\Program Files\Java\jdk-24\bin
D:\Program Files\Java\jdk-24\bin

macOS/Linux:

1. Edit the profile file (e.g., .bash_profile, .bashrc, or .zshrc) using a text editor.
2. Add the following line:

```
export PATH=/Library/Java/JavaVirtualMachines/jdk-24.jdk/Contents/Home/bin:$PATH
```

3. Save the file and run source ~/.bash_profile (or the respective profile file) to apply the changes.

Installing and configuring an IDE

Now that you have installed JDK, the next step is to install and configure an Integrated Development Environment (IDE).

The following are the most common and the best IDEs available:

- **Apache NetBeans IDE:** A free, open-source IDE that is very well-suited for Java and Jakarta EE development. NetBeans is a long-standing IDE with a strong community and excellent built-in support for Jakarta EE technologies. For this book, we will be using NetBeans IDE for our examples and instructions.
- **Eclipse IDE:** A very popular, open-source IDE that has been around for a long time and has strong support for Java and Jakarta EE development. It's free to use and has a large community and plenty of plugins.
- **IntelliJ IDEA Community Edition:** Another very popular and powerful IDE. The Community Edition is free and open-source and offers excellent support for Java and good support for Jakarta EE. The paid **Ultimate** edition has even more Jakarta EE specific features, but the Community Edition is excellent for learning.

Why Apache NetBeans for this book?

While all three IDEs are excellent, NetBeans IDE is chosen as the primary IDE for this book for a few reasons that make it particularly beginner-friendly and well-suited for learning Spring Boot:

- **Excellent built-in Jakarta EE support:** NetBeans has historically been very strong in its support for Java EE (now Jakarta EE). It offers great built-in features for creating, deploying, and debugging Jakarta EE and Spring Boot applications directly within the IDE.
- **User-friendliness:** NetBeans is often praised for its ease of use, especially for beginners. Its interface is intuitive, and many common tasks can be performed with simple menu options or wizards.
- **Out-of-the-box experience:** NetBeans, especially the **Java SE** or **All** bundles, comes with many features pre-configured and ready to use for Java and Jakarta EE development. You often need less plugin installation or complex setup compared to some other IDEs to get started with Jakarta EE.
- **Strong community and documentation:** NetBeans has a supportive community and good documentation. While perhaps not as massive as Eclipse, it's still a very active and helpful community.

While we are using NetBeans in this book, please remember that the core concepts of Spring Boot and the general steps we cover are applicable regardless of the IDE you choose. If you prefer Eclipse or IntelliJ IDEA, you can still follow along with the book and adapt the IDE-specific instructions accordingly. The important thing is to have a functional IDE set up for your development journey!

Installing Apache NetBeans

1. Visit the Apache NetBeans Downloads page.
2. You can see different download options. Choose the installer for your operating system (Windows, macOS, Linux). Click the download link for the chosen bundle and your OS. This book uses the latest version **Apache-NetBeans-26.exe** for a Windows based OS.
3. Once the download is complete, run the installer file.
4. The NetBeans installer is generally very user-friendly. Follow the on-screen instructions. You are presented with options to customize the installation. For beginners, you can usually accept the default settings.
5. Wait for the installation process to finish. Once done, you should find NetBeans IDE in your applications menu or desktop shortcuts.
6. Start NetBeans IDE for the first time.

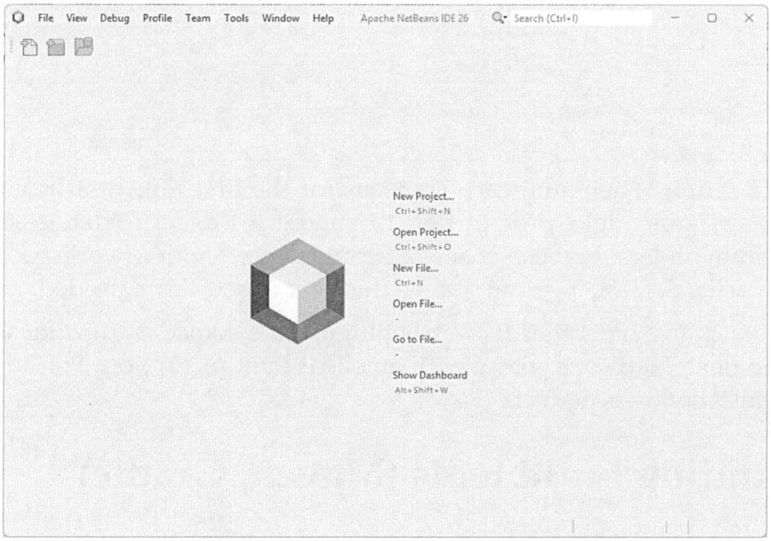

Basic IDE configuration

After installing NetBeans, here are a few basic configuration steps you might need to check:

- **JDK configuration:** Ensure NetBeans is configured to use Java Development Kit (JDK) you installed earlier in this chapter. NetBeans is generally very good at automatically detecting installed JDKs.
- **In NetBeans:** To verify or change the JDK used by NetBeans, you can go to **Tools → Java Platforms**. You can see a list of Java platforms that Apache NetBeans has detected. Make sure your JDK (version 17 or later) is listed. If not, you can click **Add Platform...** and point Apache NetBeans to your JDK installation directory.

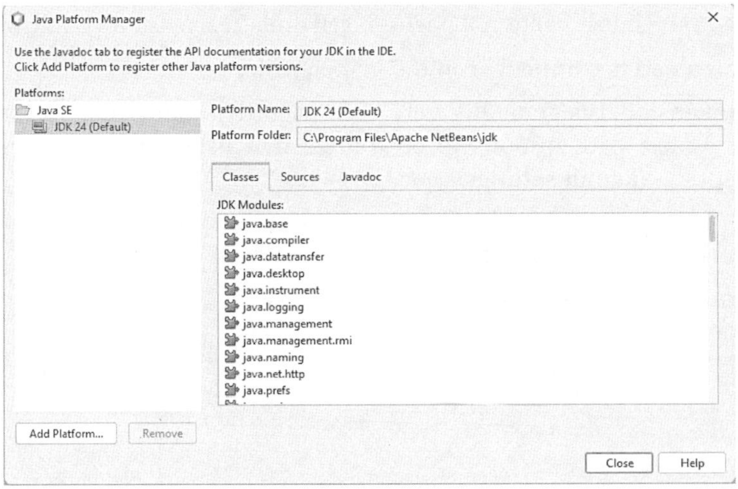

- **Workspace setup:** When you start NetBeans for the first time, it asks you to set up the initial settings and might prompt you to choose a project folder. NetBeans manages projects within folders. You can choose a default project folder (workspace) location or let NetBeans use its default. You can change this later in settings if needed.
- **Plugins:** NetBeans, like other IDEs, has plugins to enhance its functionality. For Jakarta EE development, NetBeans comes with excellent built-in support. For now, the standard NetBeans installation is perfect.

Understanding build tools (Maven, Gradle)

While NetBeans IDE provides excellent built-in support for managing Java projects using build tools, understanding build tools like Maven and Gradle as standalone entities is still valuable. NetBeans simplifies the process of using these tools within the IDE, but there are situations where understanding their purpose and basic concepts is helpful.

Therefore, in this section, we are introducing Apache Maven and Gradle, the two most popular build tools in the Java ecosystem.

Why are build tools important?

- **Dependency management:** Jakarta EE projects often rely on external libraries and frameworks (dependencies). Build tools like Maven and Gradle make it easy to declare and manage these dependencies. They automatically download the required libraries and make them available to your project. Imagine manually downloading and managing all the JAR files your project needs - build tools automate this tedious task.
- **Compilation:** Build tools compile your Java source code into bytecode (.class files).
- **Testing:** They can run automated tests to ensure your code is working correctly.
- **Packaging:** They package your application into deployable formats like WAR (Web Application Archive) or JAR (Java Archive) files, ready to be deployed to an application server.
- **Build lifecycle management:** Build tools define a standard build lifecycle (e.g., compile, test, package, install, deploy), ensuring a consistent build process across projects.

The two most popular build tools in the Java ecosystem are Maven and Gradle. Let's briefly introduce both:

- **Apache Maven:** A widely used build tool, especially in enterprise Java projects, including Jakarta EE. Maven uses a declarative approach, where you describe your project's structure and dependencies in a file called pom.xml (Project Object Model), and Maven takes care of the rest based on conventions.

  Maven and NetBeans: When you create a Maven project in NetBeans, the IDE seamlessly integrates with Maven. NetBeans provides a user-friendly interface to work with Maven projects, manage dependencies, run build goals, and more, all from within the IDE. The underlying build process is powered by Maven, but NetBeans simplifies its use significantly.
- **Gradle:** Gradle is another excellent and increasingly popular build tool, known for its flexibility and performance. Similar to Maven, NetBeans also provides good integration for Gradle projects.

  Gradle and NetBeans: Similar to Maven, NetBeans provides integrated support for Gradle. You can create, import, and manage Gradle-based Java and Jakarta EE projects directly within NetBeans. NetBeans handles the execution of Gradle tasks, dependency resolution, and other build-related operations through its IDE interface.

Which build tool to choose?

Both Maven and Gradle are excellent build tools for Jakarta EE projects.

- **Maven:** Often considered more conventional and widely used in enterprise Java, including many Jakarta EE examples and projects. Maven's convention-over-configuration approach can be simpler for beginners to get started with, and it's very well integrated into NetBeans. For this book, we are primarily going to use Maven due to its widespread use and beginner-friendliness.
- **Gradle:** Gaining popularity due to its flexibility and performance, especially for larger projects and complex builds. Gradle's DSL approach is more powerful but might have a slightly steeper initial learning curve for complete beginners.

  Recommendation for Beginners: For this book and for learning Jakarta EE as a beginner, Maven is probably an easier starting point, and it is very well supported within NetBeans. You are primarily going to interact with Maven through NetBeans's project management features.

For now, you do not need to install Maven or Gradle separately to follow along with this book using NetBeans. NetBeans handles the build tool integration for you when we create projects in later chapters.

Activating Spring Boot support in NetBeans IDE

NetBeans integrates with the official **Spring Initializr** service, which is the standard tool for generating new Spring Boot projects. However, to keep the IDE lean, this integration is provided as a plugin that you may need to install manually. Throughout this book, we use this plugin to create all our Spring Boot applications.

The most reliable method is to download the plugin file directly and install it from the **Tools → Plugins → Downloaded** tab of the NetBeans IDE.

Part 1: Download the plugin

1. Open your web browser and navigate to the official Apache NetBeans Plugin Portal: https://plugins.netbeans.apache.org/.
2. Search for **NB-SpringBoot**.

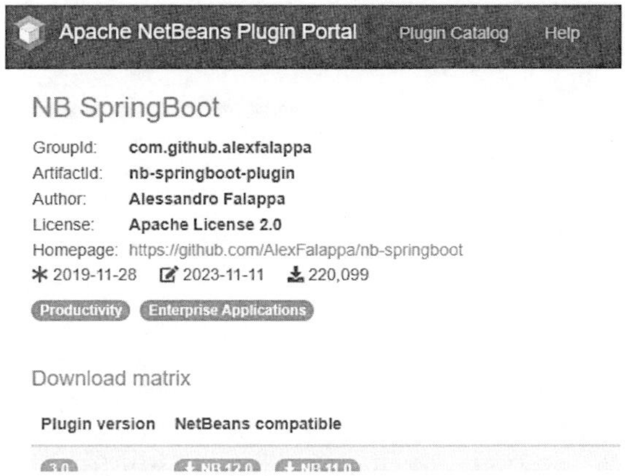

3. Find the version compatible with your NetBeans installation and download the plugin file. It will have an **.nbm extension** (e.g., NB-SpringBoot-3.1.nbm). Save this file to a memorable location, like your **Downloads** folder.

Part 2: Install the plugin in NetBeans

Follow these steps based on the installation process:

1. **Open the Plugin Manager:** In the NetBeans IDE, go to the main menu and select **Tools → Plugins**.

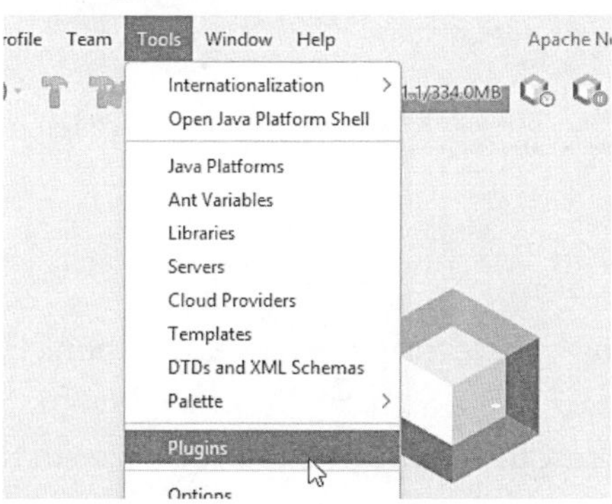

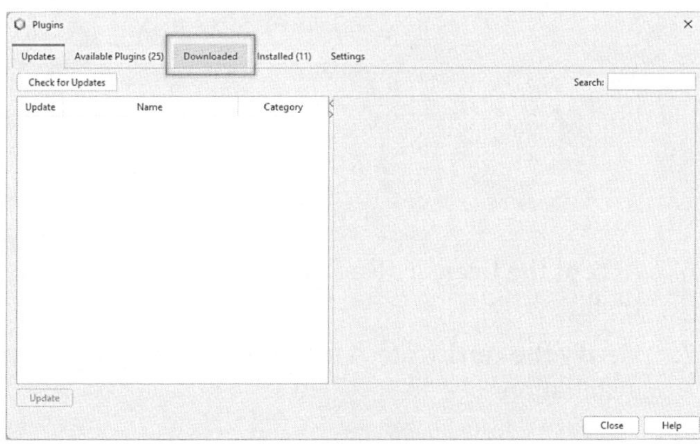

2. **Add the downloaded plugin:** In the **Plugins** dialog box, **click** on the **Downloaded** tab. Then, click the **Add Plugins...** button.
3. **Select the Plugin file:** An explorer window opens. **Navigate** to the location where you saved the .nbm file, select it, and click **Open**.

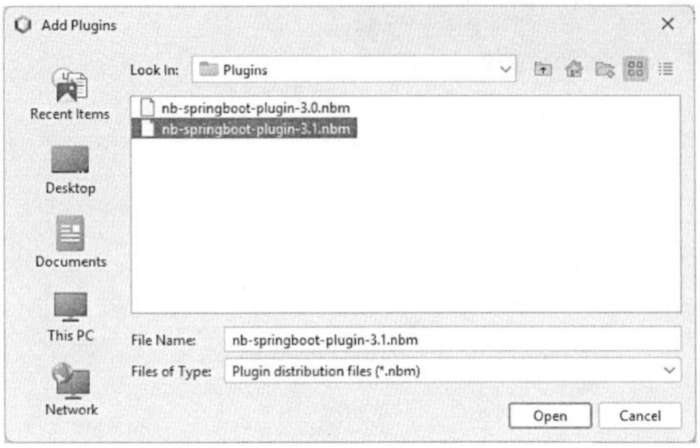

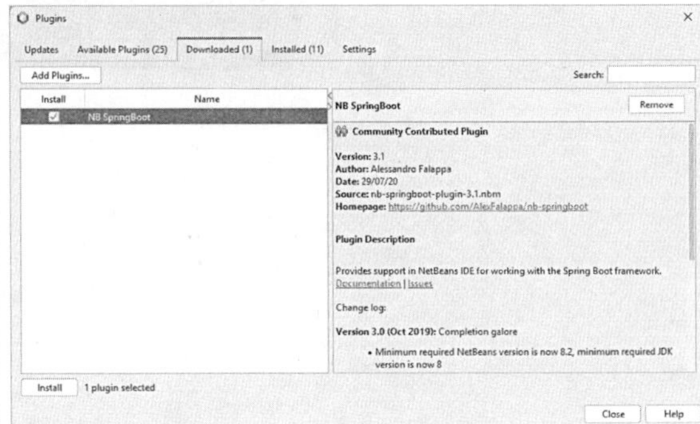

4. **Initiate the installation:** The plugin now **appears** in the list on the **Downloaded** tab. Ensure its checkbox is selected and click the **Install** button.
5. **Follow the installer wizard:** A new wizard appears to guide you. Click **Next** to begin.

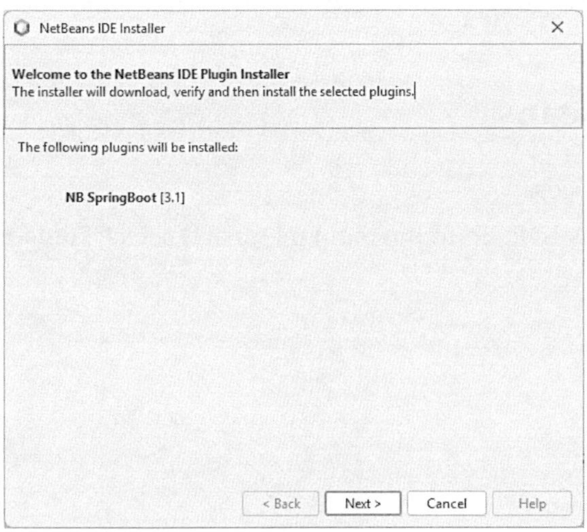

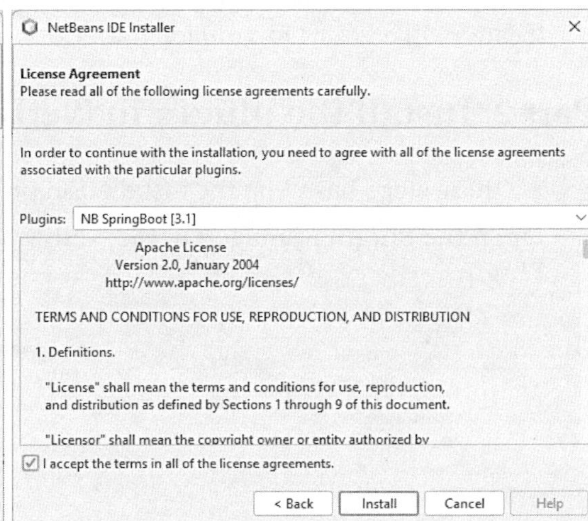

6. **Accept the license:** Read and accept the **license** terms by selecting the checkbox, then click **Install**.
7. **Verify the certificate** A security **warning** may appear. Click **Continue** to proceed with the installation.

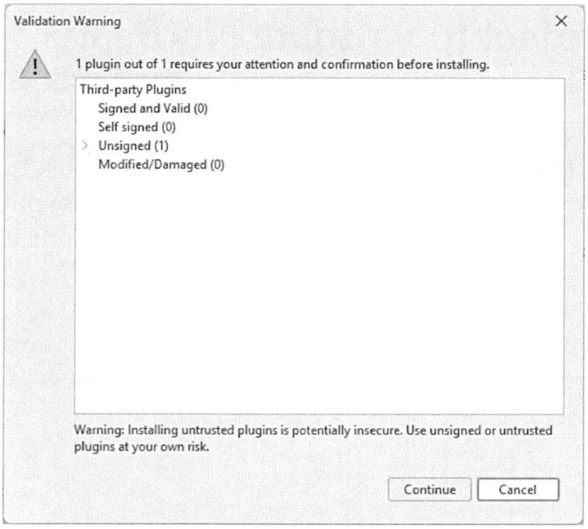

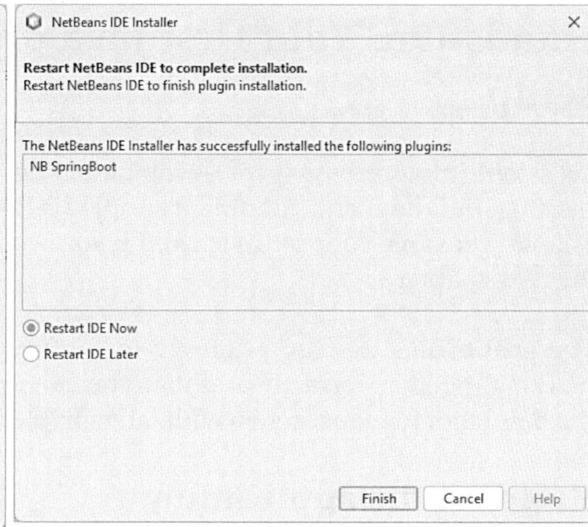

8. **Restart the IDE:** The final step requires you to restart NetBeans to activate the plugin. Ensure **Restart IDE now** is selected and click **Finish**.

Part 3: Verify the installation

After NetBeans restarts, the Spring Boot functionality is active.

1. Go to **File → New Project....**
2. In the **Choose Project** dialog box, select the **Java with Maven** category. You can now see **Spring Boot Initializr project** available in the **Projects** list, ready for you to use.

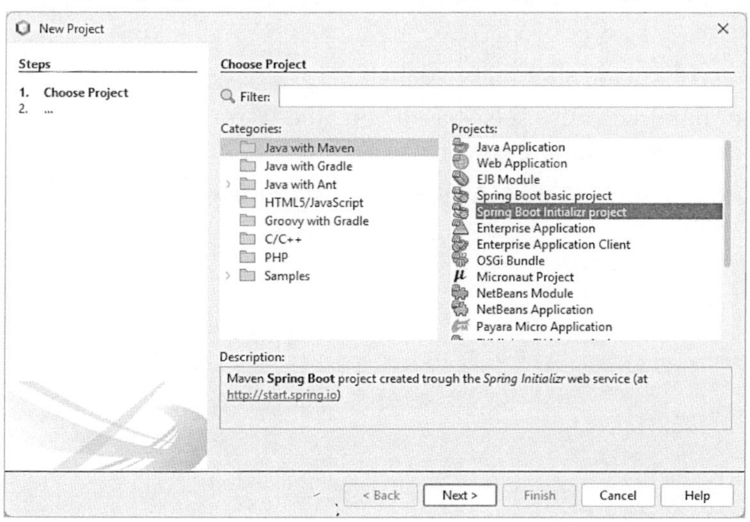

Hands-On: Your first Java project to validate NetBeans setup

Let's confirm your basic Java development environment is set up correctly. You'll do this by creating, building, and running a simple **Hello, World!** application using **Apache NetBeans**. This step ensures your setup is valid before you begin developing Spring Boot applications in the next chapter.

The goal of this exercise is purely to confirm that your JDK and NetBeans installation are working together correctly and that you can execute a basic Java program. We use Maven as the build tool for consistency with later chapters.

Building the application

Follow these steps carefully:

Create a project

1. In NetBeans, go to **File → New Project...**.
2. In the **Choose Project** dialog, select **Java with Maven** from the **Categories** list and **Java Application** from the **Projects** list. Click **Next**.
3. In the Name and Location step:
    - Set **Project Name** to **HelloWorldApp** and choose a suitable **Project Location** on your file system.
    - Set **Group Id** as **com.sharanamvaishali**.
    - **Package** automatically sets based on the Group Id and Project Name (e.g., **com.sharanamvaishali.helloworldapp**).
    - Leave the **Version** as **1.0-SNAPSHOT**. Click **Finish**.

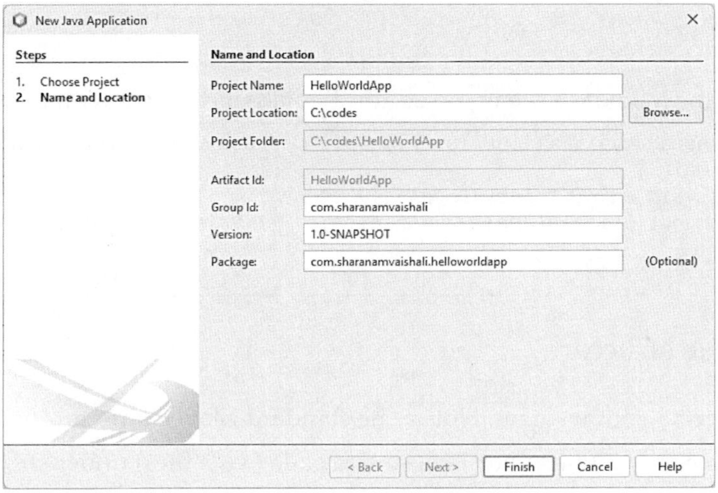

- Click **Finish**. NetBeans creates the basic project structure for your Java application using Maven.

Create a Java class

1. In the **Projects** window (usually on the left), expand the **HelloWorldApp** project node.
2. Expand **Source Packages**. You can see the package you defined (e.g., **com.sharanamvaishali.helloworldapp**).
3. Right-click on that package name and select **New → Java Class...**.
4. Enter **Main** as the **Class Name** and click **Finish**.

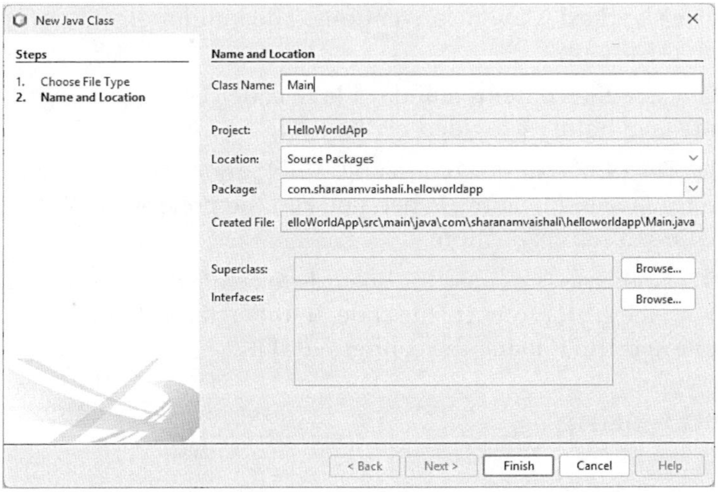

Write code

NetBeans opens the Main.java file in the editor. Replace its content with the following code:

```
package com.sharanamvaishali.helloworldapp;   // Use your actual package name here
public class Main {
public static void main(String[] args) {
        System.out.println("Hello, World!");   // Prints the message to the console
    }
}
```

Understand the structure

Look at the **Projects** window again. Notice the standard Maven structure:

- **Source Packages:** Contains your Java source code (.java files) under src/main/java.
- **Test Packages:** Contains your test code under src/test/java (we aren't using this yet).
- **Dependencies:** Lists libraries your project depends on (currently just the JDK).
- **Project Files:** Contains build-related files, most importantly pom.xml. Double-click pom.xml to see the Maven configuration NetBeans generated.

Bridging the gap: Learned concepts and application implementation

Let's connect what we just did to the concepts discussed earlier:

- **Maven conventions:** The project structure NetBeans created (src/main/java, pom.xml) directly follows standard Maven conventions. The build tool expects code and resources to be in specific locations.
- **JDK:** The Main.java file contains standard Java code. The System.out.println() method is part of the core Java library provided by the JDK.
- **Main method:** The public static void main(String[] args) method is the special entry point for any standard Java application. When you run the project, the JVM looks for this exact method signature to start execution.
- **NetBeans IDE:** NetBeans provided the wizards to create the project structure and the Java class, along with the editor to write the code. It understands the Maven project and knows how to compile and run it using the configured JDK.

Running and testing

Now, let's run the application:

1. **Run project:** Right-click on the **HelloWorldApp** project node in the **Projects** window and select **Run**.
2. **Observe output:** Look at the **Output** window, which usually appears at the bottom of the NetBeans interface. You should see output similar to this:

```
--- exec-maven-plugin:3.0.0:exec (default-cli) @ HelloWorldApp ---
Hello, World!
------------------------------------------------------------------------
BUILD SUCCESS
------------------------------------------------------------------------
```

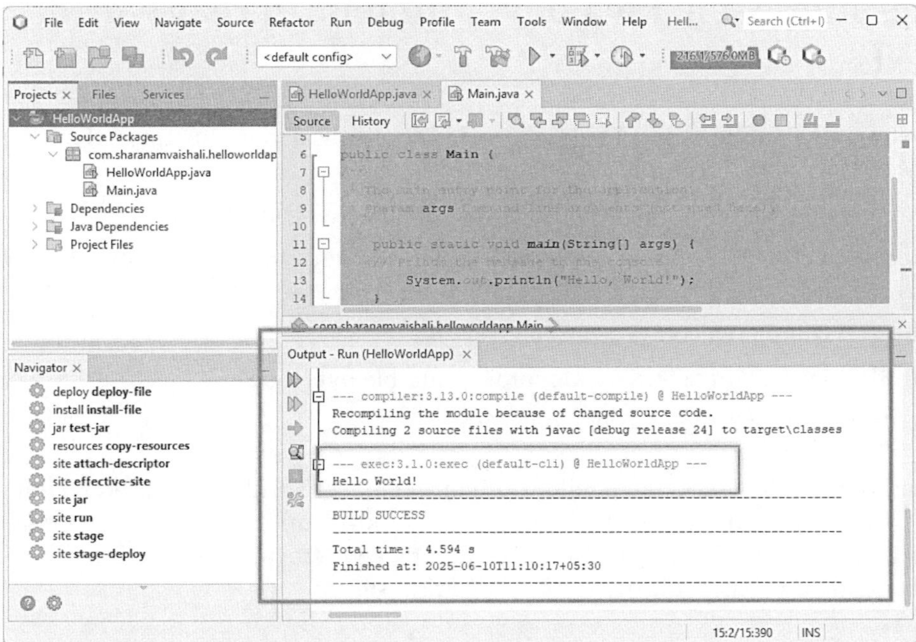

3. The key part is seeing the "Hello, World!" message printed. This confirms your application compiled and ran successfully.

Exploring application behaviour: A practical run-through

What happened behind the scenes when you clicked **Run**?

1. **Compilation:** NetBeans invoked Maven, which in turn used the Java compiler (javac from your configured JDK) to translate your Main.java source file into Java bytecode (Main.class). This .class file is placed in the target/classes directory within your project folder.

2. **Execution:** Maven (as seen in the output) then instructed the Java Virtual Machine (JVM, part of your JDK) to execute the compiled bytecode.
3. **Entry point:** The JVM loaded the Main.class file and looked for the public static void main(String[] args) method.
4. **Output:** Execution started within the main() method. The System.out.println("Hello, World!"); statement was executed, causing the text "Hello, World!" to be printed to the standard output stream, which NetBeans conveniently displays in its **Output** window.

Harnessing basic Java development in real-world contexts

While extremely simple, this "Hello, World!" application demonstrates the fundamental workflow for any Java development:

1. **Setup:** Having a working JDK and IDE (like NetBeans) configured.
2. **Project structure:** Using a build tool (like Maven) to manage project layout and dependencies.
3. **Coding:** Writing Java code within classes.
4. **Compilation:** Turning source code into executable bytecode.
5. **Execution:** Running the bytecode on a JVM.

This exact foundation - JDK, IDE, build tool, compilation, execution - is used whether you are building simple command-line tools, complex desktop applications, or the sophisticated server-side web applications with Spring Boot that we will focus on throughout the rest of this book. Mastering this basic setup is the essential first step.

Wrapping up

In this chapter, we covered the essential groundwork for modern Java development:

- **Java ecosystem:** Understood JDK, JVM, and Jakarta EE roles.
- **Spring & Spring Boot:** Introduced the core ideas behind the Spring Framework and how Spring Boot simplifies it.
- **IoC/DI:** Got a first glimpse of Inversion of Control and Dependency Injection.
- **Build tools:** Learned the purpose of Maven and Gradle.
- **Environment:** Set up JDK and NetBeans.

Congratulations on completing Chapter 1! You've successfully set up your development environment and taken the first crucial steps into the world of modern Java development by building and running your first application using NetBeans and Maven. You now have a foundational understanding of the Java ecosystem, the roles of Spring and Spring Boot, and the importance of build tools.

In the next chapter, we'll dive straight into the power of Spring Boot by creating your very first Spring Boot web application. You'll see firsthand how Spring Boot drastically simplifies setup and allows you to get a web application running with minimal effort. Get ready to say "Hello, Spring Boot!"

Chapter 2

Section 01: Launching your Spring journey - Initial setup and first steps

From Zero to Spring Hero: Your first application

What you'll learn

- Why Spring Boot?
- Key features of Spring Boot
- Essential Spring Boot starters
- How Spring Boot runs?
- What is Convention over configuration?
- Spring Initializr tool
- Understanding the main application class

Welcome to the world of Spring Boot! In the previous chapter, we set up our Java development environment and got comfortable with the basic tools. Now, we dive into what makes modern Java development so efficient and powerful: **Spring Boot**. If Spring Framework provides the core building blocks, Spring Boot is the express train that gets your application up and running with minimal fuss. Forget complex XML configurations and lengthy setup processes.

Spring Boot embraces **convention over configuration**, allowing you to focus on writing the business logic that truly matters. We explore how Spring Boot achieves this magic through features like starters and auto-configuration, enabling you to build stand-alone, production-grade applications quickly.

Why Spring Boot?

Spring Boot emerged as a solution to simplify the configuration and deployment of Spring applications. While the core Spring Framework offers immense power and flexibility, setting up a new project often involved significant boilerplate configuration (like XML files or extensive Java configuration classes) just to get started. Spring Boot takes an opinionated view of the Spring platform and third-party libraries, meaning it makes intelligent assumptions about what you need and configures things automatically, drastically reducing development time and complexity.

Its primary goals are:

- To provide a radically faster and widely accessible getting-started experience for all Spring development.
- To be opinionated out of the box, but get out of the way quickly as requirements start to diverge from the defaults.
- To provide a range of non-functional features that are common to large classes of projects (e.g., embedded servers, security, metrics, health checks, externalized configuration).
- Absolutely no code generation and no requirement for XML configuration.

Convention over configuration

This is a core principle behind Spring Boot. Instead of requiring developers to explicitly configure every detail of the application setup (the configuration part), Spring Boot makes assumptions based on common conventions. For example:

- If it finds a specific library (like **spring-boot-starter-web**) on the classpath, it assumes you want to build a web application and automatically configures an embedded server (like Tomcat) and Spring MVC.
- It assumes your application code resides in specific package structures.
- It provides sensible default configurations for databases, logging, security, etc., which you can override only when needed.

This approach significantly speeds up initial development. You define ***what*** you want to do (e.g., build a web API), and Spring Boot figures out ***how*** to set it up based on the dependencies you include and standard practices.

Key features

Three key features make Spring Boot so effective:

- **Spring Boot starters:** These are convenient dependency descriptors that you can include in your application. Adding a starter pulls in a curated set of related dependencies needed for a specific capability, simplifying dependency management. For example, adding **spring-boot-starter-web** brings in everything needed for building web applications, including RESTful applications using Spring MVC, and Tomcat as the default embedded container. Other common starters include **spring-boot-starter-data-jpa** for database persistence and **spring-boot-starter-test** for testing.
- **Auto-configuration:** This is where the magic happens. Spring Boot attempts to automatically configure your Spring application based on the JAR dependencies you have added. If **spring-boot-starter-web** is present, it automatically configures beans like DispatcherServlet, TomcatEmbeddedServletContainerFactory, etc. If you have **spring-boot-starter-data-jpa** and a database driver like H2 on the classpath, it automatically configures a DataSource and an EntityManagerFactory. Auto-configuration is non-invasive; you can always define your own configuration to override the defaults.
- **Embedded servers:** Spring Boot applications can embed a web server (like Tomcat, Jetty, or Undertow) directly within their executable JAR file. This means you don't need to deploy your application as a WAR file to an external application server. You can simply run the JAR file, and the embedded server starts automatically, making deployment much simpler, especially for microservices. It leverages the Jakarta Servlet 6.0 API for this web server integration.

Using the Spring Initializr (Web or via NetBeans)

The easiest way to start a new Spring Boot project is by using the Spring Initializr. This tool allows you to generate a basic project structure with the necessary build files (**pom.xml** for Maven or **build.gradle** for Gradle) and selected starter dependencies.

You can access it in two main ways:

1. **Web interface:**
    a. Go to **start.spring.io**.
    b. Select your build tool (Maven/Gradle), language (Java), Spring Boot version, project metadata (Group, Artifact), packaging (Jar/War), Java version (JDK 17+), and add the desired dependencies (starters).
    c. Click **GENERATE** to download a zip file containing the project structure.

2. **IDE Integration (NetBeans):** Apache NetBeans provides built-in support for creating Spring Boot projects, often integrating directly with the Spring Initializr service. This is usually the most convenient option when working within the IDE. You typically go through a wizard similar to the web interface, selecting options and dependencies, and NetBeans generates and opens the project for you.

Essential Spring Boot starters (Web, Logging)

While there are many starters available, two are fundamental for typical applications:

1. **spring-boot-starter-web:** As mentioned, this is essential for building web applications, including RESTful APIs using Spring MVC. It includes dependencies for Tomcat (by default) and core Spring MVC components. It also transitively includes **spring-boot-starter**, which provides core Boot features like auto-configuration and logging.
2. **spring-boot-starter:** This core starter includes auto-configuration support, logging, and YAML configuration support. It's included by most other starters (like -web, -data-jpa). Spring Boot uses Logback as the default logging framework, but it provides abstractions (**commons-logging**) and configuration options to manage logging easily via application.properties or application.yml.

Understanding the main application class (@SpringBootApplication)

When you generate a Spring Boot project, the Spring Initializr creates a main application class. This class typically resides in the root package and is annotated with @SpringBootApplication:

```
package com.sharanamvaishali.helloboot;
import org.springframework.boot.SpringApplication;
import org.springframework.boot.autoconfigure.SpringBootApplication;
@SpringBootApplication // <- The magic annotation!
public class HellobootApplication {
    public static void main(String[] args) {
        SpringApplication.run(HellobootApplication.class, args); // <- Boots the app
    }
}
```

The **@SpringBootApplication** annotation is a convenience annotation that combines three other annotations:

- **@EnableAutoConfiguration:** Enables Spring Boot's auto-configuration mechanism.
- **@ComponentScan:** Enables component scanning within the current package and its sub-packages. This finds beans annotated with @Component, @Service, @Repository, @Controller, @RestController, etc.

- **@Configuration:** Allows registering extra beans in the context or importing additional configuration classes. Though primarily associated with Java-based configuration, it marks the class as a source of bean definitions.

The main method uses **SpringApplication.run()** to launch the application. This bootstraps the Spring application context, performs auto-configuration, starts the embedded server (if applicable), and makes the application ready.

The application.properties / application.yml file

Spring Boot centralizes application configuration in a file named application.properties or application.yml, located in the src/main/resources directory. This file allows you to configure various aspects of your application without writing code or XML.

- **application.properties:** Uses standard Java properties file format (key=value pairs).

```
server.port=8080
logging.level.org.springframework=DEBUG
spring.application.name=MySpringBootApp
```

- **application.yml:** Uses YAML (YAML Ain't Markup Language) format, which is often more readable for hierarchical data.

```
server:
  port: 8080
logging:
  level:
    org:
      springframework: DEBUG
spring:
  application:
    name: MySpringBootApp
```

Spring Boot provides hundreds of common application properties for configuring servers, data sources, logging, security, actuators, and much more. You can find a comprehensive list in the Spring Boot documentation. The filename dictates the format used.

How Spring Boot runs?

When you include a web starter like **spring-boot-starter-web**, Spring Boot automatically includes an embedded servlet container. By default, this is Tomcat.

Here's the flow:

1. You run the main() method in your @SpringBootApplication class.
2. SpringApplication.run() bootstraps the Spring context.

3. Auto-configuration detects the web starter.
4. It configures and starts the embedded servlet container (e.g., Tomcat) on a default port (usually **8080**). It uses the Jakarta Servlet 6.0 API standard for this integration.
5. Spring MVC's DispatcherServlet is configured to handle incoming web requests.
6. Your application is now running and listening for requests on the specified port.

Because the server is embedded within your application JAR, you can run it like any other Java application (java -jar your-app.jar). There's no need for a separate server installation or complex deployment procedures for simple cases.

Hands-on: Hello, Spring Boot!

In this hands-on section, we build our very first Spring Boot application. The goal is simple: create a minimal web application that responds with a "Hello, Spring Boot!" message when accessed through a web browser. This exercise verifies that our basic Spring Boot setup is working correctly and demonstrates the core concepts of starters, auto-configuration, and handling web requests.

Building the application

We use the Spring Initializr via the NetBeans IDE to create and set up our project.

Generate project via NetBeans Spring Initializr

1. In NetBeans, go to **File → New Project…**.
2. In the **Choose Project** dialog, select **Java with Maven** from the **Categories** list and **Spring Boot Initializr project** from the **Projects** list.

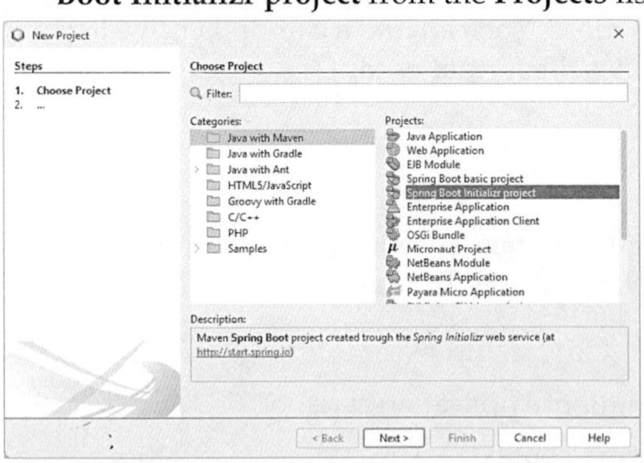

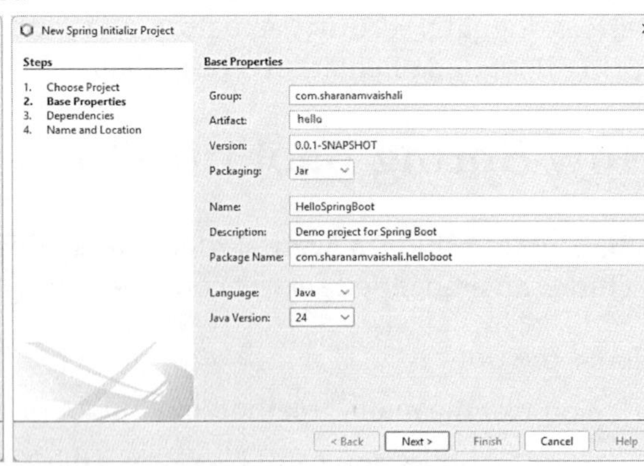

3. Click **Next**. In the **Base Properties** step:
   - o Set **Group** to **com.sharanamvaishali** and **Artifact** to **hello**.
   - o Keep the **Version** as it is (i.e. **0.0.1-SNAPSHOT**) and ensure **Packaging** is **Jar**.
   - o Set **Name** to **HelloSpringBoot** and **Package Name** to **com.sharanamvaishali.helloboot**.
   - o Select **Java** from the **Language** list and the appropriate **Java Version** (e.g., **24**).
4. Click **Next**. In the **Dependencies** step:
   - o Select the appropriate **Spring Boot Version** (e.g., **4.0.0 (SNAPSHOT)**).
   - o In the **Available** dependencies list, find and select **Spring Web**.
5. Click **Next**. In the **Name and Location** step:
   - o Set **Project Name** to **HelloSpringBootDrive**.
   - o Choose a suitable **Project Location**.

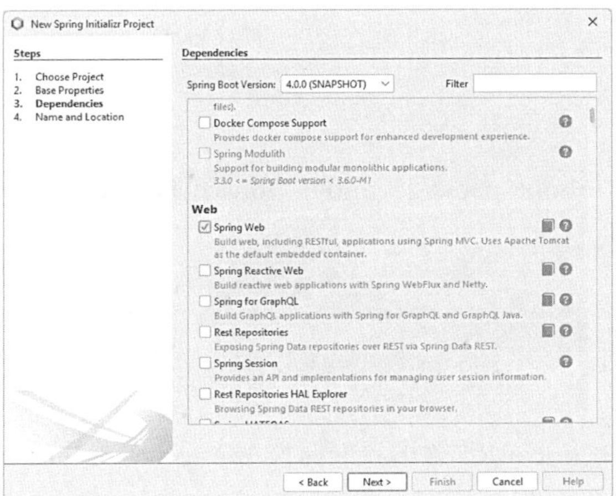

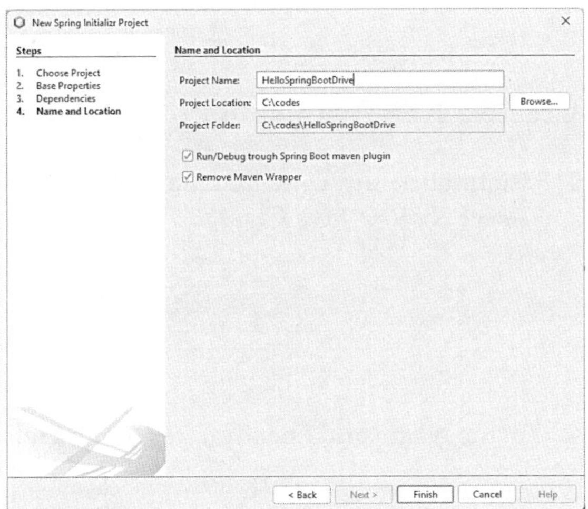

6. Click **Finish**. NetBeans generates the project structure and downloads dependencies.

Explore the project structure

NetBeans automatically opens the project. Let's explore the structure in the **Projects** window:

- **Source Packages:** Contains **com.sharanamvaishali.helloboot** with the main **HelloSpringBootApplication.java**.
- **Dependencies:** Shows the included **JARs**, notably **spring-boot-starter-web**.
- **Project Files:** Contains **pom.xml** (the Maven build file).

- Inside **src/main/resources**, you find **application.properties**.

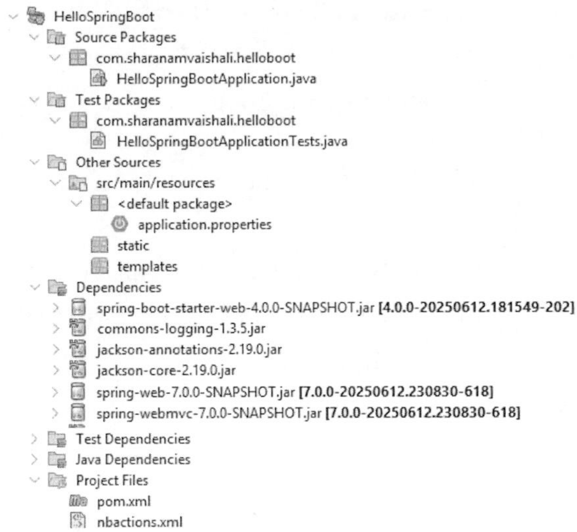

Create a REST controller

1. Right-click the **com.sharanamvaishali.helloboot** package under **Source Packages** and select **New → Java Class...**.

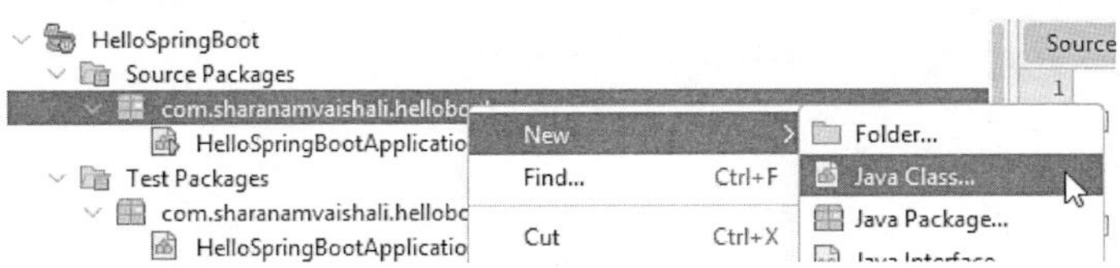

2. In the **Name and Location** step, enter **HelloController** as the **Class Name** and click **Finish**.

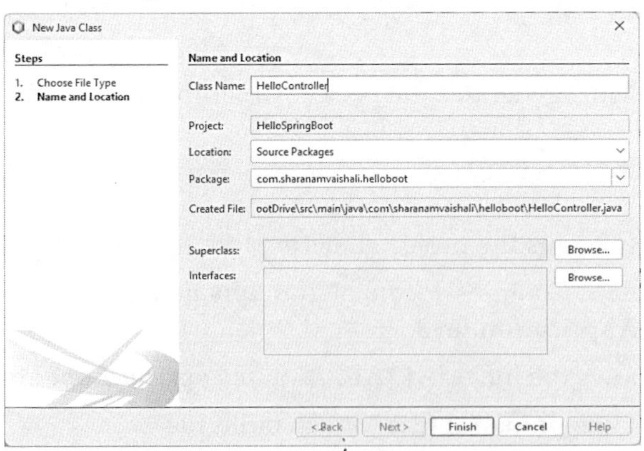

3. Open the HelloController.java file and replace its content with the following code:

```
package com.sharanamvaishali.helloboot;
import org.springframework.web.bind.annotation.GetMapping;
import org.springframework.web.bind.annotation.RestController;
@RestController // Marks this class as a request handler
public class HelloController {
    @GetMapping("/") // Maps HTTP GET requests for "/" to this method
    public String sayHello() {
        return "Hello, Spring Boot!";
    }
}
```

Code explanation

- **@RestController:** This annotation combines @Controller and @ResponseBody. It tells Spring that this class handles web requests and that the return value of methods should be bound directly to the web response body (no view template is needed here).
- **@GetMapping("/"):** This annotation maps HTTP GET requests for the root path (/) to the sayHello() method. When someone accesses http://localhost:8080/, this method executes.
- **sayHello():** This method simply returns the **String** "Hello, Spring Boot!". Because of @RestController, this string becomes the HTTP response body.

Bridging the gap: Learned concepts and application implementation

Let's connect what we built to the concepts discussed earlier:

- **Spring web starter:** Adding the **Spring Web** dependency via the Initializr brought in spring-boot-starter-web. This triggered Spring Boot's auto-configuration.
- **Auto-configuration:** Because the web starter is present, Spring Boot automatically configured an embedded Tomcat server and set up Spring MVC's DispatcherServlet to handle incoming requests. We didn't need to configure these manually.
- **@SpringBootApplication:** The main method in HelloSpringBootApplication uses this annotation, enabling component scanning (which finds our HelloController) and auto-configuration. SpringApplication.run() starts the embedded Tomcat server.
- **@RestController & @GetMapping:** These annotations define how web requests are handled. @RestController marks HelloController as a request handler whose return values are written directly to the response. @GetMapping("/") specifically routes GET requests for the root path to our sayHello() method.
- **Embedded server:** When we run the application, the embedded Tomcat server starts automatically, listening on port **8080** by default.

Running and testing

1. **Run the application from NetBeans**
   a. Right-click the **HelloSpringBootApplication.java** file in the **Projects** window.
   b. Select **Run File**.

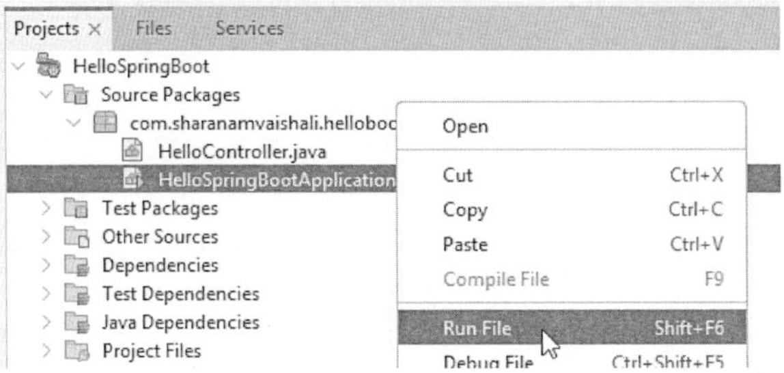

   c. Observe the **Output** window in NetBeans. You see logs indicating Spring Boot starting up, including lines showing Tomcat starting on port **8080**.

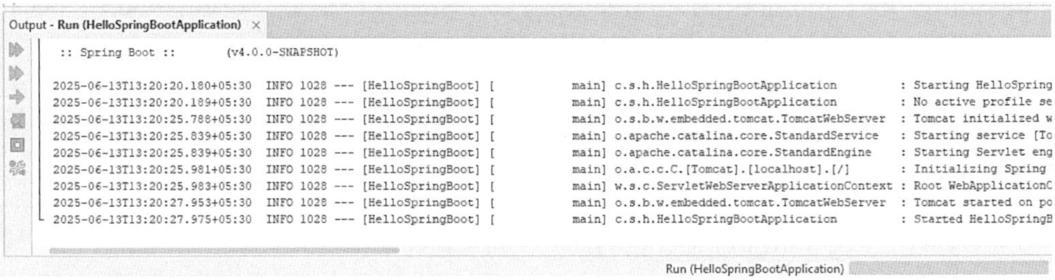

2. **Access via Web Browser**
   a. Open your web browser (like Chrome, Firefox, or Edge).
   b. Navigate to the URL: **http://localhost:8080**.
   c. The browser displays the text "**Hello, Spring Boot!**".

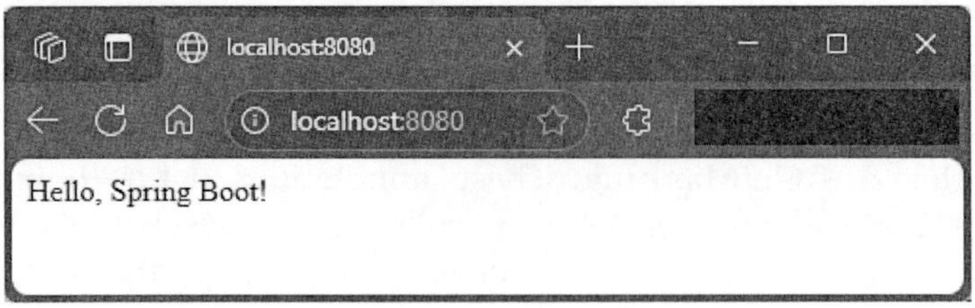

Exploring application behaviour: A practical run-through

Here's what happened behind the scenes when you accessed http://localhost:8080:

1. Your browser sent an HTTP GET request to the server running on localhost at port 8080, requesting the root path (/).
2. The embedded Tomcat server received this request.
3. Tomcat passed the request to Spring MVC's DispatcherServlet.
4. DispatcherServlet consulted its mappings and found that GET requests for / are handled by the sayHello() method in the HelloController bean (thanks to @GetMapping("/")).
5. Spring called the sayHello() method.
6. The method returned the **String** "Hello, Spring Boot!".
7. Because HelloController is annotated with @RestController, Spring MVC knew to write this string directly into the HTTP response body.
8. DispatcherServlet sent the HTTP response (with status code 200 OK and the string in the body) back to Tomcat.
9. Tomcat sent the response back to your browser.
10. Your browser rendered the received text: **Hello, Spring Boot!**.

Harnessing Spring Boot Starters and Auto-configuration in real-world contexts

This simple "Hello, World!" example showcases the power of Spring Boot's core features:

- **Rapid development:** We created a functioning web application with just a few lines of code and minimal configuration, thanks to starters and auto-configuration.
- **Simplified dependency management:** The spring-boot-starter-web brought in all necessary web libraries automatically.
- **Reduced boilerplate:** We didn't need XML configuration or complex setup classes. @SpringBootApplication, @RestController, and @GetMapping provided a concise way to define the application and its behavior.
- **Standalone applications:** The embedded server allows us to run the application directly from its JAR file, simplifying deployment.

In real-world scenarios, developers leverage these features to quickly set up various application types:

- Building REST APIs for web frontends or mobile apps.

- Creating microservices.
- Developing traditional server-side web applications with template engines like Thymeleaf (*Chapter 11 - Creating Views with Thymeleaf*).
- Integrating with databases using **spring-boot-starter-data-jpa** (*Chapter 5 - Introduction to Persistence*).

By simply adding the appropriate starter and providing minimal configuration (usually in application.properties), developers can bootstrap complex functionalities swiftly.

Wrapping up

This chapter introduced you to the core ideas and benefits of Spring Boot:

- Spring Boot simplifies Spring application development through **convention over configuration**.
- **Starters** manage dependencies for specific functionalities (e.g., web, data).
- **Auto-configuration** automatically sets up beans based on classpath dependencies.
- **Embedded servers** (like Tomcat) allow running applications as standalone JARs.
- The **Spring Initializr** (web or IDE) helps generate project skeletons.
- @SpringBootApplication is the key annotation for bootstrapping.
- application.properties or .yml centralizes configuration.
- @RestController and @GetMapping handle web requests easily.

Congratulations! You've successfully built and run your first Spring Boot web application. You've seen firsthand how Spring Boot streamlines development with starters, auto-configuration, and embedded servers. This foundation is crucial as we move forward.

In the next chapter, we delve deeper into the heart of the Spring Framework: understanding Spring Beans and the powerful concept of Dependency Injection, which form the bedrock of building modular and maintainable applications with Spring.

Chapter 3

Section 01: Launching your Spring journey - Initial setup and first steps

Wiring up your application: Dependency Injection with Spring

What you'll learn

- Spring IoC container
- Stereotype annotations
- Constructor Injection
- Java-based configuration
- What are Spring Beans?
- Dependency Injection
- @Autowired
- Bean scopes

Welcome back! In the previous chapter, you created your first Spring Boot application and saw how quickly you can get a web application up and running. Now, it's time to dive deeper into the fundamental concepts that make Spring so powerful: the Inversion of Control (IoC) container and Dependency Injection (DI). Understanding these principles is crucial for building robust, scalable, and maintainable applications with Spring.

Modern software development thrives on modularity and flexibility. Imagine building a complex system like an online store. You have components for managing users, products, orders, and payments. These components need to work together seamlessly.

Traditionally, a component might create the other components it needs directly. This creates tight coupling - changes in one component often force changes in others, making the system rigid and hard to test. Spring's core philosophy revolves around managing these components (called **beans**) and their relationships (**dependencies**) for you through a mechanism called the IoC container, promoting loose coupling and easier development.

Deep dive into the Spring IoC container (ApplicationContext)

At the heart of the Spring Framework lies the Inversion of Control (IoC) container. But what does "Inversion of Control" mean?

Normally, you control the creation and lifecycle of objects in your application. For instance, if OrderService needs a ProductRepository, the OrderService code might explicitly create an instance of ProductRepository using new ProductRepository().

With IoC, this control is **inverted**. Instead of your objects controlling the instantiation and linking of their dependencies, the Spring IoC container takes over this responsibility. You simply define your components (beans) and declare their dependencies, and the container **injects** these dependencies when needed.

The primary interface for the Spring IoC container is ApplicationContext. It is responsible for:

- **Instantiating beans:** Creating the objects you define.
- **Configuring beans:** Setting properties and satisfying dependencies.
- **Assembling beans:** Managing the relationships between beans.
- **Managing the lifecycle of beans:** Handling the entire lifecycle from creation to destruction.

You usually don't interact with ApplicationContext directly in a typical Spring Boot application. Instead, you leverage annotations and configuration to implicitly use its power. Spring Boot automatically creates and configures an appropriate ApplicationContext for you based on your project setup and dependencies.

What are Spring beans? (Managed objects)

In simple terms, a **Spring bean** is an object that is instantiated, assembled, and otherwise managed by the Spring IoC container. These are the fundamental building blocks of any Spring application.

Instead of you creating objects using the **new** keyword everywhere, you declare beans, and the Spring container manages them.

How does the container know which objects to manage? You typically tell Spring about your beans in one of the following ways:

- **Annotation-based configuration:** Using stereotype annotations on your classes.
- **Java-based configuration:** Using methods annotated with **@Bean** within configuration classes.
- **XML-based configuration** (Less common in modern Spring Boot applications).

We focus primarily on annotation-based and Java-based configuration in this book.

Stereotype annotations

The easiest way to declare a class as a Spring bean is by using stereotype annotations. These are annotations placed on a class definition that signal its role in the application to the Spring container. Spring automatically scans your project's classpath for classes marked with these annotations and registers them as beans in ApplicationContext.

The core stereotype annotations include:

- **@Component:** This is the generic stereotype annotation. It indicates that the annotated class is a "component" - a candidate for auto-detection when using annotation-based configuration and classpath scanning.
- **@Service:** This annotation is a specialization of **@Component**. It indicates that the annotated class holds business logic. It doesn't provide any extra behaviour over **@Component** by default, but it helps in clearly defining the application's layers and can be targeted by Aspect-Oriented Programming (AOP) features.
- **@Repository:** This annotation is also a specialization of **@Component**. It is used to indicate that the class fulfills the role of a repository (also known as Data Access Object or DAO). Its primary purpose is to handle data access operations. Spring provides exception translation features for repositories annotated with **@Repository**, converting platform-specific persistence exceptions (like SQLExceptions) into Spring's unified DataAccessException hierarchy.
- **@Controller:** Another specialization of **@Component**, this annotation indicates that the class serves as a controller in a web application (typically in the context of Spring MVC, which we explore in ***Chapter 10 - Handling web Requests with Spring MVC***). It marks the class as a web request handler.

You can use **@Component** for any managed bean, but using the specialized annotations (**@Service**, **@Repository**, **@Controller**) makes your code more readable and allows Spring to apply specific behaviors if needed.

Dependency Injection: Decoupling components

Dependency Injection (DI) is the **process** by which the IoC container fulfills the dependencies of a bean. Instead of a bean creating or looking up its dependencies, the container **injects** them into the bean. This design principle helps achieve loose coupling between components.

Consider our OrderService needing a ProductRepository. With DI:

- Both OrderService and ProductRepository are declared as Spring beans (e.g., using **@Service** and **@Repository**).
- OrderService declares that it **needs** an instance of ProductRepository.
- The Spring container sees this dependency, finds the managed ProductRepository bean, and provides (injects) it into the OrderService instance when it creates it.

This decouples OrderService from the specific implementation details and creation logic of ProductRepository. OrderService just needs some implementation that fulfills the ProductRepository contract. This makes the code easier to test (you can inject mock repositories) and maintain.

Spring supports several types of dependency injection:

Constructor Injection (Preferred)

With constructor injection, the container invokes a class constructor with arguments representing the dependencies. The dependencies are provided as constructor parameters:

```
@Service
public class OrderService {
    private final ProductRepository productRepository;
    private final UserRepository userRepository;
    // Dependencies are injected via the constructor
    public OrderService(ProductRepository productRepository,
                        UserRepository userRepository) {
        this.productRepository = productRepository;
        this.userRepository = userRepository;
    }
    // ... methods using repositories ...
}
```

Why preferred?

- **Immutability:** Dependencies can be declared as **final**, ensuring they cannot be changed after the object is constructed.
- **Guaranteed dependencies:** The object is guaranteed to have its mandatory dependencies upon creation. It cannot exist in an incomplete state.
- **Clarity:** Clearly signals the required dependencies of the class just by looking at the constructor signature.
- **Testability:** Makes it very easy to instantiate the class manually in unit tests by providing mock dependencies to the constructor.

Starting with Spring 4, if a class has only one constructor, the **@Autowired** annotation on the constructor is optional. Spring automatically uses that constructor for injection.

Setter Injection

Setter injection involves the container calling setter methods on your bean after invoking a no-argument constructor or a no-argument static factory method to instantiate the bean:

```
@Service
public class OrderService {
    private ProductRepository productRepository;
    private UserRepository userRepository;
    // Default constructor (usually implicit)
    public OrderService() {
    }
    // Setter method for dependency injection
    @Autowired // Annotation often required here
    public void setProductRepository(ProductRepository productRepository) {
        this.productRepository = productRepository;
    }
    // Setter method for dependency injection
    @Autowired // Annotation often required here
    public void setUserRepository(UserRepository userRepository) {
        this.userRepository = userRepository;
    }
    // ... methods using repositories ...
}
```

Setter injection is primarily used for optional dependencies where reasonable default values can be assigned within the class. It can also be useful for re-configuration or re-injection later, although this is less common.

Field Injection (Use with caution)

Field injection uses annotations directly on the fields to indicate dependencies:

```
@Service
public class OrderService {
    @Autowired
    private ProductRepository productRepository;
    @Autowired
    private UserRepository userRepository;
    // No constructor or setters needed for injection
    // ... methods using repositories ...
}
```

Why use with caution?

- **Hides dependencies:** Dependencies are not clearly visible from the class's public contract (constructors or setters).
- **Harder to test:** Instantiating the class manually in unit tests becomes difficult, as you need to use reflection to set the private fields or rely on a Spring testing context.
- **Encourages poor design:** Can make it easy to add too many dependencies without considering the class's responsibilities.
- **Immutability issues:** Cannot easily make fields **final**.

While concise, field injection often leads to less testable and less clear code compared to constructor injection. It's generally recommended to avoid it in favor of constructor injection for mandatory dependencies.

Resolving dependencies: @Autowired

The **@Autowired** annotation marks a constructor, field, setter method, or config method as needing to be autowired by Spring's dependency injection facilities.

When Spring encounters **@Autowired**, it attempts to find a matching bean in the ApplicationContext to inject. The matching usually happens **by type**.

- **On a constructor:** Spring tries to find beans matching the types of the constructor parameters. As mentioned, if there's only one constructor, **@Autowired** is optional.
- **On a setter method:** Spring tries to find a bean matching the type of the setter method's parameter.
- **On a field:** Spring tries to find a bean matching the type of the field.

What if multiple beans match the required type?

If more than one bean of the same type exists, Spring throws an exception because it cannot determine which one to inject. You can resolve this ambiguity using:

- **@Primary:** Mark one of the bean definitions as the primary candidate.
- **@Qualifier:** Use the **@Qualifier** annotation along with **@Autowired** to specify the exact bean name to inject.

For example:

```
public interface MessageService {
    String getMessage();
}
@Service("emailService") // Bean name specified
public class EmailService implements MessageService { ... }
@Service("smsService") // Another bean of the same type
public class SmsService implements MessageService { ... }
@Component
public class NotificationManager {
    private final MessageService messageService;
    // Use @Qualifier to specify which MessageService bean to inject
    public NotificationManager(@Qualifier("smsService") MessageService
                               messageService) {
        this.messageService = messageService;
    }
    // ...
}
```

What if no matching bean is found?

By default, **@Autowired** implies that the dependency is required. If Spring cannot find a matching bean, it throws an exception during application startup. You can mark a dependency as optional:

```
@Service
public class OptionalDependencyDemo {
    // Use required=false for optional dependencies
    @Autowired(required = false)
    private OptionalService optionalService;
    // Alternatively, use Java'8 java.util.Optional
    private final Optional<MandatoryService> mandatoryService;
    public OptionalDependencyDemo(Optional<MandatoryService>
                                  mandatoryService) {
       this.mandatoryService = mandatoryService;
    }
    public void doSomething() {
        if (optionalService != null) {
```

```
            optionalService.performAction();
        }
        mandatoryService.ifPresent(MandatoryService::performAction);
    }
}
```

Using java.util.Optional with constructor injection is often the cleanest way to handle optional dependencies.

Java-based configuration: @Configuration and @Bean

Besides stereotype annotations (**@Component**, **@Service**, etc.), you can define beans explicitly using Java-based configuration. This is useful for:

- Defining beans for third-party classes where you cannot add stereotype annotations.
- Creating beans with more complex instantiation logic.
- Centralizing some bean definitions.

You achieve this using the **@Configuration** and **@Bean** annotations:

- **@Configuration:** Annotate a class with **@Configuration** to indicate that its primary purpose is as a source of bean definitions. These classes themselves are managed by the container.
- **@Bean:** Annotate a method within a **@Configuration** class with **@Bean**. This signals that the method instantiates, configures, and initializes a new object to be managed as a Spring bean. The returned object is registered in ApplicationContext. The name of the method typically serves as the bean name by default.

For example:

```
import org.springframework.context.annotation.Bean;
import org.springframework.context.annotation.Configuration;
// Example: Defining beans for external classes or with custom logic
@Configuration
public class AppConfig {
    @Bean // Defines a bean named 'dataSource'
    public DataSource dataSource() {
        // Example: Configuring a data source programmatically
        HikariDataSource dataSource = new HikariDataSource();
        dataSource.setDriverClassName("org.h2.Driver");
        dataSource.setJdbcUrl("jdbc:h2:mem:testdb");
        dataSource.setUsername("sa");
        dataSource.setPassword("");
        return dataSource;
    }
```

```
    @Bean // Defines a bean named 'simpleService'
    public SimpleService simpleService(DataSource dataSource) {
        // A bean method can accept dependencies (other beans) as parameters
        // Spring automatically injects the 'dataSource' bean here
        return new SimpleServiceImpl(dataSource, "Initialized via @Bean");
    }
}
```

Spring automatically detects **@Configuration** classes and processes the **@Bean** methods within them to populate the ApplicationContext.

Bean scopes (Singleton, Prototype)

When you define a bean, you also define its **scope**. The scope determines the lifecycle and visibility of the bean instance. The most common scopes are:

- **singleton:** (Default) Only **one** shared instance of the bean definition is managed by the Spring IoC container. Every request for a bean with a matching ID results in the container returning that one specific instance. This is ideal for stateless services, repositories, and configuration objects.
- **prototype:** A **new** object instance is created every time a request is made for that specific bean. This is suitable for stateful objects where each collaborator needs its own independent instance.

Other scopes exist (e.g., **request**, **session**, **application** in web contexts), but **singleton** and **prototype** are the most fundamental.

You can specify the scope using the **@Scope** annotation:

```
@Service
@Scope("prototype") // Each injection gets a new instance
public class StatefulService {
    private String state;
    // ... getters and setters ...
}
```

By default, all beans declared via stereotype annotations or **@Bean** methods are **singletons**.

Hands-on: Wiring components together

Let's apply these concepts by modifying the "Hello, Spring Boot!" application from ***Chapter 2 - From Zero to Spring Hero: Your first application***. We create a dedicated service to provide the greeting message and inject this service into our controller using constructor injection.

The goal of this exercise is to refactor our simple web application to use Dependency Injection. We will create a GreetingService bean responsible for generating a greeting message and inject it into the RestController we created previously. This demonstrates how components are decoupled and wired together by the Spring container.

Building the application

We continue working with the project created in ***Chapter 2 - From Zero to Spring Hero: Your first application***.

Create a GreetingService Interface

1. In the **Projects** window of NetBeans, expand your project (**HelloSpringBoot**).
2. Right-click the main package node (e.g., **com.sharanamvaishali.helloboot**) under **Source Packages** and select **New → Java Package...**.

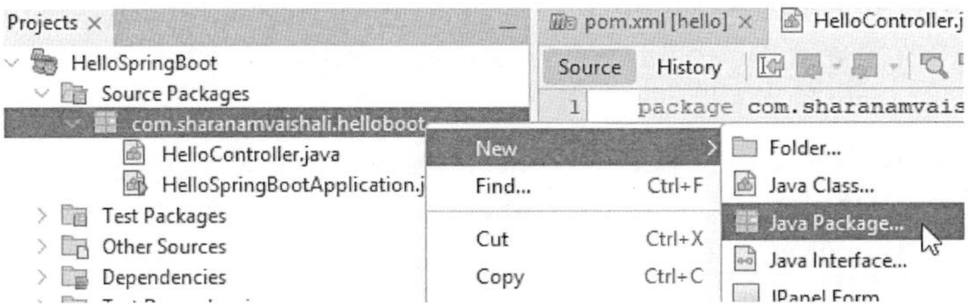

3. Enter **com.sharanamvaishali.helloboot.service** as the **Package Name** and click **Finish**.

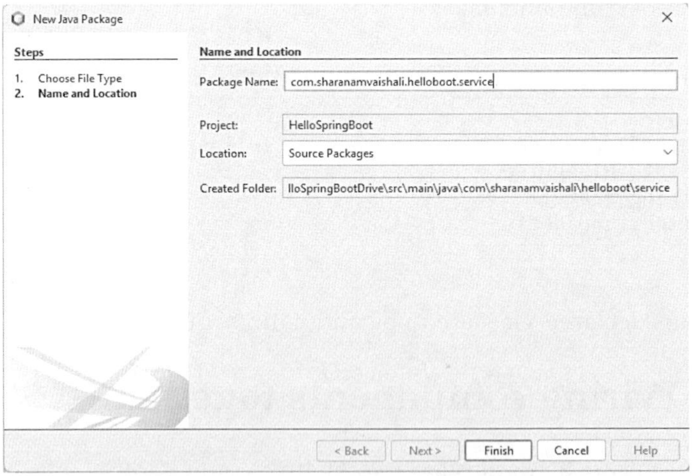

4. Right-click the new **com.sharanamvaishali.helloboot.service** package and select **New → Java Interface...**.

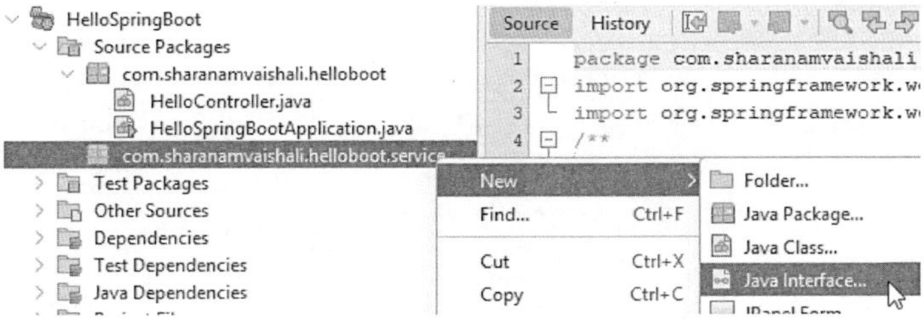

5. Enter **GreetingService** as the **Class Name** and click **Finish**.

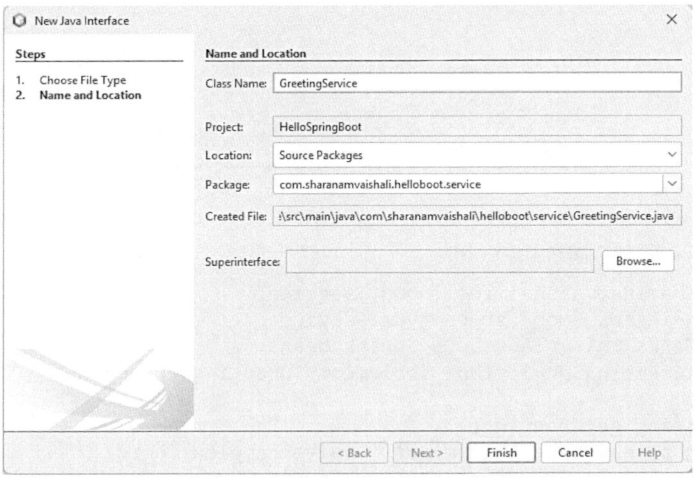

6. Open the GreetingService.java file and add a method signature:

```
package com.sharanamvaishali.helloboot.service;
public interface GreetingService {
    String getGreeting();
}
```

Create a GreetingService Implementation

1. Right-click the **com.sharanamvaishali.helloboot.service** package and select **New → Java Class....**
2. Enter **GreetingServiceImpl** as the **Class Name** and click **Finish**.

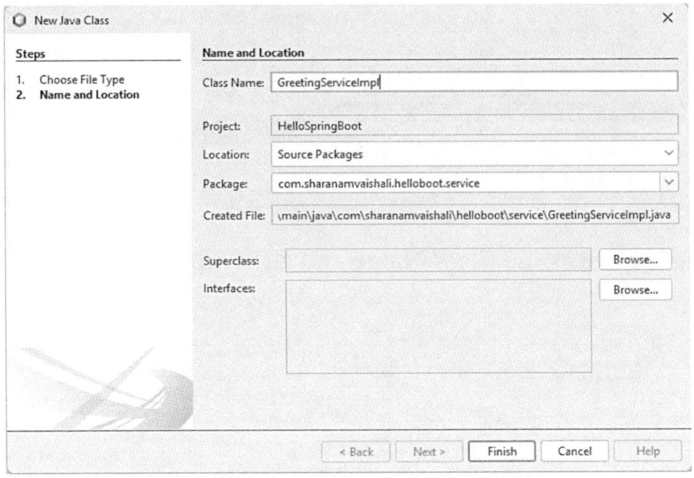

3. Open GreetingServiceImpl.java and implement the interface. Annotate the class with **@Service** to make it a Spring bean:

```
package com.sharanamvaishali.helloboot.service;
import org.springframework.stereotype.Service;
@Service // Marks this class as a Spring bean
public class GreetingServiceImpl implements GreetingService {
    @Override
    public String getGreeting() {
        // In a real app, this might involve complex logic
        return "Hello from the Greeting Service!";
    }
}
```

Modify the RestController

1. Navigate to the controller class created in ***Chapter 2 - From Zero to Spring Hero: Your first application*** (e.g., HelloController.java in the **com.sharanamvaishali.helloboot** package).
2. Add a private final field for the GreetingService.
3. Add a constructor that accepts GreetingService as a parameter and assigns it to the field. Spring automatically handles the **@Autowired** part for single constructors.
4. Store the injected service instance in the private final field.
5. Modify the handler method (e.g., sayHello) to call the getGreeting() method on the injected service and return its result.
6. The updated controller should look similar to this:

```
package com.sharanamvaishali.helloboot;
import com.sharanamvaishali.helloboot.service.GreetingService; // Import the service
import org.springframework.web.bind.annotation.GetMapping;
```

```
import org.springframework.web.bind.annotation.RestController;
@RestController
public class HelloController {
    // Field to hold the injected service
    private final GreetingService greetingService;
    // Constructor for Dependency Injection
    // @Autowired is implicit here as it's the only constructor
    public HelloController(GreetingService greetingService) {
        this.greetingService = greetingService;
    }
    @GetMapping("/")
    public String sayHello() {
        // Call the method on the injected service instance
        return greetingService.getGreeting();
    }
}
```

Code explanation:

- **private final GreetingService greetingService;:** This declares a **private and final field** named greetingService of type GreetingService.
  - **private:** This means greetingService can only be accessed from within the HelloController class, promoting encapsulation.
  - **final:** This means that once greetingService is initialized (which happens in the constructor), its reference cannot be changed. This is a good practice for dependency injection as it ensures the dependency is set only once.
- **public HelloController(GreetingService greetingService) { . . . }:** This is the **constructor** for the HelloController class.
  - It takes an argument of type GreetingService.
  - This is a prime example of **Dependency Injection (DI)**. When Spring creates an instance of HelloController, it automatically looks for a bean of type GreetingService in its application context and injects it into this constructor.
  - If a class has only one constructor, Spring's @Autowired annotation is implicitly applied to it, meaning you don't need to explicitly write @Autowired above the constructor.
  - Inside the constructor, this.greetingService = greetingService; assigns the injected GreetingService instance to the greetingService field of the HelloController class.
- **return greetingService.getGreeting();:** Inside the sayHello() method, this line calls the getGreeting() method on the greetingService instance (which was injected by Spring). Whatever String the getGreeting() method returns will be the response sent back to the client.

Bridging the gap: Learned concepts and application implementation

Let's connect the steps we took with the concepts learned:

- **@Service:** By annotating GreetingServiceImpl with **@Service**, we told the Spring IoC container to manage this class as a bean. Spring scans the project, finds this annotation, and creates an instance of GreetingServiceImpl.
- **Constructor Injection:** We added a constructor to HelloController that accepts a GreetingService parameter. This signals to Spring that HelloController depends on a GreetingService.
- **@Autowired (Implicit):** When Spring creates the HelloController bean, it sees the constructor dependency. It looks for a bean of type GreetingService in its context (it finds our GreetingServiceImpl bean). Because it's the only constructor, Spring automatically uses it for injection (autowiring), creating the GreetingServiceImpl instance and passing it to the HelloController constructor.
- **Decoupling:** HelloController now depends on the GreetingService interface, not the concrete GreetingServiceImpl class. This is loose coupling - we could create a different implementation of GreetingService (perhaps fetching the greeting from a database) and, as long as it's registered as a bean (maybe using **@Primary** or **@Qualifier** if multiple exist), the controller would work without modification.

Running and testing

1. Run the main application class (e.g., HelloSpringBootApplication.java) by right-clicking it and selecting **Run File**.
2. Observe the console output. You can see the familiar Spring Boot startup logs.

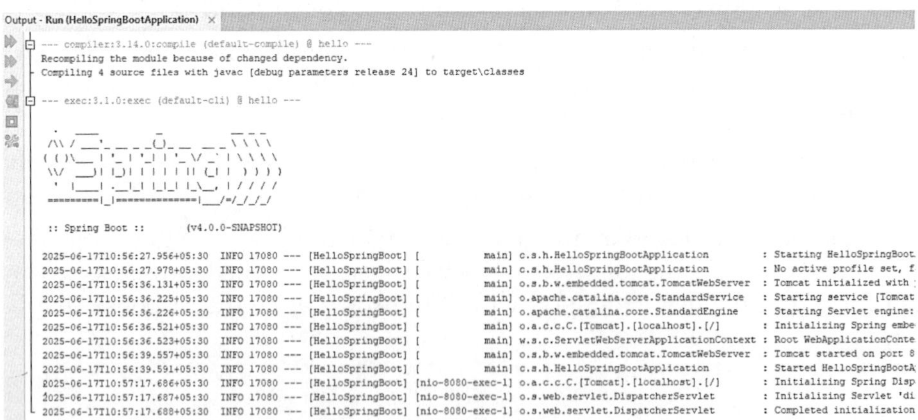

3. Open a web browser and navigate to **http://localhost:8080**.
4. You can now see the message: **Hello from the Greeting Service!** displayed on the page. This confirms that the controller received the request, used the **injected** service instance to get the greeting, and returned it as the response.

Exploring application behaviour: A practical run-through

Here's what happens behind the scenes when you run the application and make a request:

1. **Startup & component scan:** Spring Boot starts, creating the ApplicationContext. It scans the classpath (packages like **com.sharanamvaishali.helloboot** and its subpackages) for classes annotated with **@Component**, **@Service**, **@Repository**, **@Controller**, **@Configuration**, etc.
2. **Bean creation:** It finds GreetingServiceImpl annotated with **@Service** and HelloController annotated with **@RestController** (which includes **@Controller**, a type of **@Component**). It decides to create singleton instances of these beans.
3. **Dependency resolution & injection:** When creating the HelloController bean, Spring inspects its constructor. It sees a dependency on GreetingService. It looks up beans matching this type in the context and finds the GreetingServiceImpl bean instance it created earlier.
4. **Autowiring:** Spring **injects** the GreetingServiceImpl instance into HelloController by calling its constructor. The HelloController bean is now fully initialized with its dependency.
5. **Request handling:** When you access **http://localhost:8080**, the embedded Tomcat server receives the request. Spring MVC routes the request to the sayHello() method in the HelloController instance.
6. **Service call:** Inside sayHello(), the code greetingService.getGreeting() executes. This calls the method on the **injected** GreetingServiceImpl instance.
7. **Response:** GreetingServiceImpl returns the string "**Hello from the Greeting Service!**". The controller returns this string, which Spring MVC writes as the HTTP response body back to your browser.

Harnessing Dependency Injection in real-world contexts

Dependency Injection (DI) isn't just an academic concept; it's fundamental to building modern, maintainable applications:

- **Modularity:** DI encourages breaking down your application into smaller, focused components (beans) with clear responsibilities.
- **Loose coupling:** Components interact through interfaces or well-defined contracts, reducing dependencies on specific implementations. This makes the system more flexible and easier to change.
- **Testability:** DI makes unit testing significantly easier. You can easily create mock implementations of dependencies (like GreetingService) and inject them into the class under test (like HelloController) without needing a running Spring container.
- **Maintainability & refactoring:** Changes within one component are less likely to break others if the contract (interface) remains the same. Refactoring becomes simpler.
- **Managing complexity:** In large applications, manually managing the creation and wiring of hundreds of objects would be incredibly complex and error-prone. Spring's IoC container handles this reliably.

You use DI constantly when building Spring applications, injecting services into controllers, repositories into services, configuration properties into components, and so on. It forms the backbone of how different parts of your application collaborate.

Wrapping up

- The **Spring IoC container** (ApplicationContext) manages the lifecycle and dependencies of objects called **beans**.
- **Beans** are typically declared using stereotype annotations like **@Component**, **@Service**, **@Repository**, or **@Controller**.
- **Dependency Injection (DI)** is the process where the container provides beans with the dependencies they need.
- **Constructor Injection** is the preferred DI method for mandatory dependencies, promoting immutability and testability.
- **@Autowired** signals a dependency injection point, usually resolved by type.
- **@Configuration** and **@Bean** allow for Java-based bean definitions.
- Bean **scopes** (like **singleton** and **prototype**) control the number of instances created.

- DI leads to **loosely coupled**, **modular**, and more **testable** applications.

Congratulations! You've grasped the core concepts of the Spring IoC container and Dependency Injection – the foundation upon which the entire Spring ecosystem is built. You've seen how Spring manages your objects (beans) and wires them together, allowing you to focus on business logic rather than boilerplate plumbing. You practiced this by injecting a service bean into a controller, demonstrating loose coupling in action.

Let's proceed to our culmination chapter which guides you through building your first complete, standalone Spring application from scratch. You will build a simple command-line tool that reinforces your understanding of the Spring container, component scanning, and dependency injection.

Chapter 4

Section 01: Launching your Spring journey - Initial setup and first steps

Culmination: Building a Command-Line Quote Generator

What you'll learn

- Component scanning
- Dependency Injection
- Loose coupling
- CommandLineRunner

Congratulations on mastering the foundational concepts of the Spring Framework! You have learned about the core philosophy of Inversion of Control, seen how Dependency Injection works, and created your first Spring Boot web application. Now, it is time to put that theory into practice.

This chapter guides you through building your first complete, standalone Spring application from scratch. We will build a simple command-line tool that reinforces your understanding of the Spring container, component scanning, and dependency injection. This project intentionally leaves out web servers and databases to focus purely on how Spring manages and wires components together, a critical skill for any Java developer.

PRD: Quote of the day application

Before writing code, it is crucial to understand the requirements. For our project, the requirement is straightforward.

- **Requirement:** Create a console application that, when run, prints a random famous quote to the screen.
- **Key design principle:** The most important design consideration is that the source of the quotes should be easily swappable in the future without changing the main application logic. This means the part of our application that uses a quote should not know or care if the quote comes from a hardcoded list, a text file, or a remote web service. This is a classic scenario for applying the principle of loose coupling.

Hands-on: Developing the Quote Generator

In this hands-on section, we will build the application from the ground up. The primary focus is on how Spring discovers our components and automatically wires them together to form a functional application.

The goal of this exercise is to build a simple command-line application that prints a random quote. We will create two main components:

- A **service** responsible for providing the quotes.
- A **runner** that executes on startup to display a quote.

This exercise demonstrates Spring's core value proposition in a clean, simple context.

Building the application

Create a project

First, we need a new Spring Boot project:

1. In NetBeans, go to **File → New Project...**.
2. In the **Choose Project** dialog, select **Java with Maven** from the **Categories** list and **Spring Boot Initializr project** from the **Projects** list.
3. Click **Next**. In the **Base Properties** step:
    - Set **Group** to **com.sharanamvaishali** and **Artifact** to **quote**.
    - Keep the **Version** as it is (i.e. **0.0.1-SNAPSHOT**).

- Ensure **Packaging** is **Jar**.
- Set **Name** to **QuoteApp** and **Package Name** to **com.sharanamvaishali.quoteapp**.
- Select **Java** from the **Language** list and the appropriate **Java Version** (e.g., **24**).

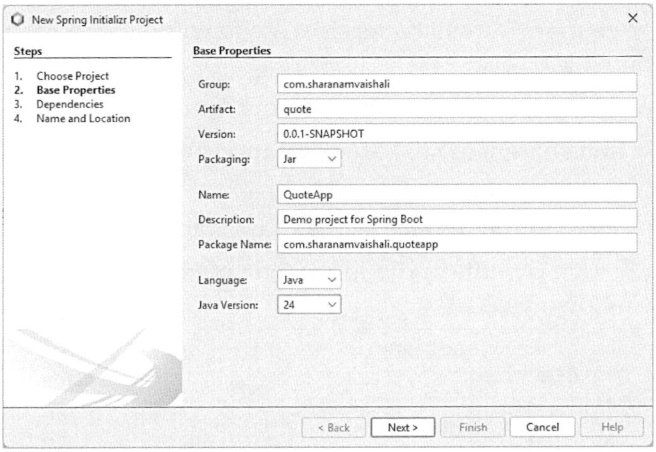

4. Click **Next**. In the **Dependencies** step:
   - Select the appropriate **Spring Boot Version** (e.g., **4.0.0 (SNAPSHOT)**).
   - In the **Available** dependencies list, find and select **Spring Web**.
5. Click **Next**. In the **Name and Location** step:
   - Set **Project Name** to **QuoteAppDrive**.
   - Choose a suitable **Project Location**.

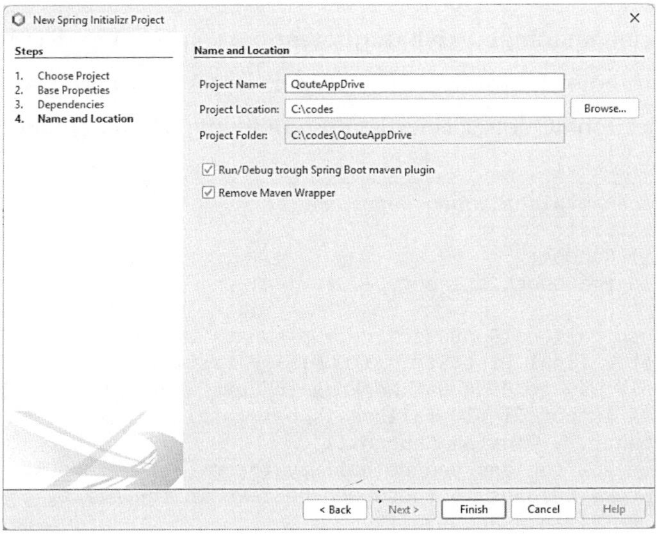

6. Click **Finish**. NetBeans generates the project structure and downloads dependencies.

Define the QuoteService Interface

An interface defines a contract for what a service can do without specifying *how* it does it. This is the key to loose coupling:

1. In the **Projects** window of NetBeans, expand your **QuoteApp** project.
2. Right-click the **com.sharanamvaishali.quoteapp** package and select **New → Java Interface....**
3. In the dialog box, enter **QuoteService** as the **Class Name** and click **Finish**.
4. Open the QuoteService.java file and add a single method signature to it. Replace the file content with the following code:

```
package com.sharanamvaishali.quoteapp;
public interface QuoteService {
    String getQuote();
}
```

Code explanation:
This interface declares a single method, getQuote(). Any class that claims to be a QuoteService must provide an implementation for this method.

Create an Implementation for the Service

Now, we create a concrete class that fulfills the QuoteService contract. This class will contain our list of quotes:

1. Right-click the **com.sharanamvaishali.quoteapp** package and select **New → Java Class....**
2. In the dialog box, enter **InspirationalQuoteService** as the **Class Name** and click **Finish**.
3. Open the InspirationalQuoteService.java file and replace its content with the following code:

```
package com.sharanamvaishali.quoteapp;
import java.util.List;
import java.util.Random;
import org.springframework.stereotype.Service;
@Service
public class InspirationalQuoteService implements QuoteService {
    private static final List<String> QUOTES = List.of(
        "The only way to do great work is to love what you do. - Steve Jobs",
        "Success is not final, failure is not fatal: it is the courage to continue
        that counts. - Winston Churchill",
        "Believe you can and you're halfway there. - Theodore Roosevelt",
        "The future belongs to those who believe in the beauty of their
        dreams. - Eleanor Roosevelt"
```

```
    );
    private final Random random = new Random();
    @Override
    public String getQuote() {
        return QUOTES.get(random.nextInt(QUOTES.size()));
    }
}
```

Code explanation:

- **@Service:** This is a stereotype annotation that tells Spring this class is a special component. Spring will create an instance of this class (a bean) and manage it in its container.
- **implements QuoteService:** This class promises to fulfill the contract defined by our QuoteService interface.
- **getQuote():** This is the implementation of the method. It simply selects a random quote from our hardcoded List.

Create a CommandLineRunner Component

We need a component that runs when the application starts. Spring Boot provides a convenient interface called CommandLineRunner for this exact purpose:

1. Right-click the **com.sharanamvaishali.quoteapp** package and select **New → Java Class...**.
2. Enter **QuoteApplicationRunner** as the **Class Name** and click **Finish**.
3. Open the QuoteApplicationRunner.java file and replace its content with the following code:

```
package com.sharanamvaishali.quoteapp;
import org.springframework.boot.CommandLineRunner;
import org.springframework.stereotype.Component;
@Component
public class QuoteApplicationRunner implements CommandLineRunner {
    private final QuoteService quoteService;
    public QuoteApplicationRunner(QuoteService quoteService) {
        this.quoteService = quoteService;
    }
    @Override
    public void run(String... args) throws Exception {
        System.out.println("--- Your Inspirational Quote of the Day ---");
        System.out.println(quoteService.getQuote());
        System.out.println("-------------------------------------------");
    }
}
```

Code explanation:

- **@Component:** This is a generic stereotype annotation that marks this class as a Spring-managed bean.

- **implements CommandLineRunner:** This tells Spring Boot that this bean has a run() method that should be executed after the application context is loaded.
- **private final QuoteService quoteService;:** This declares that our runner has a dependency—it **needs** a QuoteService to do its job.
- **public QuoteApplicationRunner(QuoteService quoteService):** This is a constructor that accepts a QuoteService. This is the constructor injection point. When Spring creates an instance of QuoteApplicationRunner, it will see this constructor and know it needs to find a QuoteService bean to pass into it.
- **run(String... args):** This is the method from the CommandLineRunner interface. The logic inside this method is what executes when the application starts. Here, we call the getQuote() method on our injected service and print the result to the console.

Running and testing

Let's see our application in action:

1. In the **Projects** window, right-click the **QuoteApp** project and select **Run**.
2. Observe the **Output** window in NetBeans. After the Spring Boot startup logs, you see a random quote printed neatly to the console.

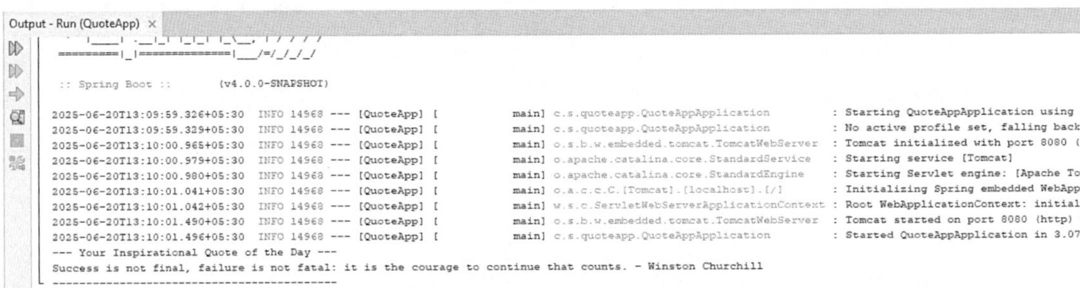

3. Run the application again. A different quote appears. This confirms our random selection logic is working.

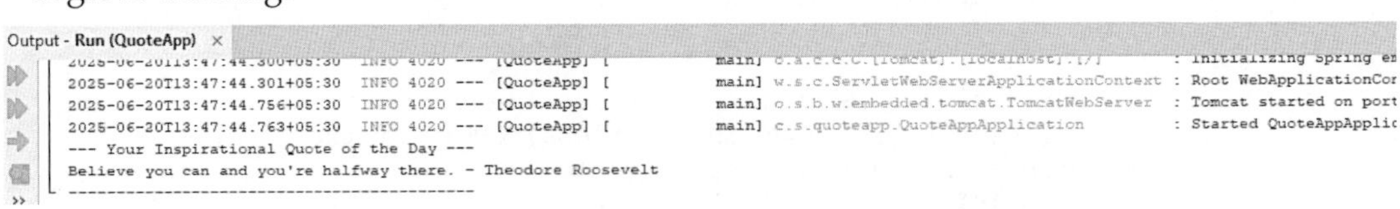

Bridging the gap: Learned concepts and application implementation

This simple application beautifully demonstrates the core concepts from the previous chapters.

- **Component scanning:** When the application starts, Spring scans the **com.sharanamvaishali.quoteapp** package. It finds the InspirationalQuoteService class annotated with @Service and the QuoteApplicationRunner class annotated with @Component. It then creates instances (beans) of both classes to manage in its IoC container.
- **Dependency injection:** Spring sees that QuoteApplicationRunner has a constructor that requires a QuoteService bean. It then looks in its container, finds the InspirationalQuoteService bean (which matches the QuoteService interface), and automatically "injects" or provides that instance to the runner's constructor. This is constructor injection in action.
- **Loose coupling:** QuoteApplicationRunner does not know or care about the InspirationalQuoteService class specifically. It only depends on the QuoteService interface. We could create FunnyQuoteService and, without changing a single line of code in the runner, Spring could inject that new service instead. This makes our application flexible and easy to maintain.

Exploring application behaviour: A practical run-through

What just happened behind the scenes is the magic of Spring. When you clicked **Run**, NetBeans compiled the code and started the Java Virtual Machine, executing the main() method in QuoteAppApplication.java. This started the Spring Boot application:

1. Spring scanned the project's classpath for components.
2. It found InspirationalQuoteService and QuoteApplicationRunner.
3. It detected that QuoteApplicationRunner needed QuoteService in its constructor.
4. It found that the InspirationalQuoteService bean satisfied this dependency.
5. Spring first created an instance of InspirationalQuoteService.
6. Then, it created an instance of QuoteApplicationRunner, passing the service instance into its constructor.
7. Finally, because QuoteApplicationRunner is a CommandLineRunner, Spring automatically executed its run method, which printed the quote to your console.

Harnessing Core Spring in real-world contexts

The simple pattern you just built—defining behaviour in a service component and injecting that service into another component that uses it—is the absolute foundation of virtually all Spring applications.

While our example is a command-line tool, this exact same pattern is used to build:

- **Background job processors:** A runner could kick off a complex task like processing a large file.
- **Data import/export tools:** A tool that reads from a CSV file and injects a service to save data to a database.
- **Scheduled tasks**: Using a different annotation (@Scheduled), a service method can be configured to run periodically (e.g., every night at 2 AM).
- **The Service layer of web applications:** In a web application, a controller will inject a service to handle business logic, just like our runner injected the QuoteService.

Wrapping up

This chapter was a major step in your journey. You built a complete application that reinforces the most critical Spring concepts. Here are the key takeaways:

- You created a standalone Spring Boot application without web dependencies.
- You used the @Component and @Service annotations to mark classes as Spring-managed beans.
- You implemented constructor-based dependency injection to wire components together.
- You learned how to use the CommandLineRunner interface to execute code on application startup.
- You practiced the principle of loose coupling by depending on an interface (QuoteService) rather than a concrete implementation.

Excellent work! You have successfully built a complete, non-trivial Spring application that showcases the power and simplicity of the Spring IoC container. You have moved from theory to practice and now have a solid mental model of how Spring discovers, instantiates, and wires your application components together. This pattern of services and components is one you will use time and time again.

Now that you have a firm grasp of the core container, it is time to address a fundamental need of almost every real-world application: persistence. In the next part of this book, we will explore how to store and retrieve data from a database using the Jakarta Persistence API (JPA) and its leading implementation, Hibernate. You'll learn about the challenges of storing Java objects in relational databases and how technologies like the Jakarta Persistence API (JPA) and Hibernate provide powerful solutions. Get ready to connect your Spring Boot application to a database!

Chapter 5

Section 02: Persistence with Hibernate and Spring Data JPA

Introduction to Persistence

What you'll learn

- Persistence challenges
- Object-Relational Mapping (ORM)
- Jakarta Persistence API (JPA)
- Hibernate: The leading JPA implementation
- Choosing your database
- Setting up the database connectivity

Welcome to the part of our journey where our application gets a memory. So far, the applications we have hinted at or built have a fleeting existence; when they stop, all the data they worked with vanishes. In the real world, applications need to store information permanently, whether it's a list of users, products in a catalogue, or tasks in a to-do list. This is where persistence comes in. But storing Java objects, with their complex relationships and behaviours, into the rigid, tabular structure of a relational database is not a straightforward task.

This chapter introduces the concepts and tools, specifically the Jakarta Persistence API (JPA) and Hibernate, that solve this very problem, allowing you to save your application's data reliably and efficiently.

The challenge of storing objects in relational databases

In an object-oriented language like Java, we model our world using objects. A Book object might have attributes like a **title** and an **author**, and it could have relationships, such as a list of Review objects associated with it. Relational databases, on the other hand, think in terms of tables, rows, and columns. A books table would have columns like **title** and **author_name**.

The fundamental differences in these two models lead to a problem known as the **Object-Relational Impedance Mismatch**. How do you represent an object hierarchy with inheritance in a flat table structure? How do you manage the "has-a" or "is-a" relationships between objects using foreign keys? Manually writing Java Database Connectivity (JDBC) code to translate between these two worlds is tedious, error-prone, and results in a lot of boilerplate code that is difficult to maintain.

Object-Relational Mapping (ORM) as a solution

This is where Object-Relational Mapping (ORM) comes to the rescue. ORM is a programming technique for converting data between the object-oriented model used in our Java application and the relational model used by the database.

An ORM framework acts as a powerful translator, automating the work of mapping object attributes to table columns and managing object relationships. This allows developers to work with Java objects naturally, while the ORM framework handles the complex SQL operations behind the scenes.

Introduction to Jakarta Persistence API (JPA)

To avoid being locked into a single ORM vendor, the Java community created a standard specification called the Jakarta Persistence API, or JPA. JPA, as part of the Jakarta EE platform, is not a tool or a framework itself; it is a set of guidelines, interfaces, and annotations (@Entity, @Id, etc.) that define the standard way to perform ORM in Java.

By writing our code against the JPA specification, we can switch between different ORM frameworks with minimal code changes, ensuring our application remains portable.

Key concepts defined by JPA include:

- **Entity:** A simple Java class that is "mapped" to a table in the database.
- **EntityManager:** An interface for interacting with the persistence context, allowing us to save, update, find, and delete entities.

- **Persistence context:** A set of managed entity instances where changes are tracked. When a transaction is committed, these changes are written to the database.

Introducing Hibernate: The leading JPA implementation

While JPA defines the **what** (the API), we still need a tool that provides the **how** (the implementation). Hibernate is the most mature, feature-rich, and widely used implementation of the Jakarta Persistence API. When we use JPA annotations in our Spring Boot application, Hibernate is the engine working in the background to translate our object operations into SQL commands for the database.

Choosing your database

Spring Boot makes it easy to connect to various databases, and for development, you have several convenient choices:

- **In-memory databases (H2):** These databases run entirely in your computer's memory. They are incredibly fast to start up and require no external installation, making them perfect for development, running tests, and quick prototypes. The downside is that all data is lost when the application shuts down.
- **File-based databases (Apache Derby Embedded):** These databases store data in a file, typically within your project's directory. They provide persistence between application restarts without needing a separate database server process, offering a simple middle ground.
- **Server databases (MySQL, PostgreSQL, etc.):** These are the robust, scalable, and feature-rich databases you would use in a production environment. They run as separate server processes that your application connects to over a network.

Setting up database connectivity with Spring Boot

One of Spring Boot's most powerful features is auto-configuration. To connect to a database, you typically do not need to write complex configuration code. Instead, you perform two main steps:

1. Add the necessary dependencies for your chosen database and for data access.
2. Define the connection properties (like the database URL, username, and password) in the **application.properties** file.

Spring Boot detects these dependencies and properties and automatically configures everything needed to connect your application to the database, including a connection pool and the Hibernate JPA implementation.

Hands-on: Setting up persistence dependencies and configuration

In this hands-on section, we will modify the project from the previous ***Chapter 3 - Wiring up your application: Dependency Injection with Spring*** to include persistence capabilities. We will add the required Spring Data JPA and Hibernate dependencies and configure our application to connect to an H2 in-memory database. We will also prepare (but leave disabled) the configurations for connecting to external MySQL database to see how easy it is to switch between them.

Building the application

We will continue working with the project created in ***Chapter 3 - Wiring up your application: Dependency Injection with Spring***.

Add the Spring Boot Starter for Data JPA dependency

The **spring-boot-starter-data-jpa** dependency brings in everything we need for persistence, including Spring Data, Hibernate, and the standard JPA APIs:

1. In the **Projects** window, expand your project. Right-click **Dependencies** and select **Add Dependency....**

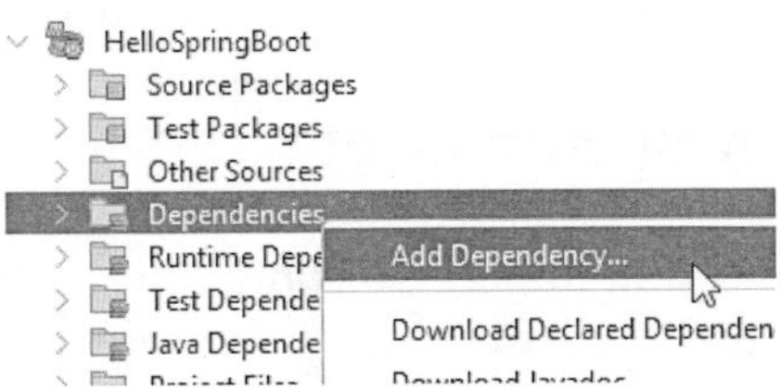

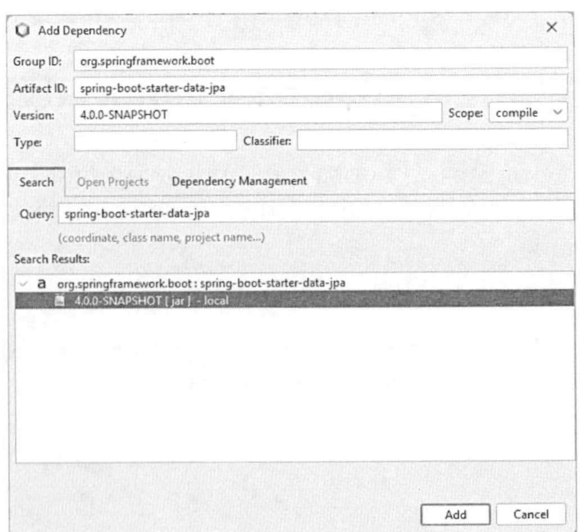

2. In the **Add Dependency** dialog box, enter **spring-boot-starter-data-jpa** in the **Query** textbox. NetBeans searches for the dependency. Select the entry under the **org.springframework.boot:spring-boot-starter-data-jpa** group and click **Add**.
3. The starter for data JPA JAR file now appears under **Dependencies**.

Add the H2 Database dependency

Next, we need the specific JDBC driver for the H2 database:

1. Right-click **Dependencies** and select **Add Dependency....**
2. In the **Query** textbox, enter **h2**. Select the entry **com.h2database:h2**. Click **Add**.
3. The H2 driver JAR file appears under **Dependencies**.

Configure H2 and JPA settings in application.properties

Now, we tell Spring Boot how to connect to our H2 database and how Hibernate should behave:

1. In the **Projects** window, navigate to **Other Sources → src/main/resources → <default package>**.

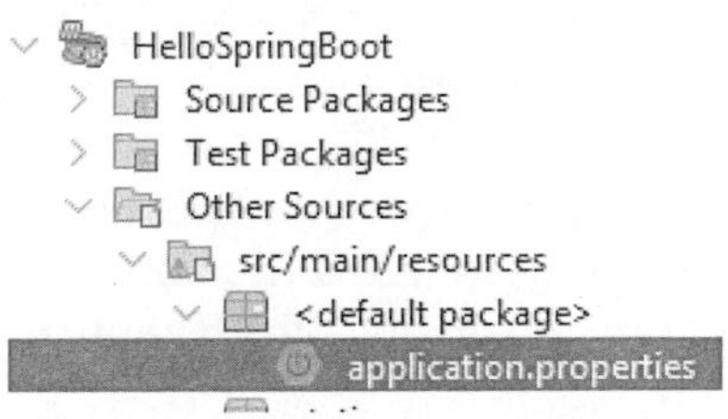

2. Open the application.properties file and add the following lines to the file:

```
# H2 Database Configuration
spring.datasource.url=jdbc:h2:mem:testdb
spring.h2.console.enabled=true
# JPA/Hibernate Configuration
spring.jpa.hibernate.ddl-auto=update
spring.jpa.show-sql=true
```

Let's break down these properties:

- **spring.datasource.url:** The JDBC connection string for the H2 database. It tells Spring to use an in-memory (**mem**) database named **testdb**.
- **spring.h2.console.enabled:** This incredibly useful property enables a web-based database console, allowing us to view the database contents and run SQL queries directly from our browser.

- **spring.jpa.hibernate.ddl-auto:** This tells Hibernate how to manage the database schema. We set it to **update**, which means Hibernate will create or update the database tables based on our entity classes when the application starts. Other common values are **create-drop** (creates the schema on startup and drops it on shutdown), **validate** (checks if the tables match the entities), and **none** (does nothing). Using **update** or **create-drop** is great for development but should be avoided in production in favor of **validate** or **none**.
- **spring.jpa.show-sql:** This property is helpful for debugging, as it instructs Hibernate to print the SQL statements it generates to the console.

Running and testing

Let's run the application to verify that our persistence layer is correctly configured:

1. Ensure that only the H2 dependencies and properties are active in your project.
2. Right-click your project in the **Projects** window and select **Run**.

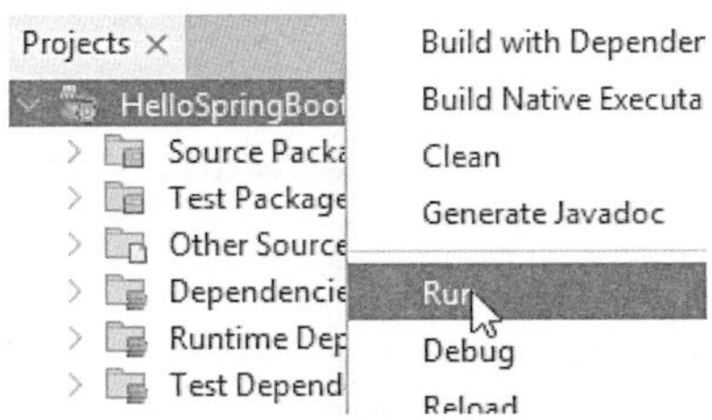

3. Observe the **Output** window. You can see log messages from Hibernate as it initializes. Look for lines indicating a connection to the **jdbc:h2:mem:testdb** database and the use of the **H2Dialect**. You will not see any errors, which confirms the setup is successful.

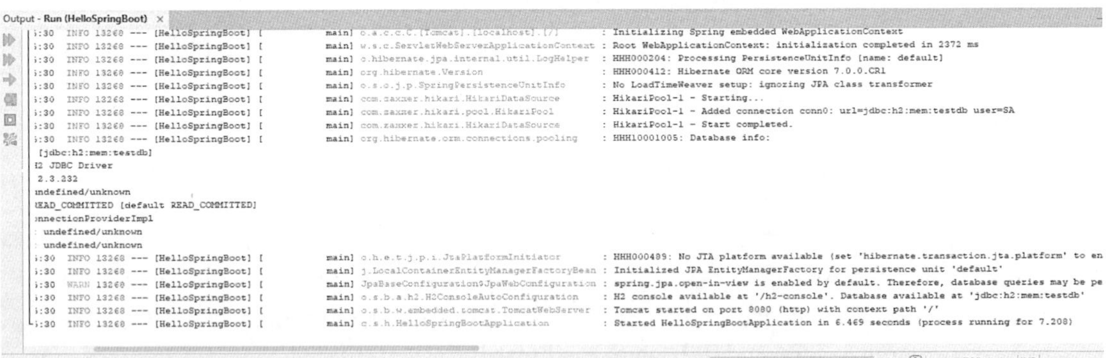

4. Now, open a web browser and navigate to **http://localhost:8080/h2-console**.

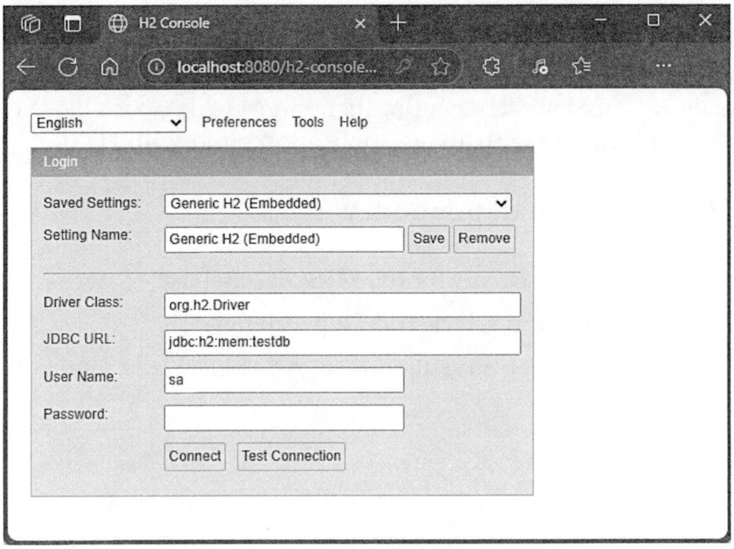

5. On the H2 Console login page, ensure the **JDBC URL** field matches the one in your properties file: **jdbc:h2:mem:testdb**. Leave the username as **sa** and the password blank.
6. Click **Connect**. You are connected to your application's live, in-memory database. Since we have not defined any entity classes yet, the schema will be empty, but the ability to connect confirms that our entire persistence stack is up and running.

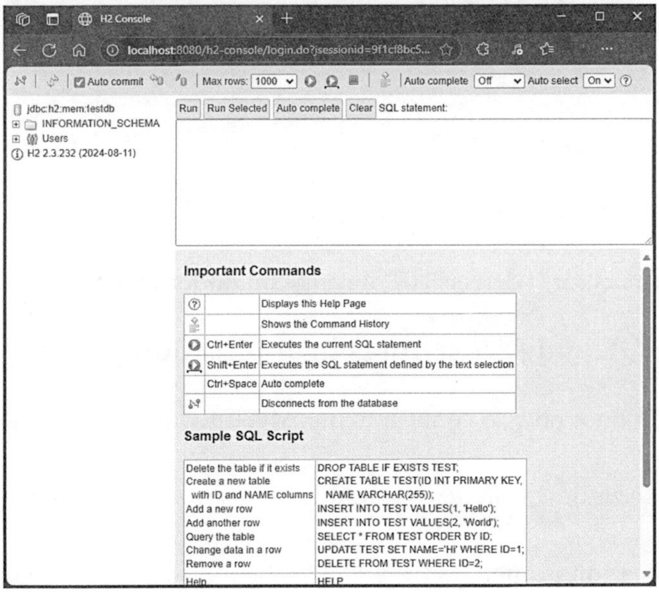

Prepare configuration for MySQL

To show how easily we could switch to a production-grade database like MySQL, let's add its configuration. We will continue with above application build with H2 database connectivity.

Add the MySQL Database dependency

Next, we need the specific JDBC driver for the MySQL database:

1. Right-click **Dependencies** and select **Add Dependency....**
2. In the **Query** textbox, enter **mysql-connector-j**. Select the entry **com.mysql:mysql-connector-j**. Click **Add**.

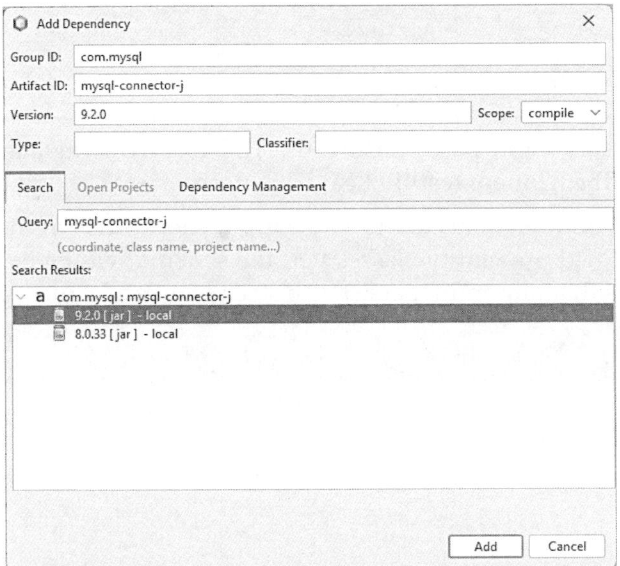

3. The MySQL Connector/J driver JAR file appears under **Dependencies**.

Configure MySQL and JPA settings in application.properties

Now, we tell Spring Boot how to connect to our MySQL database and how Hibernate should behave:

1. In the **Projects** window, navigate to **Other Sources → src/main/resources → <default package>**.
2. Open the **application.properties** file and add the following lines to the file:

```
# -- MySQL Configuration --
```

```
spring.datasource.url=jdbc:mysql://localhost:3306/bookstore_db?useSSL=false
                      &serverTimezone=UTC
spring.datasource.username=<Your MySQL User>
spring.datasource.password=<Your MySQL Password>
# -- JPA/Hibernate Configuration --
spring.jpa.hibernate.ddl-auto=update
```

3. Comment out the H2 properties.

> To use this, you must have a MySQL server running, have created a database (e.g., **bookstore_db**), and have a user with the correct permissions.
>
> Replace **<YOUR MySQL User>** and **<YOUR MySQL Password>** with your actual MySQL user and password.

Running and testing

Let's run the application to verify that our persistence layer is correctly configured:

1. Ensure that only the MySQL Connector/J dependencies and properties are active in your project.
2. Right-click your project in the **Projects** window and select **Run**.
3. Observe the **Output** window. You will not see any errors, which confirms the setup is successful.

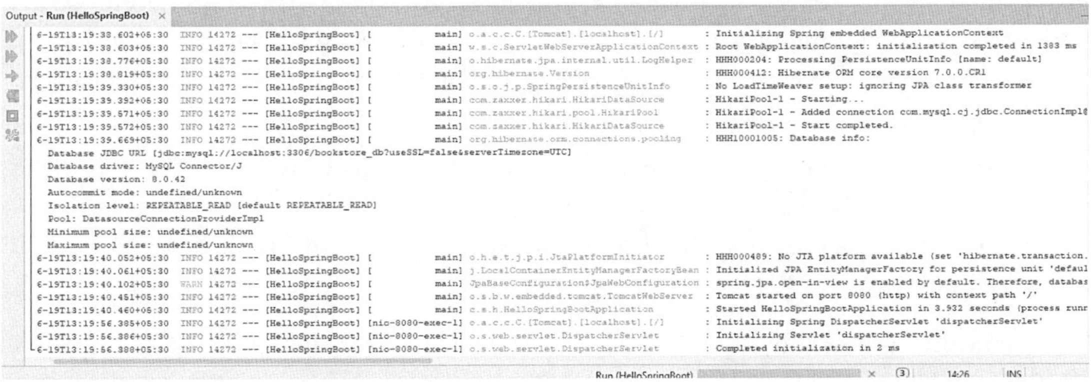

Bridging the gap: Learned concepts and application implementation

This hands-on exercise directly translates our theoretical discussion into a working setup:

- **JPA and Hibernate APIs:** Adding the **spring-boot-starter-data-jpa** dependency pulled in all the necessary libraries for persistence without us having to find and manage them individually.
- **Database drivers:** By including the **com.h2database:h2** dependency, we made the H2 JDBC driver available on the application's classpath. Spring Boot detects this and knows how to communicate with an H2 database. If we had activated the MySQL configuration, its corresponding **mysql-connector-j** driver would be used instead.
- **Configuration:** All the critical details for our database connection—the URL, the driver (often inferred by Spring Boot but can be set explicitly), and the Hibernate dialect—are neatly organized in the **application.properties** file. This demonstrates Spring Boot's powerful convention-over-configuration approach, where it makes intelligent defaults but allows us to override them easily.

Exploring application behaviour: A practical run-through

When you click Run, Spring Boot's auto-configuration springs into action. It scans the classpath, finds the Spring Data JPA starter and the H2 driver or the mysql-connector-j driver, and reads the application.properties file. Based on this information, it automatically:

1. Configures a DataSource, which manages a pool of database connections for efficiency.
2. Identifies Hibernate as the JPA provider.
3. Creates and configures a Hibernate EntityManagerFactory, which is the core factory responsible for creating EntityManager instances for our application to use.
4. Enables the H2 console at the **/h2-console** web endpoint (If H2 database is used and connected).

The application is now fully equipped to perform database operations, waiting for us to define the data model.

Harnessing multi-database configuration in real-world contexts

The ability to easily switch database configurations is not just a convenience; it is a critical practice in modern software development.

- **Portability:** Your application is not tied to a specific database vendor. It can be deployed across various environments that may use different database systems.
- **Environment-specific setups:** You can use a fast, in-memory H2 database for local development and automated tests, but deploy the exact same application code to a production environment that connects to a robust PostgreSQL or MySQL database.
- **Simplified onboarding**: New developers can get the project running on their machine without having to install and configure a full database server, simply by using the default H2 or Derby profile.

This flexibility is a cornerstone of building professional, maintainable applications with Spring Boot.

Wrapping up

This chapter laid the essential foundation for data persistence in our application. You have bridged the conceptual gap between Java objects and database tables and configured the tools to do the heavy lifting for you.

- The Object-Relational Impedance Mismatch is the core problem ORM solves.
- JPA is the standard Java API for persistence, while Hibernate is the leading implementation.
- Spring Boot drastically simplifies database setup with the spring-boot-starter-data-jpa and auto-configuration.
- All database connection details are managed within the application.properties file.
- Using an in-memory database like H2 is ideal for rapid development and testing.

Congratulations on configuring the persistence layer! You have successfully integrated a database into your Spring Boot application and can now connect to it and see it live through the H2 console. The groundwork is complete.

In the next chapter, ***Mapping Your Data with JPA Entities***, we will build on this setup by creating our first JPA @Entity class. You will see firsthand how Hibernate uses this class to automatically generate a database table, truly bringing your application's data model to life.

Chapter 6

Section 02: Persistence with Hibernate and Spring Data JPA

Mapping your data with JPA Entities

What you'll learn

- What is an entity?
- Defining persistence objects
- Mapping primary keys
- Mapping basic attributes
- Handling date/time
- Understanding relationships
- Embedding objects
- Using Lombok

In the world of modern Java development, especially when building applications that interact with databases, bridging the gap between your application's object-oriented structure and the relational database's tabular structure is a common challenge. This is where Object-Relational Mapping, or ORM, comes into play. Jakarta Persistence API, often abbreviated as JPA, provides a standard, powerful way to define how your Java objects map to database tables. Hibernate, which you explore in this book, is the most widely used implementation of JPA. This chapter delves into the core concepts of JPA entities, showing you how to define the very foundation of your application's data layer.

The Entity class (@Entity) - Defining persistent objects

At the heart of JPA is the concept of an **entity**. An entity is a lightweight, persistent domain object. In simple terms, it is a regular Java class that corresponds to a table in your database. When you mark a Java class as a JPA entity, you tell the JPA provider (like Hibernate) that instances of this class can be stored in and retrieved from a database.

You designate a class as an entity by annotating it with **@jakarta.persistence.Entity**. This annotation signifies that the class represents a database table and that its instances are persistent. By default, the name of the database table will be the same as the class name. For example, a class named **Book** annotated with **@Entity** typically maps to a table named **Book**:

```
import jakarta.persistence.Entity;
// Other imports as needed
@Entity
public class Book {
    // fields and methods
}
```

Mapping the Primary Key (@Id, @GeneratedValue strategies)

Every table in a relational database requires a **primary key**, a column or set of columns that uniquely identifies each row. Similarly, every JPA entity must define a primary key. You designate a field as the primary key of an entity by annotating it with **@jakarta.persistence.Id**.

Often, database primary keys are generated automatically by the database itself. JPA provides the **@jakarta.persistence.GeneratedValue** annotation to specify the strategy for primary key generation. The **strategy** attribute of **@GeneratedValue** takes a **GenerationType** enum value. Common strategies include:

- **GenerationType.AUTO:** (Default) The JPA provider chooses the appropriate generation strategy based on the database you are using.
- **GenerationType.IDENTITY:** This strategy relies on the database's identity column feature (e.g., AUTO_INCREMENT in MySQL, IDENTITY in H2, SERIAL in PostgreSQL). The primary key is generated by the database upon insertion.
- **GenerationType.SEQUENCE:** This strategy uses a database sequence to generate primary key values. This is common in databases like Oracle and PostgreSQL. You can configure the sequence name and other properties using the @SequenceGenerator annotation.

- **GenerationType.TABLE:** This strategy uses a special database table to store and manage primary key values. While highly portable, it generally has performance overhead compared to database-native strategies. You can configure the table and column names using the @TableGenerator annotation.

For most modern applications, **IDENTITY** or **SEQUENCE** are preferred due to their efficiency and reliance on database-native mechanisms. For simplicity and common use cases, **IDENTITY** is a popular choice for beginners, especially with databases like H2 or MySQL.

For example:

```
import jakarta.persistence.Entity;
import jakarta.persistence.Id;
import jakarta.persistence.GeneratedValue;
import jakarta.persistence.GenerationType;
@Entity
public class Product {
    @Id
    @GeneratedValue(strategy = GenerationType.IDENTITY)
    private Long id;
    // other fields
}
```

Mapping basic attributes (@Column, data types, nullability)

After defining the primary key, you map the other fields of your entity class to columns in the database table. By default, every non-static, non-transient field in an entity class is mapped to a column in the corresponding table. The column name usually matches the field name.

You can customize this mapping using the **@jakarta.persistence.Column** annotation. This annotation provides several attributes to fine-tune column properties:

- **name:** Specifies the exact name of the database column if it differs from the field name.
- **length:** Defines the length of the column for String types.
- **nullable:** A boolean indicating whether the column can store NULL values (defaults to **true**). Set this to **false** for non-nullable columns.
- **unique:** A boolean indicating whether the column must contain unique values (defaults to **false**). Set this to **true** for columns that should have unique entries, such as an ISBN number.
- **precision:** Used for numeric types to define the total number of digits.
- **scale:** Used for numeric types to define the number of digits after the decimal point.

Here is an example demonstrating **@Column**:

```
import jakarta.persistence.Entity;
import jakarta.persistence.Id;
import jakarta.persistence.GeneratedValue;
import jakarta.persistence.GenerationType;
import jakarta.persistence.Column;
@Entity
public class User {
    @Id
    @GeneratedValue(strategy = GenerationType.IDENTITY)
    private Long id;
    @Column(name = "user_name", length = 100, nullable = false)
    private String name;
    @Column(unique = true, nullable = false)
    private String email;
    // other fields
}
```

JPA automatically handles the mapping of standard Java primitive types and their wrapper classes (like **int**, **long**, **String**, **boolean**, **double**, etc.) to appropriate database data types.

Mapping Temporal types (JPA 3.1 Date/Time handling - LocalDate, LocalDateTime)

Handling dates and times is a common requirement in applications. Jakarta Persistence API 3.1 (part of Jakarta EE 10) fully embraces the Java 8 Date and Time API, making it much easier to work with modern date/time types like **LocalDate**, **LocalDateTime**, and **Instant**.

You typically do not need special annotations for these types; JPA providers like Hibernate automatically map them to appropriate database date/time types.

- **LocalDate:** Maps to a database **DATE** type (year, month, day).
- **LocalTime:** Maps to a database **TIME** type (hour, minute, second).
- **LocalDateTime:** Maps to a database column that stores both date and time (year, month, day, hour, minute, second, nanosecond) without time zone information.
- **Instant:** Maps to a database column that stores a point in time on the timeline, suitable for UTC (Coordinated Universal Time) semantics.

For example:

```
import jakarta.persistence.Entity;
import jakarta.persistence.Id;
import jakarta.persistence.GeneratedValue;
import jakarta.persistence.GenerationType;
```

```
import java.time.LocalDate;
import java.time.LocalDateTime;
@Entity
public class Event {
    @Id
    @GeneratedValue(strategy = GenerationType.IDENTITY)
    private Long id;
    private String name;
    private LocalDate eventDate; // Maps to a date column
    private LocalDateTime eventTimestamp; // Maps to a timestamp column
    // Getters and setters
}
```

Mapping Relationships

Relational databases are all about relationships between tables. JPA allows you to model these relationships directly within your Java entities. This section provides a conceptual overview of two common relationship types: Many-to-One and One-to-Many.

Many-To-One (@ManyToOne)

A Many-to-One relationship indicates that many instances of one entity can be associated with a single instance of another entity. For example, many **Book** entities can be associated with one **Author** entity. In the database, this is typically represented by a foreign key in the "many" side's table pointing to the primary key of the "one" side's table. You annotate the field on the "many" side with **@jakarta.persistence.ManyToOne**.

For example:

```
import jakarta.persistence.Entity;
import jakarta.persistence.Id;
import jakarta.persistence.GeneratedValue;
import jakarta.persistence.GenerationType;
import jakarta.persistence.ManyToOne;
@Entity
public class Book {
    @Id
    @GeneratedValue(strategy = GenerationType.IDENTITY)
    private Long id;
    private String title;
    @ManyToOne
    private Author author; // Many books can have one author
    // Getters and setters
}
@Entity
public class Author {
```

```
    @Id
    @GeneratedValue(strategy = GenerationType.IDENTITY)
    private Long id;
    private String name;
    // Getters and setters, usually a collection of books here (not shown here)
}
```

One-to-Many (@OneToMany)

A One-to-Many relationship is the inverse of Many-to-One. One instance of an entity can be associated with multiple instances of another entity. For example, one **Author** can write many **Book** entities. You annotate the field on the "one" side with **@jakarta.persistence.OneToMany**. This annotation is typically used with collections.

For example:

```
import jakarta.persistence.Entity;
import jakarta.persistence.Id;
import jakarta.persistence.GeneratedValue;
import jakarta.persistence.GenerationType;
import jakarta.persistence.OneToMany;
import java.util.Set; // Or List, etc.
@Entity
public class Author {
    @Id
    @GeneratedValue(strategy = GenerationType.IDENTITY)
    private Long id;
    private String name;
    // 'author' is the field in the Book entity that owns the relationship
    @OneToMany(mappedBy = "author")
    private Set<Book> books; // One author can have many books
    // Getters and setters
}
```

Other relationship types include:

- **One-to-One (@OneToOne):** One instance of an entity is associated with exactly one instance of another entity.
- **Many-to-Many (@ManyToMany):** Many instances of one entity are associated with many instances of another entity. This typically requires an intermediate join table in the database.

Embedding objects (@Embeddable, @Embedded)

Sometimes, you have a set of attributes that logically belong together but do not warrant their own separate database table. For instance, an address (street, city, zip code) might be a component of a **Customer** entity, but you do not need a separate **Address** table. JPA provides a way to embed such objects within an entity using **@Embeddable** and **@Embedded**.

- **@jakarta.persistence.Embeddable:** You annotate a class with **@Embeddable** to mark it as a class whose instances can be embedded within other entities. It does not have its own identity or table.
- **@jakarta.persistence.Embedded:** You annotate a field within an entity class with **@Embedded** to indicate that the field's type is an embeddable class. The attributes of the embedded object are stored as columns in the embedding entity's table.

For example:

```
import jakarta.persistence.Embeddable;
import jakarta.persistence.Embedded;
import jakarta.persistence.Entity;
import jakarta.persistence.Id;
import jakarta.persistence.GeneratedValue;
import jakarta.persistence.GenerationType;
@Embeddable
public class Address {
    private String street;
    private String city;
    private String zipCode;
    // Getters, setters, constructors
}
@Entity
public class Customer {
    @Id
    @GeneratedValue(strategy = GenerationType.IDENTITY)
    private Long id;
    private String name;
    @Embedded
    private Address shippingAddress;
    @Embedded
    // Can embed multiple instances of the same embeddable
    private Address billingAddress;
    // Getters, setters, constructors
}
```

The columns for **street**, **city**, and **zipCode** (for both shipping and billing addresses) would all appear in the **Customer** table.

Hands-on: Creating your first JPA Entity (Book)

This hands-on exercise guides you through defining a simple **Book** entity class. This entity maps to a database table and includes a primary key and basic attributes, all configured according to Jakarta Persistence specifications.

The goal of this exercise is to create a JPA entity that represents a book. This involves defining its properties (like ID, title, and author) and annotating them correctly so Hibernate can understand how to persist this object to a database table.

Building the application

Generate project

1. In NetBeans, go to **File → New Project...**.
2. In the **Choose Project** dialog, select **Java with Maven** from the **Categories** list and **Spring Boot Initializr project** from the **Projects** list.
3. Click **Next**. In the **Base Properties** step:
   - Set **Group** to **com.sharanamvaishali** and **Artifact** to **mapping**.
   - Keep the **Version** as it is (i.e. **0.0.1-SNAPSHOT**).
   - Ensure **Packaging** is **Jar**.
   - Set **Name** to **PersistenceSetupApp** and **Package Name** to **com.sharanamvaishali.bookstore.domain**.
   - Select **Java** from the **Language** list and the appropriate **Java Version** (e.g., **24**).
4. Click **Next**. In the **Dependencies** step:
   - Select the appropriate **Spring Boot Version** (e.g., **4.0.0 (SNAPSHOT)**).
   - In the **Available** dependencies list, find and select **Spring Web**.
5. Click **Next**. In the **Name and Location** step:
   - Set **Project Name** to **PersistenceSetupAppDrive**.
   - Choose a suitable **Project Location**.
6. Click **Finish**. NetBeans generates the project structure and downloads dependencies.

Add the Spring Boot Starter for Data JPA

1. In the **Projects** window, expand your project.

2. Right-click **Dependencies** and select **Add Dependency....**
3. In the **Add Dependency** dialog box, enter **spring-boot-starter-data-jpa** in the **Query** textbox. NetBeans searches for the dependency. Select the entry under the **org.springframework.boot:spring-boot-starter-data-jpa** group and click **Add**.
4. The starter JAR file now appears under **Dependencies**.

Add the H2 Database Dependency

Next, we need the specific JDBC driver for the H2 database:

1. Right-click **Dependencies** and select **Add Dependency....**
2. In the **Query** textbox, enter **h2**. Select the entry **com.h2database:h2**. Click **Add**.
3. The H2 driver JAR file appears under **Dependencies**.

Configure H2 and JPA settings in application.properties

Now, we tell Spring Boot how to connect to our H2 database and how Hibernate should behave:

1. In the **Projects** window, navigate to **Other Sources → src/main/resources → <default package>**.
2. Open the application.properties file and add the following lines to the file:

```
spring.datasource.url=jdbc:h2:mem:testdb
spring.h2.console.enabled=true
spring.jpa.hibernate.ddl-auto=update
```

Create a Book Entity

1. Right-click the **com.sharanamvaishali.bookstore.domain** package and select **New → Java Class....**
2. Enter **Book** as the **Class Name** and click **Finish**.
3. Open the Book.java file. Add the necessary imports and define the class as shown below. This includes annotating the class with @Entity, defining fields for **id**, **title**, and **author**, and annotating **id** with @Id and @GeneratedValue:

```
package com.sharanamvaishali.bookstore.domain;
import jakarta.persistence.Entity;
import jakarta.persistence.GeneratedValue;
import jakarta.persistence.GenerationType;
import jakarta.persistence.Id;
import jakarta.persistence.Column;
@Entity  // Marks this class as a JPA entity, mapping to a database table
```

```
(defaulting to 'Book' or 'BOOK').
public class Book {
    @Id   // Marks this field as the primary key of the entity.
    @GeneratedValue(strategy = GenerationType.IDENTITY)  // Configures
//the primary key to be generated by the database (identity column).
    private Long id;
   @Column(nullable = false, length = 255)  // Maps to a
//database column; specifies it cannot be null and has max length.
    private String title;
    @Column(nullable = false, length = 100)  // Maps to a database
//column; specifies it cannot be null and has max length.
    private String author;
    @Column(unique = true, nullable = false, length = 17) // Maps
//to a database column; must be unique, non-null, and specific length.
    private String isbn;
    @Column(name = "publication_year")  // Maps to a database column;
//customizes column name to 'publication_year'.
    private Integer publicationYear;
    // Constructors
    public Book() {
    }
    public Book(String title, String author, Integer publicationYear, String isbn) {
        this.title = title;
        this.author = author;
        this.publicationYear = publicationYear;
        this.isbn = isbn;
    }
    // Getters and Setters
    public Long getId() {
        return id;
    }
    public void setId(Long id) {
        this.id = id;
    }
    public String getTitle() {
        return title;
    }
    public void setTitle(String title) {
        this.title = title;
    }
    public String getAuthor() {
        return author;
    }
    public void setAuthor(String author) {
        this.author = author;
    }
    public Integer getPublicationYear() {
        return publicationYear;
    }
    public void setPublicationYear(Integer publicationYear) {
        this.publicationYear = publicationYear;
```

```
    }
    public String getIsbn() {
        return isbn;
    }
    public void setIsbn(String isbn) {
        this.isbn = isbn;
    }
    @Override
    public String toString() {
        return "Book{" + "id=" + id + ", title='" + title + '\'' +
               ", author='" + author + '\'' + ", publicationYear=" + publicationYear
               + ", isbn='" + isbn + '\'' + '}';
    }
}
```

Code explanation

- **@Entity:** This crucial annotation tells JPA that this Book class is a persistent entity and will be mapped to a database table. By default, the table name will be Book (or BOOK, depending on database naming conventions and Hibernate settings).
- **@Id:** Marks the id field as the primary key for the Book entity.
- **@GeneratedValue(strategy = GenerationType.IDENTITY):** Specifies that the database will automatically generate the value for the id field when a new Book is saved. IDENTITY is commonly used with databases that support auto-incrementing columns.
- **@Column(nullable = false, length = 255):** This annotation customizes the mapping of the title field to a database column.
    - **nullable = false:** Indicates that the title column in the database cannot contain null values.
    - **length = 255:** Sets the maximum length for the title column to 255 characters.
- **@Column(name = "publication_year"):** Demonstrates how to explicitly set a different column name in the database (here, publication_year) if you prefer it over the default field name (publicationYear).
- **@Column(unique = true, nullable = false, length = 17):** For the isbn field, **unique = true** ensures that no two books can have the same ISBN in the database, enforcing data integrity. **nullable = false** prevents null ISBNs, and **length = 17** sets a specific length.

Bridging the gap: Learned concepts and application implementation

In this exercise, you directly applied the core concepts of JPA entity mapping:

- The @Entity annotation on the **Book** class clearly maps this Java object to a corresponding table in the database.

- The @Id and @GeneratedValue(strategy = GenerationType.IDENTITY) annotations on the **id** field define the primary key and specify that the database manages its generation.
- The @Column annotations are used to customize column properties like nullability and length for **title** and **author**, and to specify a custom column name (**publication_year**) for the **publicationYear** field.

When the application starts, Hibernate (the JPA provider) reads these annotations and uses them to understand the desired database schema.

Running and testing

Since you configured H2, running the application automatically creates the **BOOK** table based on your **Book** entity:

1. Ensure your application.properties file in src/main/resources has the H2 configuration.
2. Right-click your main application class (e.g., **PersistenceSetupAppApplication.java**) in the **Projects** window and select **Run File**.
3. Observe the console logs. You see messages from Hibernate indicating schema validation or updates.

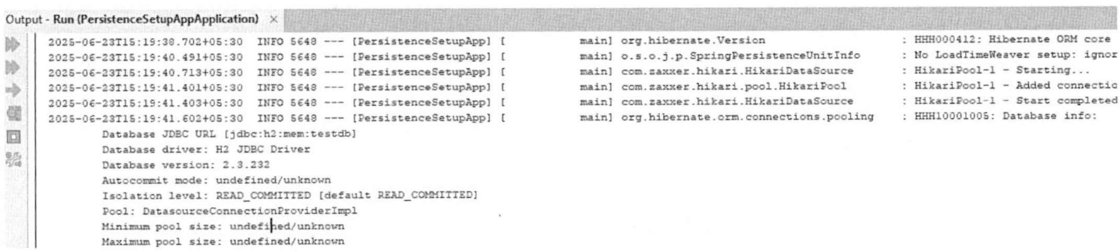

4. Open your web browser and navigate to **http://localhost:8080/h2-console**.
5. Ensure the JDBC URL matches what you configured (**jdbc:h2:mem:testdb**), leave the User **Name** as **sa**, and **Password** blank. Click **Connect**.
6. In the H2 console, you now see a **BOOK** table listed in the left-hand schema tree. Click on it to view its structure (columns like **ID, TITLE, AUTHOR, PUBLICATION_YEAR**).

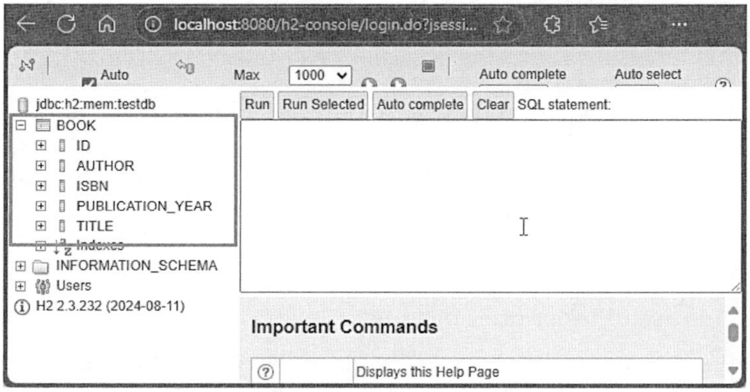

Exploring application behaviour: A practical run-through

When you run your Spring Boot application with the Book entity defined, here is what happens behind the scenes:

- **Spring Boot auto-configuration:** Spring Boot detects the presence of spring-boot-starter-data-jpa and h2 dependencies. It automatically configures Hibernate as the JPA provider and sets up an in-memory H2 database connection.
- **JPA entity scanning:** Hibernate, guided by Spring Boot, scans your application's classpath for classes annotated with **@Entity**. It finds your **Book** class in **com.sharanamvaishali.bookstore.domain**.
- **Schema generation (DDL auto):** Because you set **spring.jpa.hibernate.ddl-auto** to **update** in **application.properties**, Hibernate compares your entity definitions with the current database schema. Since this is likely the first run for the **BOOK** table, Hibernate generates and executes the necessary SQL Data Definition Language (DDL) statements (e.g., CREATE TABLE BOOK (id BIGINT NOT NULL AUTO_INCREMENT, author VARCHAR(100) NOT NULL, isbn VARCHAR(17) NOT NULL UNIQUE, publication_year INTEGER, title VARCHAR(255) NOT NULL, PRIMARY KEY (id))) to create the **BOOK** table with the columns corresponding to your **Book** entity's fields and their specified constraints.
- **H2 console:** The H2 console, enabled via **spring.h2.console.enabled=true**, provides a web-based interface to interact with your in-memory database. This allows you to visually confirm that the table was created correctly and inspect its structure, verifying that JPA successfully mapped your Java entity to its database counterpart.

This process highlights how Hibernate, acting as the JPA implementation, translates your object-oriented entity definitions into relational database schema, effectively managing the persistence layer based on standard JPA annotations.

Using Lombok

While not a part of JPA itself, Lombok is a popular library that can significantly reduce boilerplate code in Java applications, especially for entity classes. It uses annotations to automatically generate getters, setters, constructors, **equals()**, **hashCode()**, and **toString()** methods during the compilation phase. This keeps your entity classes cleaner and more readable.

Lombok annotations useful for entities include:

- **@lombok.Data:** A convenient shortcut that bundles **@ToString**, **@EqualsAndHashCode**, **@Getter** on all fields, **@Setter** on all non-final fields, and **@RequiredArgsConstructor**.
- **@lombok.NoArgsConstructor:** Generates a constructor with no arguments. This is often required by JPA providers.
- **@lombok.AllArgsConstructor:** Generates a constructor with arguments for all fields in the class.

For example:

```
import jakarta.persistence.Entity;
import jakarta.persistence.Id;
import jakarta.persistence.GeneratedValue;
import jakarta.persistence.GenerationType;
import lombok.Data;
import lombok.NoArgsConstructor;
import lombok.AllArgsConstructor;
@Entity
@Data // Generates getters, setters, equals, hashCode, toString
@NoArgsConstructor // Generates no-argument constructor
@AllArgsConstructor // Generates constructor with all fields
public class Product {
    @Id
    @GeneratedValue(strategy = GenerationType.IDENTITY)
    private Long id;
    private String name;
    private double price;
}
```

These JPA annotations are standard and work across different SQL database implementations supported by Hibernate. This means the entity definition you create functions consistently whether you are using MySQL, PostgreSQL, H2, or another relational database, as long as Hibernate supports it. This portability is a key advantage of JPA.

To use Lombok, you need to add it as a dependency in your **pom.xml** and install the Lombok plugin in your IDE (NetBeans has good support).

Hands-on: Creating Book entity using Lombok

This hands-on exercise guides you through defining a simple Book entity class with the added benefit of Lombok to reduce boilerplate code.

The goal of this exercise is to create a JPA entity that represents a book which leverages Lombok to keep your entity class clean and concise.

We will continue with the above **PersistenceSetupApp** project.

Add the Lombok dependency

1. Right-click **Dependencies** and select **Add Dependency....**
2. In the **Query** textbox, enter **lombok**. Select the entry **org.projectlombok:lombok**. Click **Add**.
3. The Lombok JAR file appears under **Dependencies**.

Changes in the Book entity

Replace the content of your Book.java file with the following code:

```
package com.sharanamvaishali.bookstore.domain;
import jakarta.persistence.Entity;
import jakarta.persistence.GeneratedValue;
import jakarta.persistence.GenerationType;
import jakarta.persistence.Id;
import jakarta.persistence.Column;
import lombok.AllArgsConstructor;
import lombok.Data;
import lombok.NoArgsConstructor;
@Entity
@Data
@NoArgsConstructor
@AllArgsConstructor
public class Book {
    @Id
    @GeneratedValue(strategy = GenerationType.IDENTITY)
    private Long id;
    @Column(nullable = false, length = 255)
    private String title;
    @Column(nullable = false, length = 100)
```

```
    private String author;
    @Column(unique = true, nullable = false, length = 17)
    private String isbn;
    @Column(name = "publication_year")
    private Integer publicationYear;
}
```

Code explanation

@Data, @NoArgsConstructor, @AllArgsConstructor are Lombok annotations. They automatically generate common methods like getters, setters, equals(), hashCode(), toString(), and necessary constructors, significantly reducing boilerplate code.

Bridging the gap: Learned concepts and application implementation

In this exercise, you directly applied the Lombok's role. By using @Data, @NoArgsConstructor, and @AllArgsConstructor, you significantly reduced the amount of boilerplate code (constructors, getters, setters, equals(), hashCode(), toString()) that you would otherwise have to write manually. This keeps your entity class clean and focused solely on its data and JPA mapping annotations, improving readability and maintainability.

When the application starts, Hibernate (the JPA provider) reads these annotations and uses them to understand the desired database schema.

Running and testing

Since you configured Lombok dependencies and made necessary changes in the Book entity, running the application automatically creates the BOOK table based on your Book entity:

1. Right-click your main application class (e.g., **PersistenceSetupAppApplication.java**) in the **Projects** window and select **Run File**.
2. Observe the console logs and then open your web browser and navigate to **http://localhost:8080/h2-console**.
3. Ensure the JDBC URL matches what you configured (jdbc:h2:mem:testdb), leave the **User Name** as **sa**, and **Password** blank. Click **Connect**.
4. You can now see a BOOK table listed in the left-hand schema tree. Click on it to view its structure (columns like ID, TITLE, AUTHOR, ISBN, PUBLICATION_YEAR).

Harnessing Jakarta Persistence Entity mapping in real-world contexts

Defining JPA entities is fundamental to any enterprise application that interacts with a relational database. It provides a clear, object-oriented way to represent your application's domain model while seamlessly ensuring its persistence in the database.

- **Defining the application's domain model in an object-oriented way:** Entities allow you to represent the core business concepts of your application (like a Book, Customer, Product, Order) as standard Java objects, leveraging the benefits of object-oriented programming (encapsulation, inheritance, polymorphism).
- **Ensuring it can be persisted to a relational database using standard Jakarta EE APIs:** By using JPA annotations, you are leveraging a widely adopted and standardized API for persistence. This ensures that your application's data layer is portable across different JPA implementations (like Hibernate) and different relational databases without significant code changes.
- **Reduced boilerplate:** Without JPA, you would have to write SQL CREATE TABLE statements, INSERT statements, and manually map result sets to Java objects. Entities and Hibernate automate this, significantly reducing boilerplate code.
- **Database agnostic:** By using JPA annotations, your entity definitions are largely independent of the specific underlying SQL database. Hibernate handles the dialect-specific SQL generation.
- **Creating a clear link between Java objects and database tables, forming the core of data management:** The entity definition is the bridge. It explicitly declares which Java class maps to which table, which fields map to which columns, and how primary keys and relationships are managed. This clear, declarative mapping simplifies data operations, allowing you to interact with data using Java objects rather than raw SQL, greatly enhancing developer productivity and application maintainability. This forms the bedrock of how your Spring Boot application will interact with and manage data in real-world scenarios.
- **Foundation for ORM:** These entities form the bedrock upon which all your data access operations (saving, retrieving, updating, deleting data) are built using higher-level abstractions like Spring Data JPA (which you will learn in the ***Chapter 7 - Simplified data access with Spring Data JPA***).

Wrapping up

- **Entities:** Represent persistent objects mapped to database tables.

- **@Entity:** Marks a class as a JPA entity.
- **@Id:** Defines the primary key field.
- **@GeneratedValue:** Automates primary key generation.
- **@Column:** Customizes column mapping (name, nullability, length).
- **Temporal Types:** Direct support for java.time classes.
- **Relationships:** Annotations for defining associations (e.g., Many-to-One).
- **Automatic schema:** Hibernate generates table schema from entities.
- **Embedded objects:** Grouping attributes with @Embeddable and @Embedded.
- **Lombok**: Reduces boilerplate code in entities.
- **JPA standard**: Annotations work across various SQL databases.

Congratulations on defining your first JPA entity! You have taken a significant step forward by learning how to define JPA entities, the very building blocks for persisting data in your Spring Boot applications. Understanding **@Entity**, **@Id**, **@GeneratedValue**, and **@Column** is crucial, as it allows you to describe your application's data model in an object-oriented way while seamlessly mapping it to a relational database. You also saw how easily this translates into actual database schema with the help of Hibernate and Spring Boot's auto-configuration, which you confirmed using the H2 console.

In the next chapter, ***Simplified data access with Spring Data JPA***, you will discover how to interact with these entities and the database using Spring Data JPA repositories, drastically simplifying your data access layer.

Chapter 7

Section 02: Persistence with Hibernate and Spring Data JPA

Simplified data access with Spring Data JPA

What you'll learn

- DAO / Repository boilerplate
- Spring Data JPA
- The JpaRepository interface
- Defining Repositories
- Query derivation
- Custom JPQL queries
- Pagination and sorting

In modern software development, interacting with a database is a fundamental requirement. For decades, developers wrote layers of code called Data Access Objects (DAOs) to handle this. This often involved writing repetitive, boilerplate code for every single database operation: opening connections, creating statements, executing queries, mapping results back to Java objects, and meticulously handling exceptions and resource cleanup. While the Jakarta Persistence API (JPA) and its EntityManager simplify this, a significant amount of boilerplate can still remain. Spring Data JPA revolutionizes this process, allowing you to create robust data access layers with surprising ease and minimal code. It's a prime example of the Spring philosophy: let the framework handle the tedious work so you can focus on your application's business logic.

The problem with boilerplate DAO / Repository code

Before frameworks like Spring Data JPA, a typical DAO implementation for a Book entity using plain JPA would look something like this:

- You would inject EntityManager, and for every query, you would manually create a Query or TypedQuery, set parameters, and execute it.
- For save or update operations, you'd call persist or merge.
- For every single entity in your application, you would write a corresponding DAO class with methods for findById, findAll, save, update, and delete.

While this is a huge improvement over raw JDBC, it's still highly repetitive. You find yourself writing the same structural code over and over again, only changing the entity type and query strings. This boilerplate is not only tedious to write but also a potential source of errors and difficult to maintain.

Spring Data JPA Repositories to the rescue

Spring Data JPA takes a different approach. It asks a simple question: What if you only had to declare your data access methods without implementing them? The core idea is to define a repository interface for each of your domain entities. You specify the methods you need, and Spring Data JPA provides the implementation automatically at runtime. This eliminates nearly all the boilerplate code associated with the data access layer, dramatically increasing productivity and reducing potential bugs.

The JpaRepository interface

The magic of Spring Data JPA starts with its repository interfaces, chief among them being **JpaRepository**. When you create your own interface that extends JpaRepository, you immediately inherit a complete set of CRUD (Create, Read, Update, Delete) methods, ready to use without writing a single line of implementation.

JpaRepository<T, ID> is a generic interface with two parameters:

- **T:** The domain type that the repository manages (e.g., **Book**).
- **ID:** The type of the primary key of the domain type (e.g., **Long**).

By extending it, your BookRepository instantly gets methods like:

- **save(S entity):** Saves a new entity or updates an existing one.

- **findById(ID id):** Retrieves an entity by its primary key.
- **findAll():** Returns all instances of the entity.
- **deleteById(ID id):** Deletes the entity with the given primary key.
- **count():** Returns the number of entities.

...and many more, including methods for batch operations, flushing, and pagination.

Defining Repository interfaces for your Entities

Creating a repository is incredibly simple. You just define an interface and extend one of the Spring Data repository interfaces. For most cases, JpaRepository is the one you want:

```
package com.sharanamvaishali.bookstore.repository;
import com.sharanamvaishali.bookstore.domain.Book;
import org.springframework.data.jpa.repository.JpaRepository;
import org.springframework.stereotype.Repository;
@Repository
public interface BookRepository extends JpaRepository<Book, Long> {
    // Spring will provide the implementation automatically!
}
```

That's it! With this simple interface, you can now inject BookRepository into other Spring components (like services or controllers) and call methods like save() and findAll(). The **@Repository** annotation is technically optional if you extend JpaRepository as Spring can deduce it, but it's good practice for clarity and consistency.

Query derivation: Creating database queries from method names

One of the most powerful features of Spring Data JPA is its **query derivation mechanism**. You can define new finder methods in your repository interface, and Spring will parse the method name to automatically create the correct database query.

The parser looks for keywords like **find...By**, **read...By**, **query...By**, **count...By**, and **get...By**, and then parses the rest of the method name as the query criteria.

Here are some examples for our Book entity:

- **Optional<Book> findByIsbn(String isbn);**
    - Finds a book by its unique ISBN. Using Optional is a good practice for methods that may not find a result.

- **List<Book> findByAuthor(String author);**
  - Finds all books by a given author.
- **List<Book> findByAuthorAndPublicationYear(String author, int year);**
  - Finds all books matching both the author and the publication year.
- **List<Book> findByTitleContainingIgnoreCase(String keyword);**
  - Finds all books whose title contains the given keyword, ignoring case.

This feature allows you to write a vast number of common queries without ever writing a line of JPQL or SQL.

Using @Query for custom JPQL

Sometimes, a query is too complex to be derived from a method name. In these cases, Spring Data JPA provides the **@Query** annotation. This allows you to write your own custom JPQL (Jakarta Persistence Query Language) or even native SQL query directly on the repository method:

```
import org.springframework.data.jpa.repository.Query;
import org.springframework.data.repository.query.Param;
public interface BookRepository extends JpaRepository<Book, Long> {
    @Query("SELECT b FROM Book b WHERE b.publicationYear > :year")
    List<Book> findBooksPublishedAfter(@Param("year") int year);
}
```

Code explanation

We define a custom JPQL query to find all books published after a certain year. The **@Param** annotation links the method parameter **year** to the named parameter **:year** in the query string.

Pagination and Sorting support

For applications that deal with large amounts of data, fetching everything at once is inefficient. Spring Data JPA has first-class support for pagination and sorting:

- **Sort:** Specifies the order in which to retrieve the data.
- **Pageable:** Contains pagination information (page number, page size) and optionally sorting information.

You can simply add a parameter of type Pageable or Sort to your repository method signature.

For example:

```
import org.springframework.data.domain.Page;
```

```
import org.springframework.data.domain.Pageable;
import org.springframework.data.domain.Sort;
public interface BookRepository extends JpaRepository<Book, Long> {
    // Method for sorting
    List<Book> findByAuthor(String author, Sort sort);
    // Method for pagination
    Page<Book> findAll(Pageable pageable);
}
```

A key advantage of using Spring Data JPA is that your repository interfaces are portable. Since they build on the standard Jakarta Persistence API, they work regardless of the underlying database you configured in ***Chapter 5 - Introduction to Persistence*** (H2, MySQL, etc.). Spring and Hibernate handle the vendor-specific SQL translation for you.

Hands-on: Creating and using a Book Repository

In this hands-on exercise, you will create a Book entity, and create a Spring Data JPA repository for it. You will then use this repository to save new books to the database and retrieve them, demonstrating the power and simplicity of this approach.

Building the application

We will now create the project to incorporate a repository.

Generate project

1. In NetBeans, go to **File → New Project...**.
2. In the **Choose Project** dialog, select **Java with Maven** from the **Categories** list and **Spring Boot Initializr project** from the **Projects** list.
3. Click **Next**. In the **Base Properties** step:
   - Set **Group** to **com.sharanamvaishali** and **Artifact** to **book**.
   - Keep the **Version** as it is (i.e. **0.0.1-SNAPSHOT**).
   - Ensure **Packaging** is **Jar**.
   - Set **Name** to **BookstoreApplication** and **Package Name** to **com.sharanamvaishali.bookstore**.
   - Select **Java** from the **Language** list and the appropriate **Java Version** (e.g., **24**).
4. Click **Next**. In the **Dependencies** step:
   - Select the appropriate **Spring Boot Version** (e.g., **4.0.0 (SNAPSHOT)**).

- In the **Available** dependencies list, find and select **Spring Web**.

5. Click **Next**. In the **Name and Location** step:
   - Set **Project Name** to **BookstoreApplicationProject**.
   - Choose a suitable **Project Location**.
6. Click **Finish**. NetBeans generates the project structure and downloads dependencies.

Add the Spring Boot Starter for Data JPA

1. In the **Projects** window, expand your project.
2. Right-click **Dependencies** and select **Add Dependency...**.
3. In the **Add Dependency** dialog box, enter **spring-boot-starter-data-jpa** in the **Query** textbox. NetBeans searches for the dependency. Select the entry under the **org.springframework.boot:spring-boot-starter-data-jpa** group and click **Add**.
4. The starter JAR file now appears under **Dependencies**.

Add the H2 Database dependency

Next, we need the specific JDBC driver for the H2 database:

1. Right-click **Dependencies** and select **Add Dependency...**.
2. In the **Query** textbox, enter **h2**. Select the entry **com.h2database:h2**. Click **Add**.
3. The H2 driver JAR file appears under **Dependencies**.

Configure H2 and JPA settings in application.properties

Now, we tell Spring Boot how to connect to our H2 database and how Hibernate should behave:

1. In the **Projects** window, navigate to **Other Sources → src/main/resources → <default package>**.
2. Open the application.properties file and add the following lines to the file:

```
spring.datasource.url=jdbc:h2:mem:testdb
spring.h2.console.enabled=true
spring.jpa.hibernate.ddl-auto=update
```

Create a Book Entity

1. Right-click the **com.sharanamvaishali.bookstore** package and select **New → Java Package...**.

2. Enter **domain** as the **Package Name** and click **Finish**.
3. Right-click the **com.sharanamvaishali.bookstore.domain** package and select **New → Java Class....**
4. Enter **Book** as the **Class Name** and click **Finish**.
5. Open the Book.java file and add the necessary imports and define the class as shown below:

```
package com.sharanamvaishali.bookstore.domain;
import jakarta.persistence.Entity;
import jakarta.persistence.GeneratedValue;
import jakarta.persistence.GenerationType;
import jakarta.persistence.Id;
import jakarta.persistence.Column;
@Entity
public class Book {
    @Id
    @GeneratedValue(strategy = GenerationType.IDENTITY)
    private Long id;
    @Column(nullable = false, length = 255)
    private String title;
    @Column(nullable = false, length = 100)
    private String author;
    @Column(unique = true, nullable = false, length = 17)
    private String isbn;
    @Column(name = "publication_year")
    private Integer publicationYear;
    public Book() {
    }
    public Book(String title, String author, String isbn, Integer publicationYear) {
        this.title = title;
        this.author = author;
      this.isbn = isbn;
        this.publicationYear = publicationYear;
    }
    public Long getId() {
        return id;
    }
    public void setId(Long id) {
        this.id = id;
    }
    public String getTitle() {
        return title;
    }
    public void setTitle(String title) {
        this.title = title;
    }
    public String getAuthor() {
        return author;
    }
```

```
    public void setAuthor(String author) {
        this.author = author;
    }
    public Integer getPublicationYear() {
        return publicationYear;
    }
    public void setPublicationYear(Integer publicationYear) {
        this.publicationYear = publicationYear;
    }
    public String getIsbn() {
        return isbn;
    }
    public void setIsbn(String isbn) {
        this.isbn = isbn;
    }
    @Override
    public String toString() {
        return "Book{" + "id=" + id + ", title='" + title + '\'' + ", author='" +
               author + '\'' + ", publicationYear=" + publicationYear + ", isbn='"
               + isbn + '\'' + '}';
    }
}
```

Create the BookRepository Interface

It's good practice to organize your classes by layer. Let's create a package for our repositories and then create the repository interface:

1. In the **Projects** window, expand your project (**BookstoreApplication**).
2. Right-click **com.sharanamvaishali.bookstore** package and select **New → Java Package....**
3. In the **New Java Package** dialog, enter **repository** as the **Package Name**, making the full name **com.sharanamvaishali.bookstore.repository**. Click **Finish**.
4. Right-click **com.sharanamvaishali.bookstore.repository** package and select **New → Java Interface....**
5. In the **New Java Interface** dialog, enter **BookRepository** as the **Interface Name**. Click **Finish**.
6. Open the BookRepository.java file and replace its content with the following code:

```
package com.sharanamvaishali.bookstore.repository;
import com.sharanamvaishali.bookstore.domain.Book;
import java.util.Optional;
import org.springframework.data.jpa.repository.JpaRepository;
import org.springframework.stereotype.Repository;
@Repository
public interface BookRepository extends JpaRepository<Book, Long> {
    Optional<Book> findByIsbn(String isbn);
```

```
}
```

Code explanation

- We declare an interface, not a class.
- It extends JpaRepository<Book, Long>, giving us a full set of CRUD operations for our Book entity, which has a primary key of type Long.
- We add a method signature for findByIsbn(String isbn). We don't provide any code for it; Spring Data will implement it for us based on the method name.

Create a CommandLineRunner to test the repository

To see our repository in action without building a web interface yet, we can use a **CommandLineRunner**. This is a special Spring Boot component whose run method is executed automatically right after the application starts:

1. Open your main application class, BookstoreApplication.java.
2. Add the following @Bean method inside the class. NetBeans will prompt you to add the necessary imports for Book, BookRepository, CommandLineRunner, and Bean:

```
package com.sharanamvaishali.bookstore;
```

```
import com.sharanamvaishali.bookstore.domain.Book;
import com.sharanamvaishali.bookstore.repository.BookRepository;
import org.springframework.boot.CommandLineRunner;
import org.springframework.boot.SpringApplication;
import org.springframework.context.annotation.Bean;
```

```
import org.springframework.boot.autoconfigure.SpringBootApplication;
@SpringBootApplication
public class BookstoreApplication {
    public static void main(String[] args) {
        SpringApplication.run(BookstoreApplication.class, args);
    }
```

```
    @Bean
    public CommandLineRunner bookInitializer(BookRepository bookRepository) {
        return args -> {
            System.out.println("--- Saving some initial books ---");
            bookRepository.save(new Book("The Hobbit", "J.R.R. Tolkien",
                                         "978-0618260300", 1937));
            bookRepository.save(new Book("1984", "George Orwell",
                                         "978-0451524935", 1949));
            bookRepository.save(new Book("Pride and Prejudice", "Jane Austen",
                                         "978-1503290563", 1813));
            System.out.println("--- Books saved ---");
            System.out.println("\n--- Finding book with ISBN 978-0451524935 ---");
            bookRepository.findByIsbn("978-0451524935")
                    .ifPresent(book -> System.out.println("Found book: " + book));
```

```
            System.out.println("\n--- Finding all books ---");
            bookRepository.findAll().forEach(book -> System.out.println(book));
            System.out.println("\n--- Hands-On complete ---");
        };
    }
}
```

Code explanation

- **@Bean:** This annotation tells Spring to create an instance of **CommandLineRunner** and manage it.
- **Dependency injection:** The method takes **BookRepository bookRepository** as a parameter. Spring sees this and automatically provides (injects) the managed BookRepository bean that it created for us.
- **Lambda expression:** We use a Java lambda expression **(args -> { ... })** to provide the implementation for the run method of the CommandLineRunner.
- **bookRepository.save():** We call the inherited save() method to persist new Book objects to the database.
- **bookRepository.findByIsbn():** We call the custom finder method we defined.
- **bookRepository.findAll():** We call the inherited findAll() method to retrieve every book record.

Running and testing

1. Ensure your H2 database settings are active in application.properties.
2. Right-click your project in the **Projects** window and select **Run**.
3. Observe the console output in NetBeans. You see logs from Hibernate creating the BOOK table, followed by the output from our CommandLineRunner:

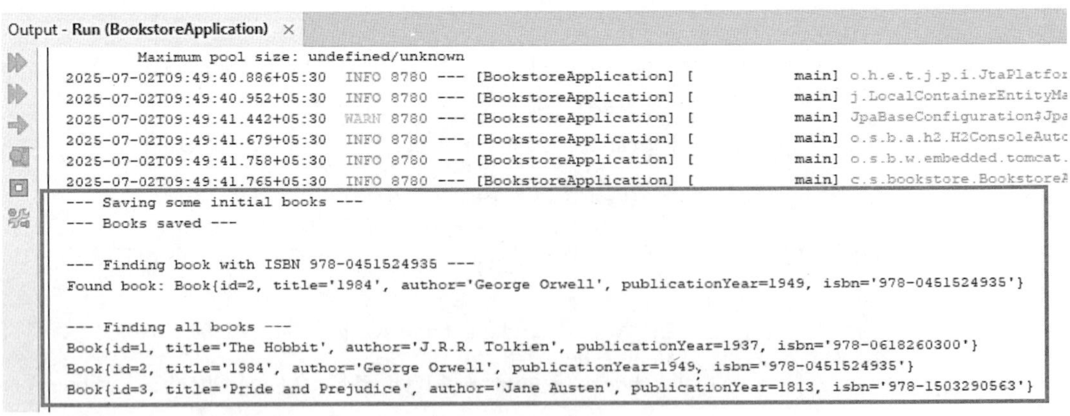

4. Access the H2 console in your browser (**http://localhost:8080/h2-console**).
5. Connect to the database and run a **SELECT * FROM BOOK;** query:

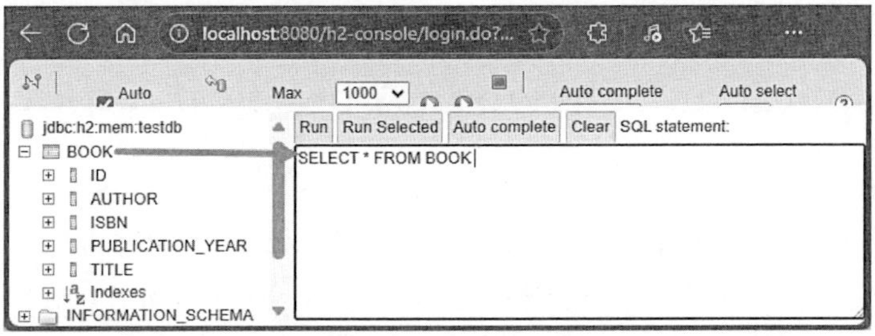

6. You can see the three book records stored neatly in the table, confirming that persistence was successful.

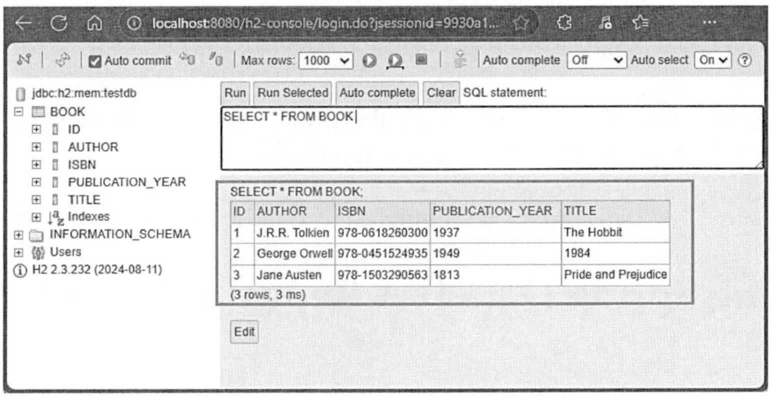

Bridging the gap: Learned concepts and application implementation

This hands-on exercise perfectly demonstrates the theory in action:

- **JpaRepository:** By extending JpaRepository, our BookRepository interface instantly gained powerful methods like save() and findAll() without any implementation code.
- **Query derivation:** We defined the findByIsbn() method signature, and Spring Data JPA generated the necessary JPQL query behind the scenes, purely based on the method name convention.
- **Dependency injection:** We saw how seamlessly Spring injected the BookRepository implementation into our CommandLineRunner, allowing us to use it immediately.

- **Abstraction:** We interacted with the database through a high-level, object-oriented repository abstraction, calling simple methods like save() instead of dealing with EntityManager or SQL.

Exploring application behaviour: A practical run-through

When the application starts:

1. Spring scans for components and finds our BookRepository interface.
2. Because it extends JpaRepository, Spring Data JPA steps in and creates a dynamic proxy implementation for this interface at runtime.
3. This proxy object is what gets injected into our CommandLineRunner.
4. When we call a method like save(book), the proxy intercepts this call, uses the JPA EntityManager to begin a transaction, persists the Book entity, and commits the transaction.
5. Similarly, when we call findByIsbn("..."), the proxy translates this into a SELECT query, executes it, and maps the result back to a Book object.

All of this complex, low-level database interaction is handled for us automatically.

Harnessing Spring Data JPA Repositories in real-world contexts

The pattern you just learned is the foundation of the data access layer in the vast majority of modern Spring applications.

- **Reduced boilerplate:** It drastically reduces the amount of repetitive data access code you need to write and maintain, saving countless hours and preventing common errors.
- **Clean and testable code:** It provides a clean, interface-based way to interact with the database, which makes your service layer easier to test (you can easily mock the repository interface).
- **Centralized logic:** It centralizes your data access logic in one place—the repository package—making your application easier to understand and navigate.

Wrapping up

This chapter introduced a powerful abstraction for data access. Let's review the key points:

- Traditional DAO patterns require writing a lot of repetitive, boilerplate code.

- Spring Data JPA allows you to create data repositories by simply defining an interface.
- Extending the JpaRepository interface provides a full suite of CRUD methods for free.
- You can create custom queries simply by adhering to a method naming convention (query derivation).
- For complex queries, the @Query annotation gives you full control with JPQL or native SQL.
- This approach significantly cleans up your codebase and boosts productivity.

Congratulations! You have successfully built a clean, powerful, and modern data access layer. You've seen how Spring can eliminate enormous amounts of boilerplate code, allowing you to define complex database interactions by simply writing an interface. Now that you can save and retrieve data, the next logical step is to ensure these operations are safe and reliable.

In the next chapter, we will dive into one of the most critical concepts in database programming: ***Managing Database Transactions***. You will learn how to use Spring's @Transactional annotation to ensure that your data remains consistent, even when multiple database operations are involved.

Chapter 8

Section 02: Persistence with Hibernate and Spring Data JPA

Managing database transactions

What you'll learn

- What is a transaction?
- ACID properties
- Declarative transaction management
- The @Transactional annotation
- Controlling transaction behaviour
- Service layer transactions

Imagine an online banking transfer. You debit one account and credit another. What if the system crashes after the debit but before the credit? One person loses money, and the other gains nothing. The bank's data becomes inconsistent and incorrect. This **all or nothing** principle is the essence of a transaction, a critical concept for any application that modifies data. In this chapter, we explore how Spring provides a simple yet powerful way to manage these operations, ensuring your data remains reliable and consistent.

What is a transaction?

At its core, a **transaction** is a single, logical unit of work that may consist of multiple operations.

To ensure data remains in a predictable and correct state, transactions adhere to a set of properties known by the acronym **ACID**:

- **Atomicity:** This property ensures that all operations within a transaction are completed successfully as a single, indivisible unit. If any part of the transaction fails, the entire transaction is rolled back, and the database is left unchanged as if the transaction never even started. It's **all or nothing**.
- **Consistency:** A transaction guarantees that the database moves from one valid state to another. It enforces all rules and constraints on the data, such as unique keys or required fields. An inconsistent transaction that would violate these rules is not allowed to be committed.
- **Isolation:** This property ensures that concurrent transactions do not interfere with each other. The operations of one transaction are hidden from other concurrent transactions until the first transaction is complete. This prevents issues like reading partially updated data.
- **Durability:** Once a transaction has been successfully committed, the changes are permanent and will survive any subsequent system failure, such as a power outage or crash.

These properties are fundamental to building reliable applications that manage critical data.

The old way: Challenges of manual transaction management

Before modern frameworks like Spring, managing transactions was a tedious and error-prone task. Using plain JDBC, you had to manually control the transaction boundaries. This involved:

- Disabling auto-commit mode on the database connection.
- Wrapping all database operations in a **try-catch** block.
- Explicitly calling **commit()** in the **try** block if everything succeeded.
- Calling **rollback()** in the **catch** block if any exception occurred.
- Ensuring the connection was properly closed in a **finally** block.

This boilerplate code cluttered the business logic and was easy to get wrong. While the Java Transaction API (JTA) offered a more robust standard, it was often complex to configure and use.

Spring's declarative transaction management

Spring revolutionized this by introducing **declarative transaction management**. Instead of manually writing transaction control code, you simply ***declare*** how you want transactions to behave. You can specify that a particular method should always run within a transaction, and Spring handles all the underlying complexity of starting, committing, or rolling back that transaction for you.

This is achieved primarily through one simple but powerful tool: the **@Transactional** annotation.

How it works: A peek behind the curtain

Spring's magic is powered by a concept called Aspect-Oriented Programming (AOP). When Spring creates a bean (like a service) that has a **@Transactional** method, it doesn't give you back the raw object. Instead, it creates a **proxy** object that wraps your original object.

This proxy intercepts calls to your methods. When a call to a **@Transactional** method comes in, the proxy performs its "magic":

1. It starts a new database transaction.
2. It calls your actual business logic method.
3. If your method finishes without throwing an error, the proxy commits the transaction.
4. If your method throws a specific type of exception, the proxy automatically rolls back the transaction.

This powerful mechanism cleanly separates your business logic from the cross-cutting concern of transaction management.

Controlling transaction behaviour

The **@Transactional** annotation has several configuration options, but two are most important for beginners:

- **Propagation:** This defines how a transactional method behaves when called from another transactional method. The default, **Propagation.REQUIRED**, is what you'll use most of the time. It means the method will join an active transaction if one exists or create a new one if it doesn't.

- **Rollback rules:** By default, Spring only marks a transaction for rollback if the method throws an unchecked exception (any RuntimeException or Error). If a method throws a checked Exception, Spring will ***commit*** the transaction. This is a crucial distinction to remember when handling errors.

Where to place @Transactional

The most common and recommended place to put the **@Transactional** annotation is on public methods in your **service layer** (@Service beans). The service layer is responsible for orchestrating business operations, which often involve one or more calls to a repository. Placing the transaction boundary at the service layer ensures that the entire business operation is atomic.

Best of all, Spring's transaction management works seamlessly with the **DataSource** you configure, abstracting away the specifics of whether you are using JDBC directly or a JPA provider like Hibernate.

Hands-on: Applying transactions to a service method

In this exercise, you will create a service that saves multiple related entities in a single operation. You will use Spring's **@Transactional** annotation to ensure this operation is atomic. To see it in action, you will then simulate an error to confirm that the transaction correctly rolls back, preventing any partial data from being saved to the database.

Building the application

We will continue modifying the project from the previous ***Chapter 7 - Simplified data access with Spring Data JPA***.

Create the BookstoreService class

1. In the **Projects** window, expand your project.
2. Right-click the **Source Packages** node and select **New → Java Package…**. Enter **com.sharanamvaishali.bookstore.service** as the **Package Name** and click **Finish**.
3. Right-click the **com.sharanamvaishali.bookstore.service** package and select **New → Java Class…**. Enter **BookstoreService** as the **Class Name** and click **Finish**.
4. Open the BookstoreService.java file and replace its content with the following code:

```
package com.sharanamvaishali.bookstore.service;
import com.sharanamvaishali.bookstore.domain.Book;
```

```
import com.sharanamvaishali.bookstore.repository.BookRepository;
import org.springframework.stereotype.Service;
import org.springframework.transaction.annotation.Transactional;
@Service
public class BookstoreService {
    private final BookRepository bookRepository;
    public BookstoreService(BookRepository bookRepository) {
        this.bookRepository = bookRepository;
    }
    @Transactional
    public void addMultipleBooks(Book book1, Book book2) {
        System.out.println("Saving first book: " + book1.getTitle());
        bookRepository.save(book1);
        // To test the rollback, uncomment the following 'if' block.
        // When active, it simulates a failure before saving the second book.
        /*
        if (true) {
            throw new RuntimeException("Simulating a critical failure!");
        }
        */
        System.out.println("Saving second book: " + book2.getTitle());
        bookRepository.save(book2);
        System.out.println("Both books saved successfully within the transaction.");
    }
}
```

Code explanation

- **@Service:** This annotation tells Spring that this class is a **service component**. Spring will create an instance of this class and manage its lifecycle, making it available for injection into other components (like controllers).
- **public BookstoreService(BookRepository bookRepository) { . . . }:** This is the **constructor** for the BookstoreService class.
    - It takes an argument of type BookRepository.
    - This is how **Dependency Injection (DI)** works in Spring. When Spring creates an instance of BookstoreService, it automatically finds and injects an instance of BookRepository (which it has also managed as a bean) into this constructor.
    - The injected BookRepository instance is then assigned to the bookRepository field of the BookstoreService class using this.bookRepository = bookRepository;.
- **@Transactional:** This annotation is placed above the addMultipleBooks() method. This is a very important part of the code for data integrity.
    - When a method is annotated with @Transactional, Spring creates a **transactional boundary** around that method's execution.
    - This means that all database operations (like bookRepository.save()) within this method will be part of a single atomic unit of work.

- If all operations complete successfully, the transaction is **committed**, and all changes are permanently saved to the database.
- If any unchecked exception (like RuntimeException) is thrown within the method, the transaction is **rolled back**, meaning all changes made within that transaction are undone, as if they never happened. This ensures data consistency.

- **public void addMultipleBooks(Book book1, Book book2) { . . . }:** This declares a **public method** named addMultipleBooks() that takes two Book objects as arguments and returns void (it doesn't return any specific value). This method's purpose is to save two books to the database as a single logical operation.
- **bookRepository.save(book1);:** This line calls the save() method on the injected bookRepository instance, passing book1 as an argument. This operation will typically persist the book1 object to the database.
- **/* if (true) { . . . } */:** This commented-out block is for **demonstration purposes**.
  - If you uncomment this block, it will unconditionally throw new RuntimeException("Simulating a critical failure!"); immediately after saving book1.
  - Because the addMultipleBooks() method is @Transactional, when this RuntimeException is thrown, Spring will detect it and **automatically roll back** the entire transaction. This means that even though book1 was saved by bookRepository.save(book1), that save operation will be undone, and book1 will not be persisted to the database. This perfectly illustrates the "all or nothing" nature of transactions.

Modify the CommandLineRunner to use the Service

Now, let's modify the **CommandLineRunner** bean (created in *Chapter 7*) to call our new transactional method. This allows us to test the service right when the application starts.

1. Open your main application class (e.g., **BookstoreApplication.java**).
2. Locate the **CommandLineRunner** bean method and Replace the entire method with the following code. We inject our new **BookstoreService** and add logic to call it:

```
package com.sharanamvaishali.bookstore;
import com.sharanamvaishali.bookstore.domain.Book;
import com.sharanamvaishali.bookstore.repository.BookRepository;
```

```
import com.sharanamvaishali.bookstore.service.BookstoreService;
```

```
import org.springframework.boot.CommandLineRunner;
import org.springframework.boot.SpringApplication;
import org.springframework.boot.autoconfigure.SpringBootApplication;
import org.springframework.context.annotation.Bean;
@SpringBootApplication
public class BookstoreApplication {
```

```
    public static void main(String[] args) {
        SpringApplication.run(BookstoreApplication.class, args);
    }
```

```
    @Bean
    public CommandLineRunner demo(BookRepository bookRepository,
                                  BookstoreService bookstoreService) {
        return (args) -> {
            System.out.println("\n--- TESTING TRANSACTIONAL SERVICE ---");
            Book bookA = new Book();
            bookA.setTitle("The Hobbit");
            bookA.setAuthor("J.R.R. Tolkien");
            bookA.setIsbn("978-0345339683");
            bookA.setPublicationYear(1937);
            Book bookB = new Book();
            bookB.setTitle("The Fellowship of the Ring");
            bookB.setAuthor("J.R.R. Tolkien");
            bookB.setIsbn("978-0618640157");
            bookB.setPublicationYear(1954);
            try {
                System.out.println("Attempting to add multiple books...");
                bookstoreService.addMultipleBooks(bookA, bookB);
            } catch (RuntimeException e) {
                System.err.println("Caught exception from service: " +
                                   e.getMessage());
                System.err.println("Transaction should be rolled back. No new books
                                   should be in the database.");
            }
            System.out.println("\n--- CHECKING DATABASE CONTENT AFTER
                                SERVICE CALL ---");
            long count = bookRepository.count();
            System.out.println("Total books in database: " + count);
            bookRepository.findAll().forEach(book -> System.out.println(" - "
                                                                       + book));
            System.out.println("--- END OF TRANSACTIONAL TEST ---\n");
        };
    }
}
```

Code explanation

- **@Bean:** This annotation indicates that the demo method will produce a bean that Spring should manage. In this case, it's a CommandLineRunner bean.
- **public CommandLineRunner demo(. . .) {:** This defines a method named demo that returns an instance of CommandLineRunner. Spring will automatically inject instances of BookRepository and BookstoreService into this method's arguments. This is another example of Spring's Dependency Injection in action. When Spring creates this CommandLineRunner bean, it will ensure these dependencies are provided.

- **return (args) -> { . . . };:** This is a lambda expression that implements the run method of the CommandLineRunner interface. The code inside this block will be executed once the Spring application context is fully loaded. The args parameter represents any command-line arguments passed to the application, though they are not used in this specific example.
- **Book bookA = new Book(); and Book bookB = new Book();:** These lines create a new Book objects named bookA and bookB and set its properties (title, author, ISBN, publication year).
- **try { bookstoreService.addMultipleBooks(bookA, bookB); }:** The try block attempts to call the addMultipleBooks() method on the bookstoreService instance, passing bookA and bookB. This is the critical part of the test: it invokes the transactional method.
- **catch (RuntimeException e) { . . . }:** This catch block handles any RuntimeException that might be thrown by the addMultipleBooks method.
  - If the commented-out throw new RuntimeException(...) line in BookstoreService is uncommented, this catch block will execute.
  - It prints an error message indicating that an exception was caught and explains that the transaction should have been rolled back, meaning no books should have been saved. This confirms the transactional behaviour.
- **bookRepository.count();:** This retrieves the total number of books currently in the database using the count() method of the bookRepository and prints it. This is crucial for verifying the transaction's effect. If the transaction was successful, the count should increase by 2 (assuming the books didn't exist before). If the transaction rolled back, the count should remain unchanged.
- **bookRepository.findAll().forEach(book -> System.out.println(" - " + book));:** This line fetches all books from the database using bookRepository.findAll() and then iterates through them, printing each book's details (assuming the Book class has a meaningful toString() method). This provides a detailed look at what's actually in the database.

In essence, this CommandLineRunner serves as a simple test harness for the BookstoreService. It demonstrates how to:

- **Inject** dependencies (BookRepository, BookstoreService) into a CommandLineRunner.
- **Create** sample data (Book objects).
- **Invoke** a transactional service method (addMultipleBooks()).
- **Handle exceptions** that might occur during the transactional operation.
- **Verify** the outcome by querying the database, showcasing whether the transaction committed successfully or was rolled back.

Running and testing

We will run the application twice to observe both the successful commit and the automatic rollback.

Test 1: Successful transaction

1. Ensure the **if (true) { throw new RuntimeException(...) }** block in BookstoreService.java is **commented out**.

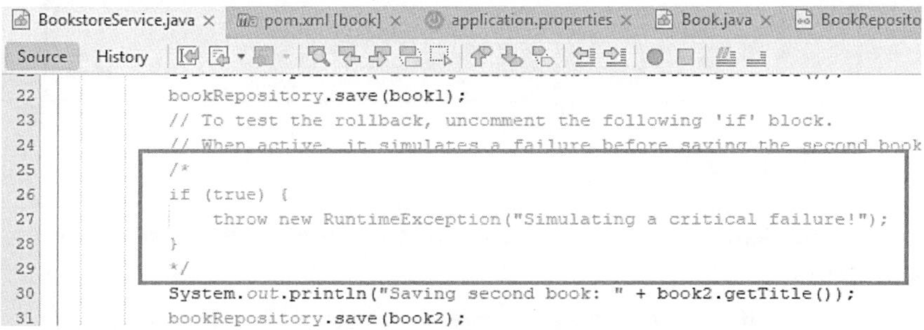

2. Right-click the project and select **Run**.
3. Observe the console output. You can see messages indicating both books were saved successfully, followed by a list of all books in the database, including the two new ones.

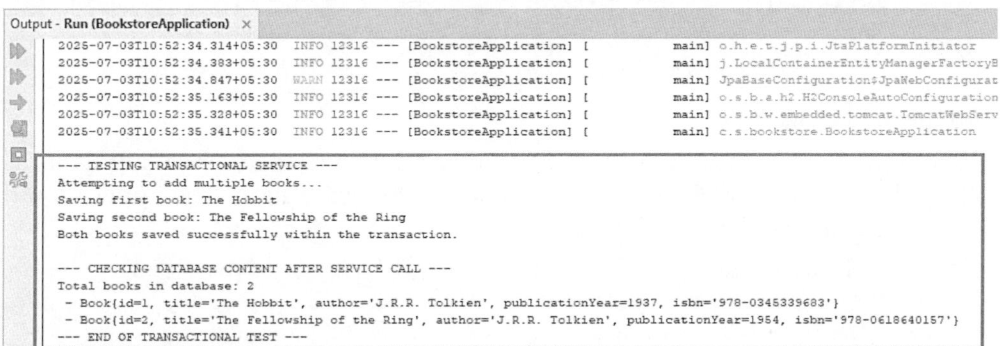

4. To be absolutely sure, access the H2 console at **http://localhost:8080/h2-console** and connect. Run **SELECT * FROM BOOK;** and you can see the two new records for **The Hobbit** and **The Fellowship of the Ring**.

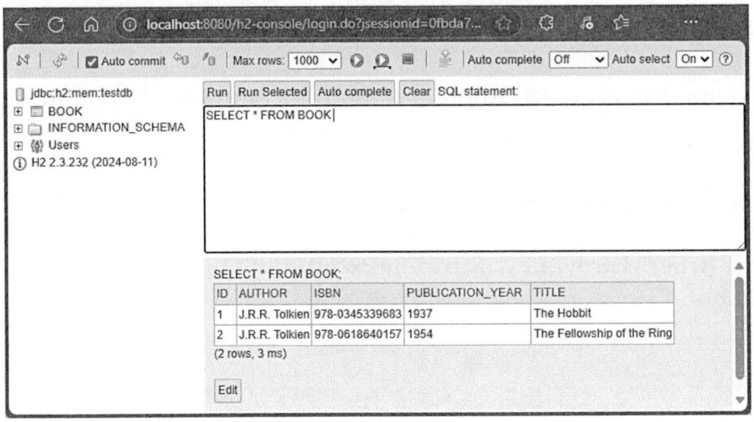

Test 2: Transaction rollback

1. Go back to BookstoreService.java and **uncomment** the **if** block that throws the RuntimeException.

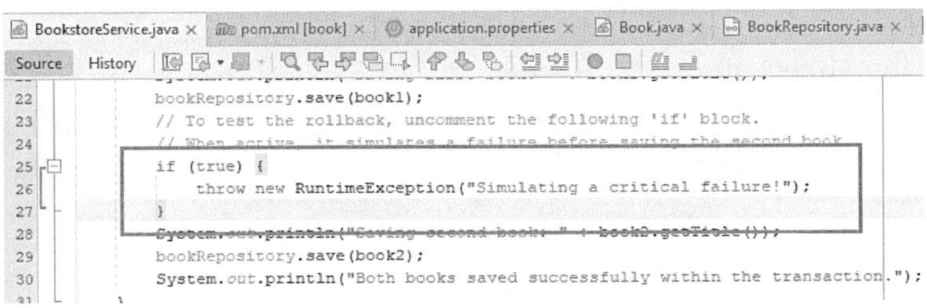

2. Run the project again.
3. Observe the console output carefully. You can see the message for saving the first book, followed by the red error message from the RuntimeException. The application doesn't save the second book.

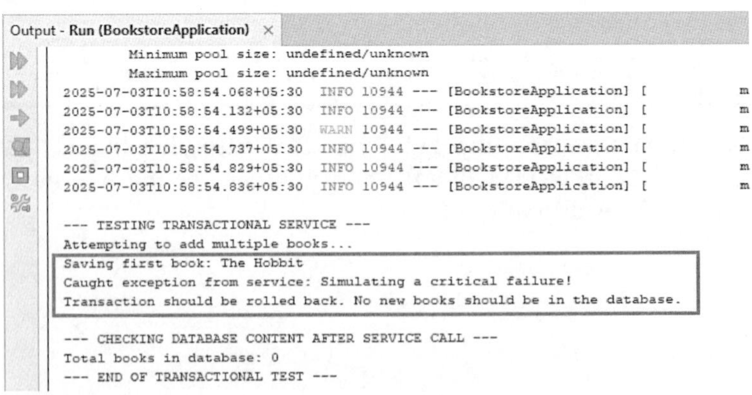

4. Most importantly, check the H2 console again. Run **SELECT * FROM BOOK;**. You neither see that **The Hobbit** nor **The Fellowship of the Ring** is in the table. Even though the first save operation completed, the subsequent exception caused the entire transaction to roll back.

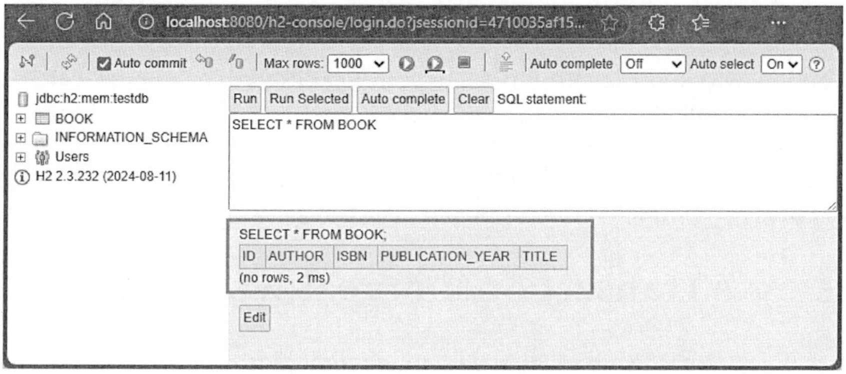

Bridging the gap: Learned concepts and application implementation

This hands-on exercise directly connects theory to practice:

- **@Service:** By annotating **BookstoreService**, we declared it as a Spring bean, making it a candidate for component scanning and dependency injection.
- **@Transactional:** We applied this annotation to the **addMultipleBooks()** method. This instructs Spring's AOP proxy mechanism to wrap this method's execution within a single database transaction.
- **Atomicity:** The two separate **bookRepository.save()** calls are now treated as one atomic unit. They either both succeed and the transaction commits, or one fails and the entire transaction rolls back, leaving the database untouched.

Exploring application behaviour: a practical run-through

In the second test, the following sequence occurred:

1. The CommandLineRunner called the proxied the addMultipleBooks() method.
2. The Spring transaction proxy intercepted the call and started a database transaction via the JPA **EntityManager**.
3. The first line of the method, **bookRepository.save(book1)**, executed successfully, saving "The Hobbit" within the *context* of the ongoing transaction.

4. The next line threw a RuntimeException.
5. The Spring proxy caught this unchecked exception and, following its default rules, immediately marked the transaction for rollback. It issued a **ROLLBACK** command to the database.
6. The database discarded all changes made during the transaction.
7. The exception was then re-thrown so that the calling code (our **try-catch** block in the runner) could handle it.

This demonstrates how **@Transactional** ensures atomicity, protecting your database from inconsistent, partially completed operations.

Harnessing @Transactional in real-world contexts

This pattern is the cornerstone of reliable data management in enterprise applications. You use it to:

- Ensure data consistency when performing multiple related database operations, like creating an order and updating inventory levels simultaneously.
- Simplify your code by removing manual transaction management.
- Apply to service layer methods that orchestrate complex business logic involving one or more database writes.

Wrapping up

Let's quickly review the key takeaways from this chapter:

- Transactions guarantee data integrity using the **ACID** (Atomicity, Consistency, Isolation, Durability) properties.
- Spring's **@Transactional** annotation provides powerful declarative transaction management.
- The magic happens through **AOP proxies** that manage the transaction lifecycle for you.
- By default, Spring transactions automatically roll back on **unchecked exceptions** (like RuntimeException).
- The best practice is to apply **@Transactional** to public methods on your **service layer beans**.

Congratulations! You have just mastered one of the most critical concepts in backend development. You now have the power to write robust service methods that protect the integrity of your application's data. By handling transactions declaratively, you can focus on writing clean business logic, confident that Spring is managing the underlying complexity.

Now that you've mastered the core components of persistence, ***Chapter 9*** is a culmination project where you'll apply everything you've learned so far—entities, repositories, and transactions—to build a complete command-line **Contact Manager** application from the ground up.

Chapter 9

Section 02: Persistence with Hibernate and Spring Data JPA

Culmination: Building a simple Contact Manager

What you'll learn

- Creating entity
- Service layer design
- Building command line runner
- Using repository
- Applying transactions

Welcome to the second culmination chapter of your journey! So far, you have tackled the core theories of persistence one by one: mapping objects to database tables with the Jakarta Persistence API (JPA), simplifying data access with Spring Data repositories, and ensuring data integrity with declarative transactions. Now it's time to assemble those individual building blocks into a single, cohesive application. This chapter is all about practice and reinforcement. You will build a complete command-line application from the ground up, solidifying your understanding of how these powerful persistence layers work together to create a robust and functional data management tool.

PRD: Command-line Contact Manager

This section outlines the requirements for the application you are about to build.

Requirement

The goal is to create a console application that enables a user to perform basic CRUD (Create, Read, Update, Delete) operations on a list of contacts. Each contact must store a name, email address, and phone number, and this data must be saved in a database to ensure it persists between application restarts.

Tools and Frameworks

To build this application, you will use the foundational tools from Section 1, combined with the persistence technologies from Section 2:

- Spring Boot (for the application context and command-line support)
- Spring Boot Data JPA Starter
- Spring Framework Core (for Dependency injection)
- Hibernate (as the JPA implementation)
- H2 database (file-based for persistence)
- Jakarta Persistence 3.1
- JDK 24, Maven, and Apache NetBeans

Hands-on: Developing the Contact Manager

In this hands-on section, we will construct the persistence and service layers for our contact manager and then wire them up to a simple command-line interface for user interaction.

The objective is to apply your knowledge of JPA entities, Spring Data repositories, and transactional services by building a functional command-line contact management application. We will focus on creating a well-structured application where the database logic is cleanly separated from the user interaction logic.

Building the application

Create a Spring Boot project

1. In NetBeans, go to **File → New Project...**.
2. In the **Choose Project** dialog, select **Java with Maven** from the **Categories** list and **Spring Boot Initializr project** from the **Projects** list.

3. Click **Next**. In the **Base Properties** step:
    - Set **Group** to **com.sharanamvaishali** and **Artifact** to **contactproject**.
    - Keep the **Version** as it is (i.e. **0.0.1-SNAPSHOT**).
    - Ensure **Packaging** is **Jar**.
    - Set **Name** to **ContactManager** and **Package Name** to **com.sharanamvaishali.contactmanager**.
    - Select **Java** from the **Language** list and the appropriate **Java Version** (e.g., **24**).
4. Click **Next**. In the **Dependencies** step:
    - Select the appropriate **Spring Boot Version** (e.g., **4.0.0 (SNAPSHOT)**).
    - In the **Available** dependencies list, find and select **Spring Web**.
5. Click **Next**. In the **Name and Location** step:
    - Set **Project Name** to **ContactManagerProject**.
    - Choose a suitable **Project Location**.
6. Click **Finish**. NetBeans generates the project structure and downloads dependencies.

Add the Spring Boot Starter for Data JPA

1. In the **Projects** window, expand your project.
2. Right-click **Dependencies** and select **Add Dependency....**
3. In the **Add Dependency** dialog box, enter **spring-boot-starter-data-jpa** in the **Query** textbox. NetBeans searches for the dependency. Select the entry under the **org.springframework.boot:spring-boot-starter-data-jpa** group and click **Add**.
4. The starter JAR file now appears under **Dependencies**.

Add the H2 Database dependency

Next, we need the specific JDBC driver for the H2 database:

1. Right-click **Dependencies** and select **Add Dependency....**
2. In the **Query** textbox, enter **h2**. Select the entry **com.h2database:h2**. Click **Add**.
3. The H2 driver JAR file appears under **Dependencies**.

Configure the application for a persistent file-based database

To ensure our data survives when the application stops, we will configure H2 to write to a file instead of running purely in memory.

1. In the **Projects** window, navigate to **Other Sources → src/main/resources → <default package>**.
2. Open the application.properties file.
3. Add the following lines to configure the H2 database, enable the web console, and set the database to update its schema automatically based on our entities.

```
spring.datasource.url=jdbc:h2:file:./contactdb;DB_CLOSE_DELAY=-1
spring.datasource.driverClassName=org.h2.Driver
spring.datasource.username=sa
spring.datasource.password=
spring.h2.console.enabled=true
spring.jpa.hibernate.ddl-auto=update
```

Code explanation

The **spring.jpa.hibernate.ddl-auto** property controls Hibernate's schema generation. The **update** value instructs Hibernate to check the database schema against your entity mappings (Contact class) when the application starts and automatically create or update the tables as needed. The book's hands-on guide for this project specifies using this setting to ensure the database is correctly initialized.

> **A Note on the "Open-in-View" Warning**
> You might see a warning: spring.jpa.open-in-view is enabled by default. For a command-line application without web pages, it's good practice to disable this. Add the following line to your application.properties file to remove the warning:
>
> ```
> spring.jpa.open-in-view=false
> ```

Create the Contact Entity

This class defines the structure of our contact data and maps it to a database table.

1. In the **Projects** window, right-click the **com.sharanamvaishali.contactmanager** package and select **New → Java Package...**.
2. Enter **com.sharanamvaishali.contactmanager.domain** as the **Package Name** and click **Finish**.
3. Right-click the **com.sharanamvaishali.contactmanager.domain** package and select **New → Java Class...**.
4. Enter **Contact** as the **Class Name** and click **Finish**.
5. Replace the content of the Contact.java file with the following code:

```
package com.sharanamvaishali.contactmanager.domain;
import jakarta.persistence.Entity;
import jakarta.persistence.GeneratedValue;
import jakarta.persistence.GenerationType;
```

```
import jakarta.persistence.Id;
@Entity
public class Contact {
    @Id
    @GeneratedValue(strategy = GenerationType.IDENTITY)
    private Long id;
    private String name;
    private String email;
    private String phone;
    public Contact() {
    }
    public Contact(String name, String email, String phone) {
        this.name = name;
        this.email = email;
        this.phone = phone;
    }
    public Long getId() {
        return id;
    }
    public void setId(Long id) {
        this.id = id;
    }
    public String getName() {
        return name;
    }
    public void setName(String name) {
        this.name = name;
    }
    public String getEmail() {
        return email;
    }
    public void setEmail(String email) {
        this.email = email;
    }
    public String getPhone() {
        return phone;
    }
    public void setPhone(String phone) {
        this.phone = phone;
    }
    @Override
    public String toString() {
        return "Contact{" + "id=" + id + ", name='" + name + '\'' + ", email='"
                        + email + '\'' + ", phone='" + phone + '\'' + '}';
    }
}
```

Code explanation

- **@Entity:** This JPA annotation marks the Contact class as a persistent entity, meaning it will be mapped to a database table.

- **@Id:** This annotation designates the id field as the primary key for the table.
- **@GeneratedValue(strategy = GenerationType.IDENTITY):** This tells the database to automatically generate the value for the id field, a common strategy for primary keys.

Create the ContactRepository Interface

This interface will provide us with all the necessary CRUD methods without writing a single line of implementation code, thanks to Spring Data JPA.

1. In the **Projects** window, right-click the **com.sharanamvaishali.contactmanager** package and select **New → Java Package....**
2. Enter **com.sharanamvaishali.contactmanager.repository** as the **Package Name** and click **Finish**.
3. Right-click the **com.sharanamvaishali.contactmanager.repository** package and select **New → Java Interface....**
4. Enter **ContactRepository** as the **Interface Name** and click **Finish**.
5. Replace the content of the ContactRepository.java file with the following code:

```
package com.sharanamvaishali.contactmanager.repository;
import com.sharanamvaishali.contactmanager.domain.Contact;
import org.springframework.data.jpa.repository.JpaRepository;
import org.springframework.stereotype.Repository;
@Repository
public interface ContactRepository extends JpaRepository<Contact, Long> {
}
```

Code explanation

- **extends JpaRepository:** By extending this interface, ContactRepository inherits a rich set of methods for data manipulation, such as save(), findById(), findAll(), and deleteById(). The generic types specify that this repository works with Contact entities, whose primary key is of type Long.
- **@Repository:** While often optional when extending JpaRepository, this annotation clearly marks the interface as a Spring bean responsible for data access.

Create the ContactService Service

The service layer contains the business logic. It will use the repository to interact with the database and its methods will be transactional to ensure data integrity.

1. In the **Projects** window, right-click the **com.sharanamvaishali.contactmanager** package and select **New → Java Package....**

2. Enter **com.sharanamvaishali.contactmanager.service** as the **Package Name** and click **Finish**.

3. Right-click the **com.sharanamvaishali.contactmanager.service** package and select **New → Java Class....**

4. Enter **ContactService** as the **Class Name** and click **Finish**.

5. Replace the content of the ContactService.java file with the following code:

```
package com.sharanamvaishali.contactmanager.service;
import com.sharanamvaishali.contactmanager.domain.Contact;
import com.sharanamvaishali.contactmanager.repository.ContactRepository;
import java.util.List;
import java.util.Optional;
import org.springframework.beans.factory.annotation.Autowired;
import org.springframework.stereotype.Service;
import org.springframework.transaction.annotation.Transactional;
@Service
public class ContactService {
    private final ContactRepository contactRepository;
    @Autowired
    public ContactService(ContactRepository contactRepository) {
        this.contactRepository = contactRepository;
    }
    @Transactional
    public Contact saveContact(Contact contact) {
        return contactRepository.save(contact);
    }
    @Transactional(readOnly = true)
    public List<Contact> getAllContacts() {
        return contactRepository.findAll();
    }
    @Transactional(readOnly = true)
    public Optional<Contact> getContactById(Long id) {
        return contactRepository.findById(id);
    }
    @Transactional
    public void deleteContact(Long id) {
        contactRepository.deleteById(id);
    }
}
```

Code explanation

- **@Service:** This marks the class as a Spring service bean, making it a candidate for dependency injection.
- **@Autowired:** We use constructor injection to get an instance of our ContactRepository, which Spring provides automatically.

- **@Transactional:** This powerful annotation is applied to our public methods. For methods that modify data (saveContact, deleteContact), it ensures the operation completes fully or not at all. For read-only methods (getAllContacts, getContactById), we add (readOnly = true) as an optimization hint for the persistence provider.

Create the CommandLineRunner

This component will be the user's entry point into our application. It will run on startup, present a menu, and use our ContactService to perform actions based on user input.

1. In the **Projects** window, right-click the **com.sharanamvaishali.contactmanager** package and select **New → Java Package....**
2. Enter **com.sharanamvaishali.contactmanager.cli** as the **Package Name** and click **Finish**.
3. Right-click the **com.sharanamvaishali.contactmanager.cli** package and select **New → Java Class....**
4. Enter **ContactManagerRunner** as the **Class Name** and click **Finish**.
5. Replace the content of the ContactManagerRunner.java file with the following code:

```
package com.sharanamvaishali.contactmanager.cli;
import com.sharanamvaishali.contactmanager.domain.Contact;
import com.sharanamvaishali.contactmanager.service.ContactService;
import java.util.Scanner;
import org.springframework.boot.CommandLineRunner;
import org.springframework.stereotype.Component;
@Component
public class ContactManagerRunner implements CommandLineRunner {
    private final ContactService contactService;
    public ContactManagerRunner(ContactService contactService) {
        this.contactService = contactService;
    }
    @Override
    public void run(String... args) throws Exception {
        Scanner scanner = new Scanner(System.in);
        while (true) {
            System.out.println("\n--- Contact Manager ---");
            System.out.println("1. Add a new contact");
            System.out.println("2. List all contacts");
            System.out.println("3. Exit");
            System.out.print("Choose an option: ");
            String choice = scanner.nextLine();
            switch (choice) {
                case "1":
                    addContact(scanner);
                    break;
                case "2":
                    listContacts();
                    break;
```

```
                case "3":
                    System.out.println("Exiting application.");
                    return;
                default:
                    System.out.println("Invalid option. Please try again.");
            }
        }
    }
    private void addContact(Scanner scanner) {
        System.out.print("Enter name: ");
        String name = scanner.nextLine();
        System.out.print("Enter email: ");
        String email = scanner.nextLine();
        System.out.print("Enter phone: ");
        String phone = scanner.nextLine();
        Contact newContact = new Contact(name, email, phone);
        contactService.saveContact(newContact);
        System.out.println("Contact saved successfully!");
    }
    private void listContacts() {
        System.out.println("\n--- All Contacts ---");
        contactService.getAllContacts().forEach(System.out::println);
        if (contactService.getAllContacts().isEmpty()) {
            System.out.println("No contacts found.");
        }
    }
}
```

Code explanation:

- **@Component:** Marks this class as a generic Spring bean.
- **implements CommandLineRunner:** This interface signals to Spring Boot that it should execute the run method after the application context is loaded.
- **Scanner:** We use a standard Java Scanner to read input from the console.
- **run() method:** This method contains the main loop of our application, displaying a menu and routing user input to the appropriate private methods (addContact, listContacts).
- **Service calls:** The private methods call our injected ContactService to perform the actual database operations.

Running and testing

Now, let's see our application in action.

1. In the **Projects** window, right-click the **ContactManager** project and select **Run**.
2. The console will start, and you can see the menu appear.

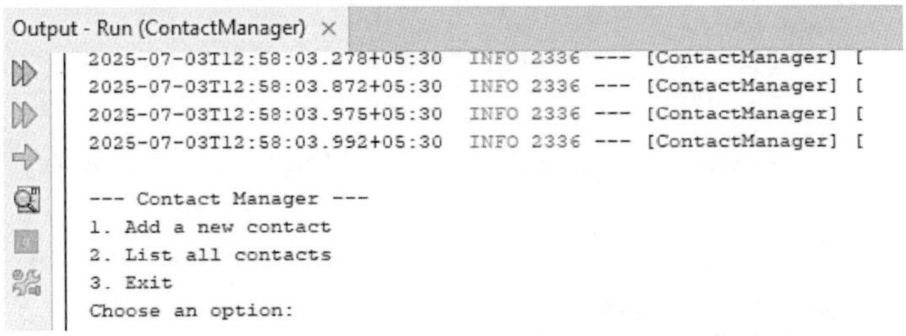

3. Select option **1** to add a new contact. Enter a name, email, and phone number when prompted.

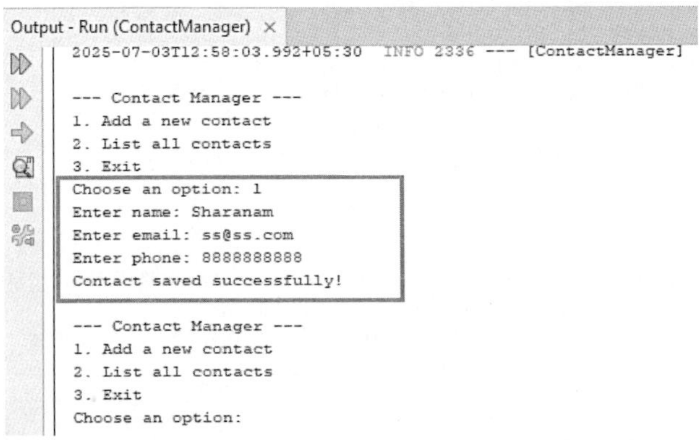

4. Select option **2** to list all contacts. You should see the contact you just added.

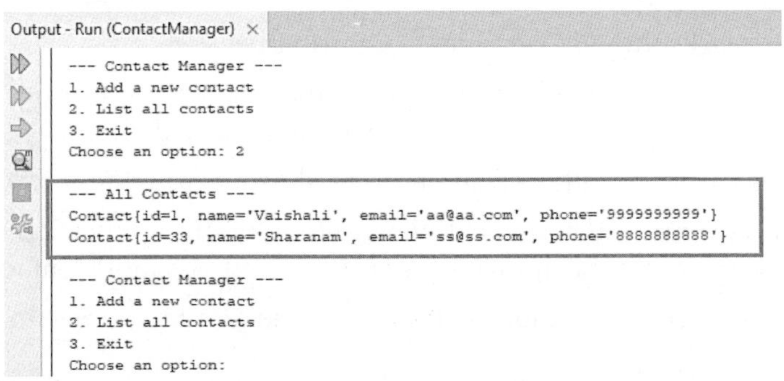

5. Add another contact.
6. Stop the application by clicking the red square button in the **Output** window.
7. Run the application again. Select option **2**. Both contacts you added should still be there, confirming that our data was persisted to the **contactdb** file.
8. To look directly at the database, open your web browser and navigate to **http://localhost:8080/h2-console**. Use the JDBC URL **jdbc:h2:file:./contactdb**.

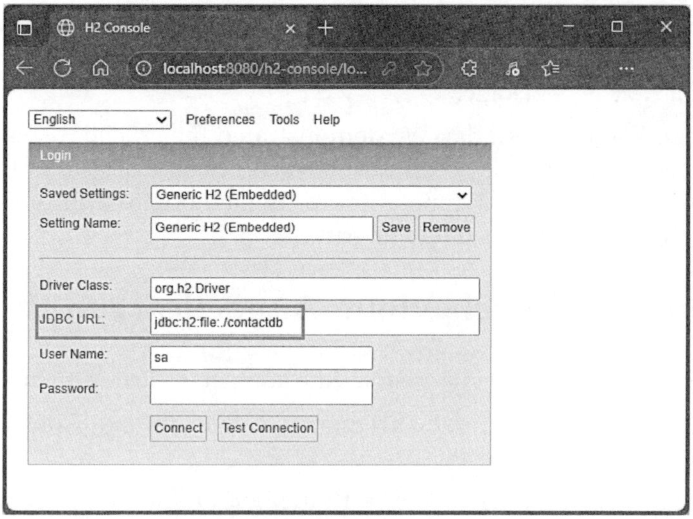

9. Click **Connect**. You can see the **CONTACT** table and can query its contents.

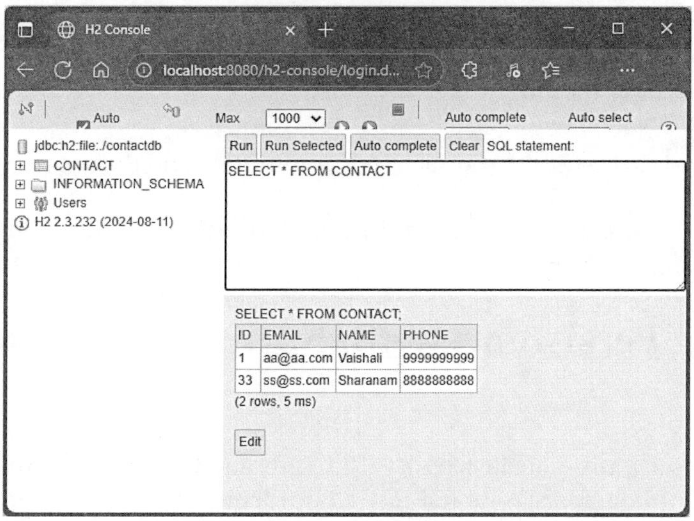

Bridging the gap: Learned concepts and application implementation

This hands-on exercise perfectly demonstrates how the concepts from the previous chapters form a complete persistence layer:

- **@Entity:** We reinforced the creation of a persistent domain object by annotating our Contact class, defining the blueprint for our database table.

- **JpaRepository:** We practiced using Spring Data JPA by creating ContactRepository. This provided a full set of CRUD operations without any implementation code, drastically simplifying our data access logic.
- **Service layer and @Transactional:** We demonstrated the crucial role of a service layer by creating ContactService. This layer encapsulates our business logic and, most importantly, we applied the @Transactional annotation to its methods to ensure that every database operation is safe and maintains data integrity.

Exploring application behaviour: A practical run-through

When you run the application and choose to add a contact, a clear sequence of events occurs.

1. Your input from the console menu triggers a call to the addContact() method in the ContactManagerRunner.
2. This method then invokes the saveContact() method on the ContactService.
3. Because this service method is marked as @Transactional, Spring starts a database transaction.
4. The service then calls the save() method on the ContactRepository implementation provided by Spring Data JPA, which in turn generates and executes the necessary SQL INSERT command.
5. If the command succeeds, the transaction is committed, and the data is permanently saved.

This entire flow, from user input to a safe, transactional database write, demonstrates the power of integrating these layers.

Harnessing Persistence with Spring in real-world contexts

The three-tier architecture you just built—CLI (presentation), Service (business logic), and Repository/Entity (data access)—is not just an academic exercise. It forms the foundational data access layer for nearly every enterprise application. Whether you are managing user data for a social media platform, product catalogues for an e-commerce site, or financial records for a bank, this pattern of using entities, repositories, and transactional services is the standard, robust, and maintainable way to interact with a database in the Spring ecosystem.

Wrapping up

This chapter was a major milestone, combining individual concepts into a working application.

Here are the key takeaways:

- **Entities** are plain Java objects annotated with @Entity that map to database tables.
- **Spring Data JpaRepository** provides full CRUD functionality out of the box, eliminating boilerplate code.
- A **Service layer** (@Service) encapsulates business logic and is the ideal place to manage transactions.
- **@Transactional** is essential for ensuring data operations are atomic and maintain integrity.
- **CommandLineRunner** is a simple and effective way to build interactive console applications with Spring Boot.
- Configuring a **file-based H2 database** is an excellent way to achieve persistence during development.

Congratulations on building your first complete persistence application! You have successfully integrated all the key components of Spring's data management stack.

With this solid foundation in handling data, you are now perfectly prepared to move on to the next exciting part of the book: building interactive web applications. In the next chapter, we will introduce the Model-View-Controller (MVC) pattern and show you how to handle web requests with Spring MVC.

Chapter 10

Section 03: Building web applications with Spring Boot

Handling Web Requests with Spring MVC

What you'll learn

- The MVC design pattern
- Spring MVC components
- Creating controllers
- Mapping HTTP requests
- Extracting request data
- Passing data to views
- Returning view names for server-side rendering

Welcome to the presentation layer! So far, you have built the core logic and data persistence layers of an application. But how does a user actually interact with it through a web browser? This is where Spring MVC comes in. It provides a powerful framework for building web applications, acting as the crucial bridge between a user's click in their browser and the business logic you've carefully crafted in your service layer. In this chapter, you'll learn how to intercept user requests, process them, and prepare data for display on a web page, turning your backend application into an interactive web experience.

Recap: Web starter and embedded Jakarta Servlet containers

As you saw in previous chapters, adding the **spring-boot-starter-web** dependency to your project is transformative. It doesn't just add a few libraries; it installs and configures a complete, ready-to-run web server directly inside your application. By default, this is Apache Tomcat, one of the most widely used **Jakarta Servlet** containers. This "just works" setup means you don't need to install a separate web server or deploy WAR files. Spring Boot handles the entire lifecycle, starting the server when your application runs and shutting it down when it stops, allowing you to focus purely on writing your application's web-facing logic.

The Model-View-Controller (MVC) design pattern

To manage the complexity of web applications, developers rely on proven design patterns. The most common and important one is **Model-View-Controller (MVC)**. It separates an application into three interconnected components:

- **Model:** Represents the application's data and business logic. In our case, this is the data retrieved from the database (like a Book object) and the service layer that processes it.
- **View:** The user interface (UI) that presents the model's data. This is typically an HTML page that the user sees in their browser.
- **Controller:** The intermediary that handles user input and interaction. It receives requests from the user, interacts with the model (e.g., calls a service to fetch data), and then selects a view to render the response.

This separation is key to building maintainable applications. It ensures that business logic is not mixed with presentation code, making the application easier to test, debug, and evolve.

Spring MVC core components

Spring MVC implements the MVC pattern using a set of powerful and loosely coupled components. While you don't always interact with them directly, understanding their roles is helpful. The process starts with **DispatcherServlet**, the front controller of Spring MVC.

Here's a simplified flow of a request:

1. An HTTP request arrives at the embedded servlet container (e.g., Tomcat).
2. The container passes the request to **DispatcherServlet**.
3. **DispatcherServlet** consults **HandlerMapping** to determine which controller method should handle this specific request (based on the URL).

4. **DispatcherServlet** calls the appropriate controller method.
5. The controller method executes your business logic, prepares the data (**Model**), and returns a logical view name.
6. **DispatcherServlet** uses **ViewResolver** to translate the logical view name into an actual **View** (like a Thymeleaf template).
7. The final rendered view (HTML) is returned as the HTTP response to the browser.

Creating web controllers: @Controller

In Spring MVC, a controller is simply a Java class annotated with **@Controller**. This stereotype annotation tells the Spring container that this class is responsible for handling web requests. When Spring Boot starts, it automatically scans for classes with this annotation and registers them as potential handlers for incoming requests.

Mapping HTTP requests

To direct a request to a specific method within your controller, you use mapping annotations. The general-purpose annotation is **@RequestMapping**, but for clarity, it's better to use its HTTP method-specific shortcuts:

- **@GetMapping:** Maps HTTP GET requests. Used for retrieving data (e.g., displaying a page or a list of items).
- **@PostMapping:** Maps HTTP POST requests. Used for creating new data (e.g., submitting a form).
- **@PutMapping:** Maps HTTP PUT requests. Used for updating existing data.
- **@DeleteMapping:** Maps HTTP DELETE requests. Used for deleting data.

You provide a URL path to the annotation, like **@GetMapping("/books")**, to specify which requests the method should handle.

Extracting request data

Controllers often need to extract information from the incoming request URL. Spring MVC makes this easy with special method parameter annotations:

- **@RequestParam:** Use this to extract values from the query string of a URL. For a URL like **/search?keyword=hibernate**, you can capture the value **hibernate** with a method parameter (@RequestParam String keyword).

- **@PathVariable:** Use this to extract values from the URL path itself. For a URL template mapped with **/books/{id}**, a request to **/books/123** can be handled by a method with the parameter (@PathVariable Long id), which would capture the value **123**.

Passing data to the view (Model)

Once a controller has processed a request and fetched the necessary data from a service or repository, it needs a way to pass this data to the view for display. This is done using a **Model** object. You simply add **Model model** as a parameter to your handler method, and Spring will provide an instance. You can then add data to it using the addAttribute() method, giving your data a name (a key) and passing the data object (the value):

```
model.addAttribute("books", allBooks);
```

The view can then access this list of books using the key **books**.

Returning view names for server-side rendering

After the controller has added all necessary data to the model, its final job is to tell Spring which view should be rendered. In server-side rendering, you do this by returning a **String** from your handler method. This string is not the final HTML; it's a ***logical view name***.

For example, returning **book-list** tells **DispatcherServlet** to find a view template named **book-list** (e.g., **book-list.html** in the case of Thymeleaf) to render the response.

Hands-on: Displaying books on a web page

In this hands-on exercise, you will build upon the **BookstoreApplication** project from ***Chapter 7 - Simplified data access with Spring Data JPA***. You will create a Spring MVC controller that fetches the list of all books from the database using BookRepository and prepares this data for display.

While we won't build the final user interface yet, you will create a placeholder HTML page and verify that your controller correctly routes browser requests to it. This confirms that the web layer is correctly configured.

Building the application

We will modify the persistence project from the previous part to add a web layer.

Verify Starter Web dependency

Ensure the pom.xml file contains the spring-boot-starter-web dependency. This was likely added in an earlier chapter but is crucial for this one:

```
<dependency>
    <groupId>org.springframework.boot</groupId>
    <artifactId>spring-boot-starter-web</artifactId>
</dependency>
```

Create a web Package

Organize your code by creating a new package for web controllers.

1. In the **Projects** window, expand your project.
2. Right-click the **Source Packages** node and select **New → Java Package....**
3. Enter **com.sharanamvaishali.bookstore.web** as the **Package Name** and click **Finish**.

Create the BookController

This class will handle web requests related to books.

1. Right-click the **com.sharanamvaishali.bookstore.web** package and select **New → Java Class....**
2. Enter **BookController** as the **Class Name** and click **Finish**.
3. Open the BookController.java file and replace its content with the following code:

```
package com.sharanamvaishali.bookstore.web;
import com.sharanamvaishali.bookstore.repository.BookRepository;
import org.springframework.stereotype.Controller;
import org.springframework.ui.Model;
import org.springframework.web.bind.annotation.GetMapping;
@Controller
public class BookController {
    private final BookRepository bookRepository;
    public BookController(BookRepository bookRepository) {
        this.bookRepository = bookRepository;
    }
    @GetMapping("/books")
    public String listBooks(Model model) {
        var books = bookRepository.findAll();
        model.addAttribute("books", books);
        return "book-list";
    }
}
```

Code explanation

- **@Controller:** This annotation tells Spring that this class is an **MVC controller**. This means it's designed to receive web requests, process them, and typically return a view name or render a response.
- **private final BookRepository bookRepository;:** This declares a private and final field named bookRepository of type BookRepository.
  - **private:** Ensures that bookRepository can only be accessed from within the BookController class.
  - **final:** Guarantees that the bookRepository reference, once assigned in the constructor, cannot be changed later. This is good practice for injected dependencies.
- **public BookController(BookRepository bookRepository) { . . . }:** This is the constructor for the BookController class.
  - It takes an argument of type BookRepository.
  - This demonstrates **Constructor Injection**, a recommended way to provide dependencies in Spring. When Spring creates an instance of BookController, it automatically finds and injects an instance of BookRepository (which it manages as a bean) into this constructor.
  - The injected BookRepository instance is then assigned to the bookRepository field of the controller.
- **@GetMapping("/books"):** This annotation, placed above the listBooks() method, maps **HTTP GET requests to the /books URL path** to this method. So, when a user navigates to http://your-app-url/books in their browser, this method will be executed.
- **public String listBooks(Model model) {:** This declares a public method named listBooks().
  - It returns a String, which in a Spring MVC controller (that returns a view name) represents the **logical name of the view** to be rendered (e.g., a Thymeleaf template named book-list.html).
  - It takes a Model object as an argument. Spring automatically provides this Model object, allowing the controller to add data that will be accessible in the view.
- **var books = bookRepository.findAll();:** This line uses the injected bookRepository to call its findAll() method. This method retrieves all Book entities from the database. The result is stored in a local variable named books. var is a Java 10+ feature for type inference, meaning the compiler infers the type of books (which would be List<Book>).
- **model.addAttribute("books", books);:** This line adds the books list (fetched from the repository) to the Model object.
  - The first argument, "books", is the **name** under which the list of books will be accessible in the view.

  - The second argument, books, is the actual List<Book> object.
  - So, in your book-list.html template, you would typically iterate over a variable named books to display the information.
- **return "book-list";:** This line returns the string "book-list". Spring's view resolver (e.g., configured for Thymeleaf) will then typically resolve this to a physical view file, such as src/main/resources/templates/book-list.html. The data added to the Model (the books list) will be available within that template.

In summary, this BookController is a simple Spring MVC controller that:

- Is responsible for handling HTTP GET requests to the /books URL.
- Uses Dependency Injection to receive an instance of BookRepository.
- Fetches all books from the database using the repository.
- Adds the retrieved list of books to the Spring Model object.
- Returns the logical view name "book-list", which Spring will then render using an appropriate view technology (e.g., Thymeleaf), displaying the book data to the user in a web page.

Create the Placeholder View

This is the HTML file that Spring will render.

1. In the **Projects** window, expand your project.
2. Right-click the **src/main/resources/templates** folder and select **New → Other...**.

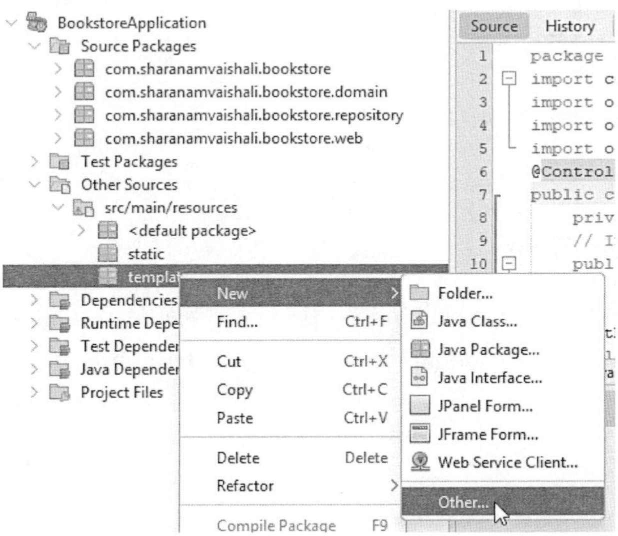

> **TIP** If the **templates** folder does not exist, create it first by right-clicking **src/main/resources**, selecting **New → Folder...**, and naming it **templates**.

3. In the **New File** dialog box, select **Other** from **Categories** section and then select **HTML File** from the **File Types** section.

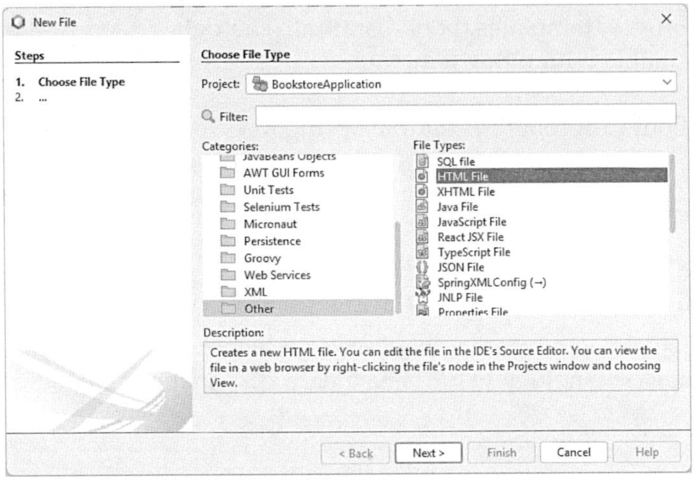

4. Click **Next**. Enter **book-list** as the **File Name** and click **Finish**.
5. Open the **book-list.html** file and add a simple title to verify it works.

```
<!DOCTYPE html>
<html>
    <head>
        <title>Book List</title>
        <meta charset="UTF-8">
    </head>
    <body>
        <h1>Book List Page (Placeholder)</h1>
    </body>
</html>
```

Running and testing

1. Run the application by right-clicking the project in NetBeans and selecting **Run**.
2. Open a web browser and navigate to the following URL: **http://localhost:8080/books**.
3. You see the placeholder page you created, with the heading **Book List Page (Placeholder)** displayed.

If you get an error like this after opening the browser and navigating through the given URL:

Then you need to add the Thymeleaf dependency (explained more in details in the ***Chapter 11: Creating Views with Thymeleaf***).

Add Thymeleaf dependency

Add spring-boot-starter-thymeleaf dependency to your pom.xml:

```
<dependency>
    <groupId>org.springframework.boot</groupId>
    <artifactId>spring-boot-starter-thymeleaf</artifactId>
</dependency>
```

Think of it like this:

- Your BookController says, "Go show the user something called 'book-list'."
- Spring Boot looks around and asks, "Okay, who knows how to show 'book-list'?"
- **Without Thymeleaf:** There's no one. No one on the team (your dependencies) knows how to translate "book-list" into actual HTML that the browser can understand and display. So, Spring Boot throws up its hands and says "Not Found!" (the 404 error).
- **With Thymeleaf:** Spring Boot sees the Thymeleaf dependency and thinks, "Ah! Thymeleaf knows how to do this. I'll pass 'book-list' to Thymeleaf, and it will find book-list.html in src/main/resources/templates/ and render it."

Therefore, adding the spring-boot-starter-thymeleaf dependency is crucial because it provides the necessary **templating engine** and its **Spring Boot auto-configuration** that allows Spring MVC to correctly resolve your book-list view name to the book-list.html file and eventually render it in the browser.

Bridging the gap: Learned concepts and application implementation

This simple exercise connects all the theoretical concepts of the chapter into a working example:

- **@Controller:** We annotated BookController with @Controller, marking it as a Spring-managed web handler.
- **Dependency injection:** BookRepository is injected through the constructor, allowing our web layer to access the data layer without being tightly coupled to its implementation.
- **@GetMapping("/books"):** This annotation maps any HTTP GET request for the **/books** URL directly to our listBooks() method.
- **Model:** The listBooks() method accepts a Model object. We use model.addAttribute("books", ...) to pass the data we fetched from the database into the model. This data is now available to the view under the name **books**.
- **Logical view name:** The method returns the string **book-list**. This tells Spring's DispatcherServlet that it should find a template named **book-list** to render the final HTML response.

Exploring application behaviour: A practical run-through

When you navigate to the **/books** URL, a specific chain of events occurs behind the scenes:

1. The embedded Tomcat server receives your browser's HTTP GET request and passes it to Spring's central DispatcherServlet.
2. DispatcherServlet then examines the URL and, thanks to your @GetMapping("/books") annotation, determines that the BookController.listBooks() method is the correct handler.
3. It invokes this method, which in turn calls the findAll() method on BookRepository to fetch data from the H2 database.
4. This data is added to the Model.
5. Finally, the returned string **book-list** instructs the ViewResolver to find and render the **book-list.html** template, sending the resulting HTML back to your browser.

Harnessing Spring MVC controllers and mappings in real-world contexts

The pattern you just implemented is the backbone of most server-side web applications built with Spring.

Controllers are the primary entry point for all user interactions. They are used to organize the web layer, handle different user actions (like viewing a list, showing a form for adding a new item, or processing that form submission), and delegate business logic to service-layer components. This clean separation of concerns is essential for building applications that are scalable, testable, and easy to maintain, from simple portfolio websites to large-scale enterprise systems.

Wrapping up

- **@Controller** classes act as the entry point for web requests.
- **@GetMapping** and other mapping annotations route requests to specific handler methods based on URL and HTTP method.
- The **Model** is a container for passing data from the controller to the view.
- Returning a **String** from a handler method specifies the logical name of the view to be rendered.
- The **spring-boot-starter-web** dependency provides an embedded servlet container and all the necessary Spring MVC components.

Congratulations! You have successfully created your first web controller and handled a live request from a browser. You've bridged the gap between your powerful backend logic and the user's screen. While the page is just a placeholder for now, you have built the essential plumbing required to serve dynamic content. In the next chapter, you will bring this page to life using Thymeleaf, a modern template engine that will allow you to dynamically render the book data you've prepared, turning your static placeholder into a rich, data-driven web page.

In the upcoming chapter, we'll take these static foundations and breathe life into them. You'll learn how to leverage **Thymeleaf**, a powerful and elegant template engine, to transform your static HTML into dynamic, data-driven views, finally bringing your book list to life directly in the browser.

Chapter 11

Section 03: Building web applications with Spring Boot

Creating Views with Thymeleaf

What you'll learn

- What are template engines?
- Introducing Thymeleaf
- Thymeleaf syntax and expressions

In the previous chapter, you successfully created a web controller that routes a browser request to a method and serves up a web page. However, that page was a static, empty placeholder. It didn't display any of the book data we worked so hard to manage in our service and repository layers. A web application isn't very useful if it can't display dynamic data.

This chapter introduces the solution: **template engines**. Specifically, you'll learn how to use **Thymeleaf**, the modern, elegant template engine that integrates seamlessly with Spring Boot, to transform your static HTML files into dynamic, data-driven views. You'll replace hardcoded content with powerful expressions that fetch data directly from your application, finally bringing your book list to life in the browser.

What are template engines?

At its core, a web application serves HTML to a user's browser. But rarely is that HTML completely static. Think of an e-commerce site; the product list, your shopping cart, and your order history all change based on data. This is where server-side rendering and template engines come into play.

A **template engine** is a tool that runs on the server and processes template files written in a specific format. These templates are mostly HTML but contain special placeholders and logic. The engine combines these templates with data from your Java code to generate the final, dynamic HTML that gets sent to the user's browser.

Spring Boot supports several template engines (like FreeMarker, Mustache, and Groovy Templates), but it has first-class, auto-configuration support for Thymeleaf, making it an excellent choice for Spring developers.

Introduction to Thymeleaf

Thymeleaf is a modern server-side Java template engine built for web and standalone environments. It's designed to be a "natural template" engine. This means a Thymeleaf HTML file is still a perfectly valid HTML file that can be correctly displayed by a browser. Designers can open a Thymeleaf template and see a static prototype without needing to run the application server. When the application runs, Thymeleaf finds its special attributes and replaces the static prototype content with dynamic data.

Adding the Thymeleaf starter

Integrating Thymeleaf into a Spring Boot project is incredibly simple. You only need to add one dependency to your pom.xml file: **spring-boot-starter-thymeleaf**.

Once this starter is on the classpath, Spring Boot's auto-configuration takes over. It automatically configures the necessary beans, including a ViewResolver that knows how to find and render your Thymeleaf templates. By default, it looks for templates in the src/main/resources/templates directory and expects them to have an **.html** extension.

Basic Thymeleaf syntax and expressions

Thymeleaf works by using special attributes in your HTML tags, all of which start with the prefix **th:**.

When Thymeleaf processes the template, it interprets these attributes, executes the logic they contain, and modifies the HTML tag accordingly. Let's look at the most common ones:

- **Variable expressions (${...}):** This is the most common expression. It's used to access data from the Spring Model. For example, if you added an attribute named **books** to the Model, you would access it in your template as ${books}.
- **th:text:** This attribute replaces the body of an HTML tag with the value of its expression. For example, <p th:text="${book.title}">Static Title</p> would result in <p>The Great Gatsby</p> if the book.title variable contained that string.
- **th:each:** This is Thymeleaf's looping mechanism, perfect for iterating over collections. You use it to repeat an HTML element for each item in a list.
- **th:if:** This attribute conditionally renders an HTML element. If the expression evaluates to **true**, the element and its children are included in the output. If **false**, they are removed.
- **Link expressions (@{...}):** This expression is used for creating URLs. It's essential for building links that are aware of the application's context path. For example, @{/books/add} ensures the link works correctly whether your app runs at the root (/**) or under a sub-path (/my-app/).

Hands-on: Displaying the book list with Thymeleaf

In this hands-on section, you will modify the web application from the previous ***Chapter 10 - Handling web requests with Spring MVC***. You will replace the static placeholder book-list.html with a dynamic Thymeleaf template that iterates over a list of Book objects and displays them in a clean HTML table.

Building the application

Verify Thymeleaf Starter dependency

Ensure the pom.xml file contains the **spring-boot-starter-thymeleaf** dependency. This was likely added in an earlier chapter:

```
<dependency>
    <groupId>org.springframework.boot</groupId>
    <artifactId>spring-boot-starter-thymeleaf</artifactId>
</dependency>
```

Updating the view template

Now, let's modify the HTML file to use Thymeleaf's syntax.

1. In the **Projects** window, navigate to **Source Packages → src/main/resources → templates**.

2. Open the **book-list.html** file. Replace its entire content with the following code:

```
<!DOCTYPE html>
<html xmlns:th="http://www.thymeleaf.org">
<head>
    <title>Book List</title>
    <meta charset="UTF-8">
    <meta name="viewport" content="width=device-width, initial-scale=1.0">
</head>
<body>
    <h1>Our Book Collection</h1>
    <table border="1">
        <thead>
            <tr>
                <th>Title</th>
                <th>Author</th>
                <th>ISBN</th>
                <th>Publication Year</th>
            </tr>
        </thead>
        <tbody>
            <tr th:each="book : ${books}">
                <td th:text="${book.title}">Book Title</td>
                <td th:text="${book.author}">Author Name</td>
                <td th:text="${book.isbn}">ISBN-13</td>
                <td th:text="${book.publicationYear}">2025</td>
            </tr>
        </tbody>
    </table>
</body>
</html>
```

Code explanation:

- **xmlns:th="http://www.thymeleaf.org":** This is the standard Thymeleaf namespace declaration. It tells the template engine (and your IDE) which attributes belong to Thymeleaf.
- **<tr th:each="book : ${books}">:** This is the core of our dynamic table. The th:each attribute iterates over the collection found in the Model with the key **books**. For each element in the collection, it creates a new local variable named **book** and renders a new <tr> (table row) element.
- **<td th:text="${book.title}">:** Inside the loop, we access properties of the **book** object. The th:text attribute replaces the placeholder text (like **Book Title**) inside the <td> tag with the actual value of book.title for the current book in the iteration. We do this for the author, ISBN, and publication year as well.

Running and testing

Let's see our dynamic page in action:

1. Ensure you have a CommandLineRunner that saves some Book objects to the database, as established in previous ***Chapter 10 - Handling web requests with Spring MVC***, so there is data to display.
2. Run the main application class from NetBeans.
3. Open a web browser and navigate to **http://localhost:8080/books**.
4. Instead of a blank page, you can now see a styled HTML table populated with the book data from your database.

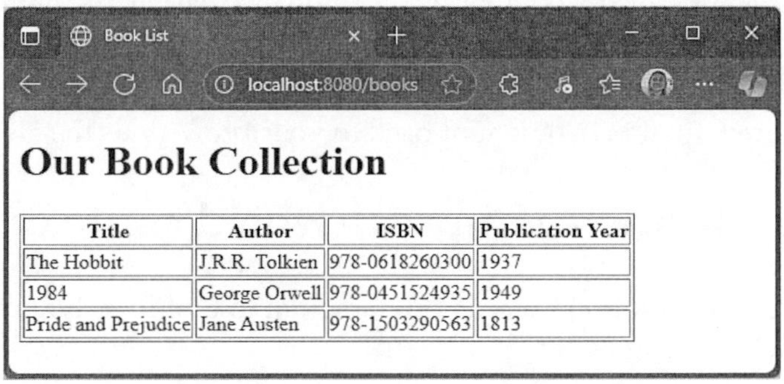

Bridging the gap: Learned concepts and application implementation

This hands-on exercise directly applies the concepts from this chapter:

- **Auto-configuration:** By adding the **spring-boot-starter-thymeleaf** dependency, you triggered Spring Boot's auto-configuration. It set up a ThymeleafViewResolver bean that tells Spring MVC how to process your templates.
- **Template location:** Spring Boot automatically looks for your template named **book-list** in src/main/resources/templates/book-list.html, matching the logical view name you returned from the controller in ***Chapter 10 - Handling web requests with Spring MVC***.
- **Dynamic data:** The Model object you populated in your BookController is the bridge to the view. The ${books} expression in the template directly pulls that List<Book> out of the Model.
- **Syntax in Action:** You used th:each to create the table rows dynamically, th:text to populate the cells with data from each book object, and @{...} to create a safe, context-aware URL.

Exploring application behaviour: A practical run-through

Here's a summary of what happens when you request the **/books** URL:

1. Spring MVC routes the request to your BookController's listBooks() method.
2. The controller calls the service/repository to fetch all Book objects from the database.
3. The controller adds this list of books to the Model under the key **books**.
4. The controller returns the logical view name **book-list**.
5. Spring's ThymeleafViewResolver identifies that **book-list** corresponds to the src/main/resources/templates/book-list.html template.
6. The Thymeleaf engine processes this file. It finds the th:each attribute, loops through the books collection from the Model, and generates an HTML <tr> for each one, filling in the <td> elements with data using th:text.
7. The fully rendered, final HTML is sent back to your browser as the HTTP response.

Harnessing Thymeleaf in real-world contexts

The pattern you learned in this chapter is fundamental to building dynamic, server-rendered web applications with Spring Boot.

- **Data display:** It's used for displaying product catalogues, user profiles, search results, dashboards, and any other data-driven content.
- **Separation of concerns:** Thymeleaf helps maintain a clean separation between your presentation layer (HTML) and your business logic (Java). Your Java controllers prepare the data, and your Thymeleaf templates decide how to display it.
- **Interactive UIs:** Combined with links and forms, Thymeleaf is the foundation for creating rich, interactive user interfaces for your web applications.

Wrapping up

- **Template engines** combine data with templates to generate dynamic HTML.
- **Thymeleaf** is a modern, natural template engine that integrates seamlessly with Spring Boot.
- Adding the **spring-boot-starter-thymeleaf** dependency is all you need for basic setup.
- Thymeleaf uses **th:** attributes like th:text, th:each, and th:if to manipulate the HTML.
- Variable expressions ${...} access data from the Spring Model.

- Link expressions @{...} create context-aware URLs.

Congratulations! You've taken a massive step forward by transforming a static page into a dynamic view. You now have a complete read-only web application that pulls data from a database and presents it cleanly to a user.

In the next chapter, we will close the loop by learning how to handle user input. You will build web forms that allow users to submit data back to the application, enabling you to create, update, and manage your data directly from the browser.

Chapter 12

Section 03: Building web applications with Spring Boot

Working with Web Forms

What you'll learn

- Anatomy of web form
- Form data submission
- Binding form data to Java objects
- Processing form submissions
- Data validation
- Handling validation results
- The Post-Redirect-Get pattern
- Thymeleaf's form handling support

So far, our web application can display a list of books from our database, which is a fantastic start. However, most web applications are interactive. Users need to be able to submit information—whether it's creating a new social media post, registering for an account, or, in our case, adding a new book to our catalogue. This is where web forms come in. They are the primary way users send data from their browser to our server-side Spring Boot application.

This chapter dives into how Spring MVC makes handling web forms straightforward and secure. We'll explore how to display forms, capture user input into our Java objects, validate that the data is correct, provide helpful feedback if it isn't, and safely save it to our database, preventing common web pitfalls like duplicate submissions.

The anatomy of a web form

At its core, a web form is a section of an HTML document containing interactive controls like text fields, buttons, and checkboxes. The process begins with two fundamental HTML tags:

- **<form>:** This tag acts as a container for all the input elements. It has two crucial attributes:
  - **action:** The URL where the form data is sent for processing.
  - **method:** The HTTP method used to send the data.
- **<input>:** This tag represents a data entry field.
  - **type:** This attribute can be **text**, **password**, **submit**, and many others.
  - **name:** This attribute is essential, as it provides the key that our Spring application uses to identify the submitted value.

Submitting form data: GET vs. POST

You can send form data using two primary HTTP methods:

- **GET:** Appends the form data directly to the URL as query parameters (e.g., **/search?query=Spring+Boot**). GET requests are suitable for non-sensitive, idempotent operations like search queries or filtering. They are bookmarkable but have limitations on data length and are not secure for sensitive information.
- **POST:** Sends the form data within the body of the HTTP request. This method is preferred for any action that creates or modifies data. It's more secure, doesn't have the same size limitations, and the data is not visible in the browser's address bar. For adding a new book, we will use POST.

Binding form data to Java objects

Manually extracting every form field from a request would be tedious and error-prone. Spring provides a powerful annotation, **@ModelAttribute**, to automatically bind incoming form data to a Java object.

When a user submits a form, Spring MVC looks at the **name** attributes of the input fields and matches them to the field names of the object annotated with @ModelAttribute. For example, an input field with **name="title"** will be automatically mapped to the **title** field of our **Book** entity. This process is called **data binding**.

Processing submissions

In our controller, we use the **@PostMapping** annotation to create a handler method that specifically listens for POST requests to a given URL. This is where we place our logic to receive the form data (bound to an object via @ModelAttribute), validate it, and then call our service layer to persist it.

Data validation with Jakarta Bean Validation

Accepting user input without validation is a significant security risk and leads to poor data quality. A user might forget to enter a title or submit an invalid ISBN. We must validate data on the server side (even if we also have client-side validation).

The Spring Boot ecosystem integrates seamlessly with Jakarta Bean Validation, the standard specification for bean validation in Java. By adding the **spring-boot-starter-validation** dependency, we can use simple annotations on our entity fields to define validation rules.

Common validation annotations include:

- **@NotEmpty:** Ensures a string field is not null and not empty.
- **@Size(min=X, max=Y):** Checks if a string's length is within a specific range.
- **@Min(value=X):** Verifies a number is not less than a specified value.
- **@Email:** Validates that a string is a well-formed email address.

To trigger this validation in our controller, we simply add the **@Valid** annotation before our @ModelAttribute object.

Handling validation results

What happens when validation fails? Spring doesn't just throw an error. Instead, it populates an object called **BindingResult** with all the validation errors. To capture these errors, we add a BindingResult parameter to our handler method, placed ***immediately*** after the @Valid annotated object:

```
public String addBook(
    @Valid @ModelAttribute("book") Book book, BindingResult bindingResult) {
    if (bindingResult.hasErrors()) {
        // If there are errors, return to the form page
        return "book-form";
    }
    // If everything is okay, save the book
```

```
        bookService.save(book);
        return "redirect:/books";
}
```

If bindingResult.hasErrors() returns **true**, we know something is wrong. In this case, we simply return the name of our form view. Spring is smart enough to re-render the form, and because we are using Thymeleaf, we can easily display the error messages next to the corresponding fields.

The Post-Redirect-Get (PRG) pattern

Notice the return statement in the successful path of the method above:

```
return "redirect:/books"
```

This is an implementation of the Post-Redirect-Get (PRG) pattern, a crucial web development practice.

Here's the problem it solves:
If you submit a form and the server simply returns a "Success" page, what happens if the user hits the browser's refresh button? The browser will resubmit the POST request, potentially creating a duplicate record in your database.

The PRG pattern prevents this.

1. **POST:** The user submits the form. The server processes it and saves the data.
2. **Redirect:** Instead of returning a view, the server sends a redirect response to the browser, telling it to go to a different URL (like the book list page).
3. **GET:** The browser makes a new GET request to the new URL.

Now, if the user refreshes the page, they are only refreshing the GET request for the book list, which is a safe, idempotent operation.

Thymeleaf's form handling support

Thymeleaf offers special attributes to make working with forms and displaying validation errors incredibly simple:

- **th:object:** Binds the entire form to a model attribute.
- **th:field:** A powerful attribute that replaces the **name**, **id**, and **value** attributes of an input. It uses the field name from th:object to correctly bind the input. For example, th:field="*{title}" links the input to the **title** property of the form-backing object.

- **th:errors:** Displays validation errors for a specific field.
- **th:if:** Conditionally renders an element. We use this to check if errors exist before trying to display them.

Hands-on: Adding a new book via a web form

In this hands-on section, we will enhance our bookstore application by adding the functionality to create new books. You will build a web form, implement server-side validation using Jakarta Bean Validation, display user-friendly error messages with Thymeleaf, and protect against duplicate submissions using the Post-Redirect-Get pattern.

Building the application

We'll continue with the project from the previous ***Chapter 11 - Creating Views with Thymeleaf***.

Add the Validation Starter dependency

First, we need to add the Spring Boot Starter Validation dependency for validation:

1. In the **Projects** window, expand your bookstore project.
2. Right-click **Dependencies** and select **Add Dependency....**
3. In the **Add Dependency** dialog box, enter **spring-boot-starter-validation** in the **Query** textbox.
4. In the search results, select the entry for **org.springframework.boot:spring-boot-starter-validation** and click **Add**.
5. The validation starter JAR file appears under **Dependencies**.

Add Validation annotations to the Book entity

Next, let's define the validation rules directly on our **Book** entity. Open the Book.java file and add @NotEmpty and @Size annotations to the **title** and **author** fields:

```
package com.sharanamvaishali.bookstore.domain;
import jakarta.persistence.Entity;
import jakarta.persistence.GeneratedValue;
import jakarta.persistence.GenerationType;
import jakarta.persistence.Id;
import jakarta.validation.constraints.NotEmpty;
import jakarta.validation.constraints.Size;
@Entity
```

```java
public class Book {
    @Id
    @GeneratedValue(strategy = GenerationType.IDENTITY)
    private Long id;
    @NotEmpty(message = "Title cannot be empty.")
    @Size(min = 2, max = 100, message = "Title must be between 2 and 100
          characters.")
    private String title;
    @NotEmpty(message = "Author cannot be empty.")
    @Size(min = 2, max = 100, message = "Author must be between 2 and 100
          characters.")
    private String author;
    private String isbn;
    private Integer publicationYear;
    public Book() {
    }
    public Book(String title, String author, String isbn, Integer publicationYear) {
        this.title = title;
        this.author = author;
      this.isbn = isbn;
        this.publicationYear = publicationYear;
    }
    public Long getId() {
        return id;
    }
    public void setId(Long id) {
        this.id = id;
    }
    public String getTitle() {
        return title;
    }
    public void setTitle(String title) {
        this.title = title;
    }
    public String getAuthor() {
        return author;
    }
    public void setAuthor(String author) {
        this.author = author;
    }
    public Integer getPublicationYear() {
        return publicationYear;
    }
    public void setPublicationYear(Integer publicationYear) {
        this.publicationYear = publicationYear;
    }
    public String getIsbn() {
        return isbn;
    }
```

```
    public void setIsbn(String isbn) {
        this.isbn = isbn;
    }
    @Override
    public String toString() {
        return "Book{" + "id=" + id + ", title='" + title + '\'' +
            ", author='" + author + '\'' + ", publicationYear=" + publicationYear
            + ", isbn='" + isbn + '\'' + '}';
    }
}
```

Code explanation

- Validation on **title** field:
    - **@NotEmpty(message = "Title cannot be empty."):**
        - This annotation ensures that the title field cannot be null and cannot be an empty string.
        - **message = "Title cannot be empty.":** This custom message will be returned to the user if the title field fails this validation rule.
    - **@Size(min = 2, max = 100, message = "Title must be between 2 and 100 characters."):**
        - This annotation enforces that the title string must have a minimum length of 2 characters and a maximum length of 100 characters.
        - **min = 2:** Specifies the minimum allowed length.
        - **max = 100:** Specifies the maximum allowed length.
        - **message = "Title must be between 2 and 100 characters.":** The custom error message for this validation rule.
- Validation on **author** Field:
    - **@NotEmpty(message = "Author cannot be empty."):** Similar to the title field, this ensures the author field is not null or an empty string.
    - **@Size(min = 2, max = 100, message = "Author must be between 2 and 100 characters."):** Again, similar to the title field, this enforces a length constraint on the author string, between 2 and 100 characters.

Create the Controller method to display the form

Now, in BookController.java, add a method to handle GET requests for the "add book" page. This method will simply prepare an empty **Book** object and pass it to the view, which will use it to structure the HTML form:

```
package com.sharanamvaishali.bookstore.web;
import com.sharanamvaishali.bookstore.repository.BookRepository;
import org.springframework.stereotype.Controller;
```

```
import org.springframework.ui.Model;
import org.springframework.web.bind.annotation.GetMapping;
@Controller
public class BookController {
    private final BookRepository bookRepository;
    public BookController(BookRepository bookRepository) {
        this.bookRepository = bookRepository;
    }
    @GetMapping("/books")
    public String listBooks(Model model) {
        var books = bookRepository.findAll();
        model.addAttribute("books", books);
        return "book-list";
    }
    @GetMapping("/books/add")
    public String showAddBookForm(Model model) {
        model.addAttribute("book", new Book());
        return "book-form";
    }
}
```

Code explanation

- **@GetMapping("/books/add"):** This annotation maps HTTP GET requests to /books/add URL to the showAddBookForm() method. This is the endpoint that users will hit when they want to add a new book (e.g., by clicking an "Add Book" button).
- **public String showAddBookForm(Model model):** Similar to listBooks(), this method returns a logical view name and receives a Model object.
- **model.addAttribute("book", new Book());:** This is the core of this method's purpose.
    - It creates a **new, empty Book object**.
    - It then adds this empty Book object to the Model with the attribute name "book".
    - **Why an empty Book object?** When you render a form for creating a new entity, the form fields need to be bound to ***something***. By providing an empty Book object, your Thymeleaf (or other template engine) form can then use this object to structure its input fields. For example, a Thymeleaf input field for the title might look like <input type="text" th:field="*{title}" />. The *{title} expression tells Thymeleaf to bind this input to the title property of the book object in the model. This is essential for:
        - **Form binding:** Allowing the template engine to correctly render form fields (e.g., for title, author, etc.).
        - **Validation error display:** If the form is submitted with invalid data and the server returns to the form, the book object (now populated with the invalid data and potentially error messages) can be used to re-populate the form fields and display validation errors next to the relevant fields.

- **return "book-form";:** This returns the logical view name "book-form". Spring will resolve this to a template file named book-form.html. This book-form.html file will contain the actual HTML form for adding/editing a book.

Create the Thymeleaf form template

We need an HTML file for our form.

1. In the **Projects** window, expand your project.
2. Right-click the **src/main/resources/templates** folder and select **New → HTML File....**
3. Enter **book-form** as the **File Name** and click **Finish**.
4. Open the newly created book-form.html and replace its content with the following code:

```
<!DOCTYPE html>
<html xmlns:th="http://www.thymeleaf.org">
    <head>
        <title>Add Book</title>
    </head>
    <body>
        <h1>Add a New Book</h1>
        <form action="#" th:action="@{/books/add}" th:object="${book}"
              method="post">
            <div>
                <label>Title:</label>
                <input type="text" th:field="*{title}" />
                <span th:if="${#fields.hasErrors('title')}" th:errors="*{title}"
                         style="color:red;">Title Error</span>
            </div><br/>
            <div>
                <label>Author:</label>
                <input type="text" th:field="*{author}" />
                <span th:if="${#fields.hasErrors('author')}" th:errors="*{author}"
                         style="color:red;">Author Error</span>
            </div><br/>
            <div>
                <label>ISBN:</label>
                <input type="text" th:field="*{isbn}" />
            </div><br/>
            <div>
                <label>Publication Year:</label>
                <input type="number" th:field="*{publicationYear}" />
            </div><br/>
            <div>
                <button type="submit">Add Book</button>
            </div>
        </form>
    </body>
</html>
```

Code explanation

- **th:action="@{/books/add}":** This is a Thymeleaf attribute that dynamically generates the action URL for the form. **@{/books/add}** is a **Thymeleaf URL expression**. It's used to create context-relative URLs. Spring Boot (and embedded servers like Tomcat) will automatically resolve this to the correct absolute URL for your application (e.g., http://localhost:8080/books/add). This ensures that your form always submits to the correct endpoint, regardless of the application's deployment context.
- **th:object="${book}":** This is a critical Thymeleaf attribute for **form binding**. **${book}** refers to the Book object that you added to the Model in your BookController's showAddBookForm() method (model.addAttribute("book", new Book());). This tells Thymeleaf that all fields within this form (that use th:field) should be bound to properties of this book object.
- **<input type="text" th:field="*{title}" />:** This is where the magic of Thymeleaf form binding happens.
  - **th:field="*{title}":** This is another essential Thymeleaf attribute for form binding.
    - ***{title}:** This is a **field expression** in Thymeleaf. It tells Thymeleaf to bind this input field to the title property of the book object (th:object="${book}") that was passed to the view.
    - **What th:field does?** When processed, th:field automatically generates the id, name, and value attributes for the <input> tag based on the bound property. For *{title}, it would typically generate something like <input type="text" id="title" name="title" value="[current value of book.title]" />. This is incredibly convenient for form handling, especially when re-displaying a form with pre-filled data or validation errors.
- **<span> for Validation errors:** These <span> tags are used to display validation error messages dynamically.
  - **th:if="${#fields.hasErrors('title')}":**
    - **th:if:** A Thymeleaf conditional attribute. The content of this <span> will only be rendered if the condition is true.
    - **#fields.hasErrors('title'):** This is a Thymeleaf **utility object** (#fields) and a method (hasErrors). It checks if there are any validation errors associated with the title field of the book object.
  - **th:errors="*{title}":** If th:if evaluates to true (i.e., there are errors for title), this attribute will automatically render the specific error messages associated with the title field. The error messages come from the @NotEmpty and @Size annotations (or custom messages you define) on your Book entity.

- **<button type="submit">Add Book</button>:** A standard HTML button that, when clicked, will submit the form data to the th:action URL using the specified method (POST in this case).

Create the Controller method to process the form

This is the most critical part. Add the following method to BookController.java to handle the POST request when the user submits the form. It includes @Valid to trigger validation and BindingResult to catch any errors:

```
package com.sharanamvaishali.bookstore.web;
import com.sharanamvaishali.bookstore.domain.Book;
import com.sharanamvaishali.bookstore.repository.BookRepository;
import jakarta.validation.Valid;
import org.springframework.stereotype.Controller;
import org.springframework.ui.Model;
import org.springframework.validation.BindingResult;
import org.springframework.web.bind.annotation.GetMapping;
import org.springframework.web.bind.annotation.ModelAttribute;
import org.springframework.web.bind.annotation.PostMapping;
@Controller
public class BookController {
    private final BookRepository bookRepository;
    public BookController(BookRepository bookRepository) {
        this.bookRepository = bookRepository;
    }
    @GetMapping("/books")
    public String listBooks(Model model) {
        var books = bookRepository.findAll();
        model.addAttribute("books", books);
        return "book-list";
    }
    @GetMapping("/books/add")
    public String showAddBookForm(Model model) {
        model.addAttribute("book", new Book());
        return "book-form";
    }
    @PostMapping("/books/add")
    public String addBook(@Valid @ModelAttribute("book") Book book,
                          BindingResult bindingResult) {
        if (bindingResult.hasErrors()) {
            return "book-form";
        }
        bookRepository.save(book);
```

```
        return "redirect:/books";
    }
}
```

Code explanation

- **@PostMapping("/books/add"):** This annotation maps HTTP POST requests to the /books/add URL to the addBook() method. This means when the form (from book-form.html) is submitted with method="post" to /books/add, this specific method will be invoked. This contrasts with @GetMapping which is used for retrieving data or displaying forms.
- **public String addBook(@Valid @ModelAttribute("book") Book book, BindingResult bindingResult):** This method, and its parameters are critical for handling form submissions and validation.
    - **@Valid**: This annotation instructs Spring to apply all validation rules defined in the Book entity (e.g., @NotEmpty, @Size) to the book object **after** it has been populated from the form data. If any validation rules are violated, errors will be stored in the BindingResult.
    - **@ModelAttribute("book") Book book:**
        - **@ModelAttribute("book"):** This annotation tells Spring to take the form data from the incoming request and bind it to a new Book object. The "book" argument here explicitly specifies the model attribute name that was used when rendering the form (i.e., th:object="${book}" in book-form.html). This ensures that the incoming data is mapped correctly to the Book object.
        - **Book book:** This declares a parameter of type Book, which will hold the populated (and potentially validated) Book object.
    - **BindingResult bindingResult**: This parameter **must immediately follow** the @ModelAttribute (or @RequestBody) parameter that is being validated. Spring will automatically populate this BindingResult object with any validation errors that occurred when @Valid was applied to the book object. If there are no errors, bindingResult.hasErrors() will return false.
- **Validation error handling:**
    - **if (bindingResult.hasErrors()) {:** This is the crucial check for validation.
        - **bindingResult.hasErrors():** This method returns true if any validation constraints defined on the Book entity were violated during the data binding and validation process.
    - **return "book-form";:** If bindingResult.hasErrors() is true, this line is executed. It returns the logical view name "book-form". **Why return to the same form?** When there are validation errors, you want to show the user the form again, but with:
        - The previously entered (invalid) data pre-filled in the fields.

        - The specific error messages displayed next to the problematic fields (as configured in book-form.html with th:if="${#fields.hasErrors('fieldName')}" and th:errors="*{fieldName}").
        - Spring MVC and Thymeleaf automatically handle this. Because the book object (containing the invalid data and error information in its BindingResult) is still available in the model implicit to the redirect or forward, the book-form.html template can access it to re-populate the fields and display errors.

- **return "redirect:/books";:** If the book is saved successfully (i.e., no validation errors), this line performs a **redirect**.
    - **"redirect:/books":** This is a special prefix in Spring MVC that tells the dispatcher servlet to issue an HTTP redirect to the client's browser. **Why redirect?** This is a crucial pattern known as **"Post/Redirect/Get" (PRG) pattern**.
        - It prevents **duplicate form submissions** if the user refreshes the page after a successful POST. If you just returned a view name, refreshing would re-POST the form, potentially creating duplicate entries.
        - It ensures that the browser's URL reflects the current state (a list of books), rather than the form submission URL.
        - After the redirect, the client's browser will make a new GET request to /books, which will trigger your listBooks() method, displaying the updated list including the newly added book.

Add a Link to the form

Finally, let's make it easy for users to get to our new form. Open book-list.html and add a link to the "add book" page:

```
<!DOCTYPE html>
<html xmlns:th="http://www.thymeleaf.org">
    <head>
        <title>Book List</title>
        <meta charset="UTF-8">
        <meta name="viewport" content="width=device-width, initial-scale=1.0">
    </head>
    <body>
        <h1>Our Book Collection</h1>
        <a th:href="@{/books/add}">Add a New Book</a>
        <br/><br/>
        <table border="1">
            <thead>
                <tr>
                    <th>Title</th>
                    <th>Author</th>
```

```
                    <th>ISBN</th>
                    <th>Publication Year</th>
                </tr>
            </thead>
            <tbody>
                <tr th:each="book : ${books}">
                    <td th:text="${book.title}">Book Title</td>
                    <td th:text="${book.author}">Author Name</td>
                    <td th:text="${book.isbn}">ISBN-13</td>
                    <td th:text="${book.publicationYear}">2025</td>
                </tr>
            </tbody>
        </table>
    </body>
</html>
```

Running and testing

Now, let's see our form in action.

1. Run your main application class from NetBeans.
2. Open your browser and navigate to **http://localhost:8080/books**. Click the **Add a New Book** link. You see the form you created.

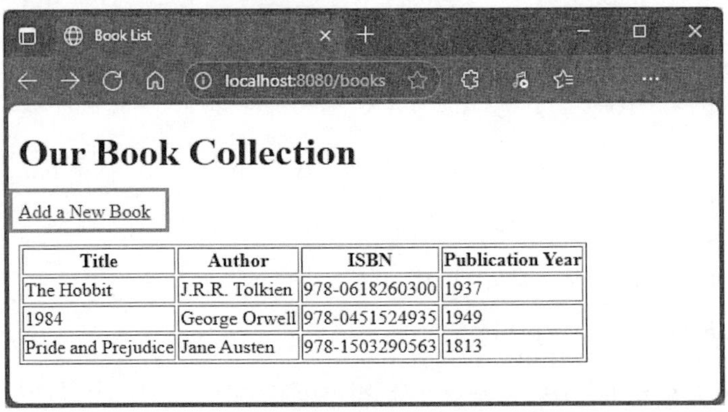

3. **Test the validation**: Click the **Add a New Book** button without filling out any fields. You can see the form reload with your red error messages displayed next to the Title and Author fields.

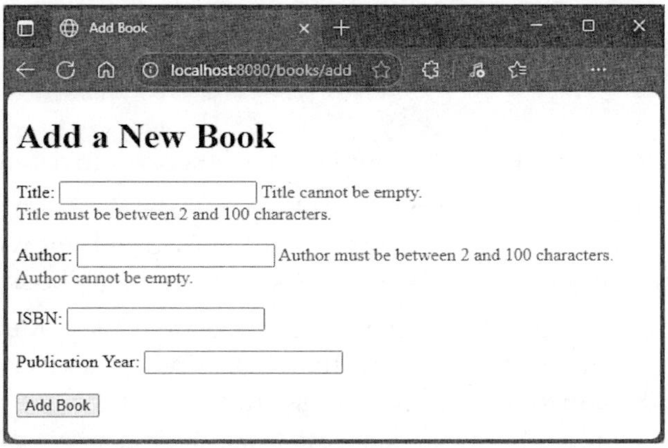

4. **Test a valid submission:** Fill out the form with valid data and click **Add Book**. You are redirected back to the main book list, and your new book appears in the table.

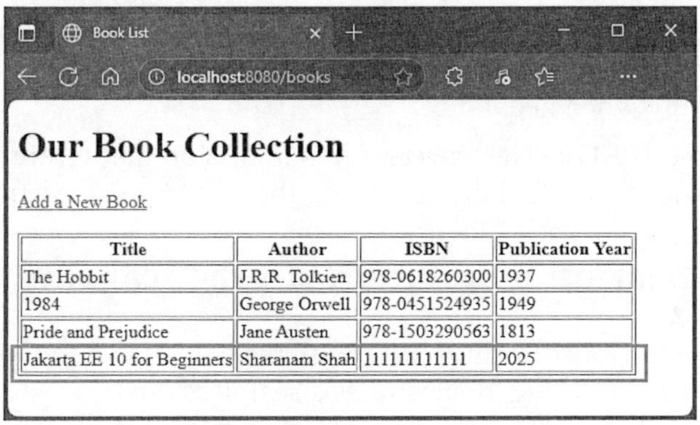

5. Check the H2 Console to confirm that the new record was successfully inserted into the **BOOK** table.

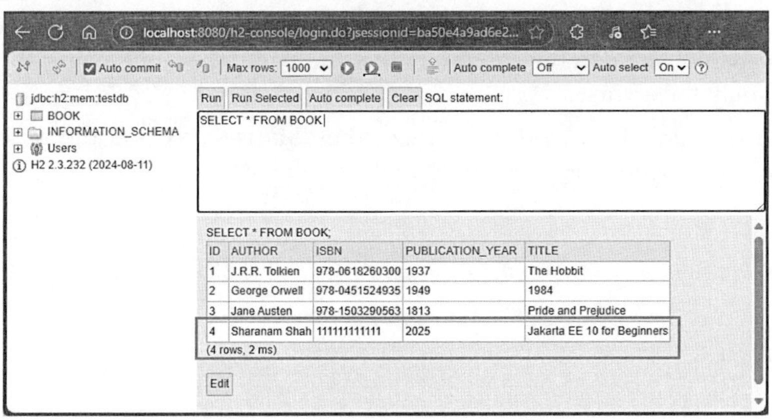

Bridging the gap: Learned concepts and application implementation

This hands-on exercise directly translates our chapter's theory into a working feature:

- **Form display and submission:** The @GetMapping("/books/add") method handles the initial request to show the form. The <form> in book-form.html with its **method="post"** and **th:action** attribute sends the data to our @PostMapping("/books/add") handler.
- **Data binding:** Spring automatically populates the Book book parameter in the addBook() method thanks to @ModelAttribute. The th:field attributes in Thymeleaf ensure the form inputs are correctly named to match the **Book** entity's fields.
- **Validation:** Adding the @NotEmpty and @Size annotations to the Book entity defined our rules. Using @Valid in the controller method signature told Spring to enforce them. We check for issues with bindingResult.hasErrors().
- **Error handling:** The th:if="${#fields.hasErrors('...')}" and th:errors attributes in our Thymeleaf template connect directly to the BindingResult object, displaying our custom error messages only when needed.
- **Post-Redirect-Get (PRG):** The successful submission path returns **"redirect:/books"**, preventing users from accidentally re-adding the same book by refreshing their browser.

Exploring application behaviour: A practical run-through

- When you submit the form, Spring MVC, with the help of Jackson for data conversion and Thymeleaf for view rendering, orchestrates a seamless flow.
- The request body containing the form data is mapped to the Book object.
- The validator checks the annotations on the Book fields.
- If there's an error, BindingResult is populated, the addBook() method returns the book-form view name, and Thymeleaf re-renders the page, this time using the BindingResult data to display the errors.
- If the data is valid, BookService is called, the data is saved via the repository, and the redirect response sends the user safely to the book list.

Harnessing Spring MVC forms and Jakarta Validation in real-world contexts

The patterns you've just implemented are fundamental to building almost any data-driven web application. This flow for creating, validating, and saving data is used everywhere, from simple contact forms to complex, multi-page wizards in large enterprise systems. Mastering this workflow provides a robust foundation for creating professional, secure, and user-friendly web interfaces.

Wrapping up

This chapter covered a lot of ground, moving your application from read-only to fully interactive. Here are the key takeaways:

- **Web forms** are built with HTML and processed on the server.
- **@PostMapping** is used to handle form submission logic.
- **@ModelAttribute** binds form data to your Java objects.
- The **Validation Starter** enables server-side validation with annotations like @NotEmpty.
- The **@Valid** annotation triggers the validation process.
- **BindingResult** captures and holds validation errors.
- Thymeleaf's **th:field** and th:errors attributes simplify form binding and error display.
- The **Post-Redirect-Get (PRG)** pattern is essential for preventing duplicate form submissions.

Congratulations! You have successfully added a critical piece of functionality to your application and learned the standard, secure way to handle data input in a Spring Boot application. You can now not only display data but also create and validate it, a huge step in your journey as a developer.

In the next chapter, we will shift gears. Instead of creating web pages for humans, we will learn how to create REST APIs. These APIs allow our application to communicate directly with other programs, like mobile apps or modern frontend frameworks, by sending and receiving data in a machine-readable format like JSON.

Chapter 13

Section 03: Building web applications with Spring Boot

Building simple REST APIs

What you'll learn

- What is an API?
- What is REST?
- REST principles
- HTTP methods in REST
- HTTP status codes for APIs
- @RestController
- JSON request/response conversion
- Returning data v/s ResponseEntity
- Handling request data
- API versioning

In today's interconnected digital world, applications rarely live in isolation. They constantly communicate, share data, and provide services to each other. This communication is the backbone of everything from your favourite mobile app fetching the latest news to complex microservice architectures powering large-scale enterprise systems. The dominant architectural style for these interactions is REST (REpresentational State Transfer), which provides a standardized way for systems to talk to each other over the web. Spring Boot makes creating these powerful and flexible REST APIs incredibly straightforward, transforming your data-driven applications into services that can be consumed by any client, anywhere.

What is an API?

An **API (Application Programming Interface)** is a set of rules and protocols that allows different software applications to communicate with each other. It defines the methods and data formats that applications can use to request and exchange information.

What is REST?

REST (REpresentational State Transfer) is an architectural style for designing networked applications. It's not a standard or a protocol, but a set of constraints that, when applied, lead to a scalable, fast, and reliable system. When an API follows these REST principles, it is called a **RESTful API**.

Key REST principles

The beauty of REST lies in its simplicity and its use of existing web standards, primarily HTTP. Understanding its core principles is key to designing effective APIs:

- **Statelessness:** Every request from a client to the server must contain all the information needed to understand and process the request. The server does not store any client context between requests. This makes the API highly scalable, as any server instance can handle any request.
- **Resources:** The key abstraction in REST is a **resource**. A resource is any piece of information that can be named, such as a user, a product, or, in our case, a book. Resources are identified by URIs (Uniform Resource Identifiers), like **/api/v1/books**.
- **Representations:** Clients interact with resources through their **representations**. A representation is a snapshot of the resource's state at a particular point in time. The most common format for these representations today is **JSON (JavaScript Object Notation)** because it is lightweight, human-readable, and easy for machines to parse.

HTTP methods in REST

REST leverages standard HTTP methods to perform operations on resources. This creates a uniform and predictable interface:

- **GET:** Retrieves a representation of a resource. This is a safe and idempotent operation, meaning it doesn't change the resource and making the same request multiple times produces the same result. (e.g., GET /api/v1/books to get a list of all books).

- **POST:** Creates a new resource. It is not safe or idempotent. (e.g., POST /api/v1/books to add a new book).
- **PUT:** Replaces an existing resource with a new representation or creates it if it doesn't exist. It is idempotent. (e.g., PUT /api/v1/books/123 to update the book with ID 123).
- **DELETE:** Removes a resource. It is idempotent. (e.g., DELETE /api/v1/books/123 to delete the book with ID 123).

HTTP status codes for APIs

Well-designed APIs use HTTP status codes to inform the client about the outcome of its request. This is crucial for error handling and a smooth user experience.

- **200 OK:** The request was successful (used for GET, PUT).
- **201 Created:** The resource was successfully created (used for POST).
- **204 No Content:** The request was successful, but there is no representation to return (used for DELETE).
- **400 Bad Request:** The server cannot process the request due to a client error (e.g., invalid JSON format, validation failure).
- **404 Not Found:** The requested resource could not be found.
- **500 Internal Server Error:** A generic error message, given when an unexpected condition was encountered on the server.

Using @RestController

In Spring MVC, the @Controller annotation is used to create web controllers that typically return a view name to be resolved by a template engine. For REST APIs, we want to return data directly in the response body, usually as JSON.

Spring provides a convenient annotation, **@RestController**, for this exact purpose. It's a stereotype annotation that combines @Controller and @ResponseBody. Applying @RestController to a class tells Spring that every method in this controller will have its return value written directly to the HTTP response body, rather than being passed to a view for rendering.

Automatic JSON request/response conversion

One of Spring Boot's most powerful features for API development is its automatic object-to-JSON conversion. When you include the **spring-boot-starter-web** dependency, it brings in the **Jackson** library, a high-performance JSON processor for Java.

When an HTTP request with a content type of **application/json** hits an endpoint, Jackson automatically deserializes the JSON payload into a Java object. Conversely, when a controller method returns a Java object, Jackson serializes it into a JSON string to be sent in the HTTP response. This all happens behind the scenes, requiring zero manual configuration.

Returning data vs. ResponseEntity

Controller methods in a @RestController can return the data object directly (e.g., List<Book>). Spring will automatically wrap it in a response with a **200 OK** status.

However, for more control over the HTTP response, it's better to return a ResponseEntity<T>. This generic class allows you to specify the response body (your data), the HTTP status code, and even HTTP headers. This is essential for properly handling different outcomes, like returning a **404 Not Found** when a resource doesn't exist or a **201 Created** after a successful creation.

Handling request data

APIs need to receive data from clients. Spring MVC provides several annotations to easily extract this information from the incoming HTTP request.

- **@RequestBody:** This annotation binds the body of the HTTP request (typically JSON) to a method parameter. Spring uses Jackson to deserialize the request body into your Java object. It's commonly used with POST and PUT requests.
- **@PathVariable:** This annotation extracts values from the URI itself. For a mapping like @GetMapping("/{isbn}"), you can use @PathVariable String isbn to capture the ISBN from the URL.
- **@RequestParam:** This is used to extract query parameters from the URL (e.g., **/books?sort=title**).

API versioning

As APIs evolve, you may need to introduce breaking changes. To avoid disrupting existing clients, it's a best practice to version your API. A common and simple strategy is to include the version number in the URI path, such as **/api/v1/books**. This allows you to deploy a new version (e.g., **/api/v2/books**) while maintaining the old one for backward compatibility.

Hands-on: Creating a REST API for Books

In this hands-on section, we will take our existing bookstore application and expose its functionality through a JSON-based REST API. You will create a controller specifically for API requests, allowing external clients to get a list of books, find a specific book by its ISBN, add a new book, and delete a book. This exercise solidifies your understanding of @RestController, request mappings, and handling data with ResponseEntity. We will use the project from *Chapter 8 - Managing database transactions*.

Building the application

Add the Validation Starter dependency

Add the Spring Boot Starter Validation dependency for validation:

1. In the **Projects** window, expand your bookstore project.
2. Right-click **Dependencies** and select **Add Dependency...**.
3. In the **Add Dependency** dialog box, enter **spring-boot-starter-validation** in the **Query** textbox.
4. In the search results, select the entry for **org.springframework.boot:spring-boot-starter-validation** and click **Add**.
5. The validation starter JAR file appears under **Dependencies**.

Add the Thymeleaf dependency

Add the Thymeleaf dependency for validation:

1. In the **Projects** window, expand your bookstore project.
2. Right-click **Dependencies** and select **Add Dependency...**.
3. In the **Add Dependency** dialog box, enter **spring-boot-starter-thymeleaf** in the **Query** textbox.

4. In the search results, select the entry for **org.springframework.boot:spring-boot-starter-thymeleaf** and click **Add**.
5. The thymeleaf JAR file appears under **Dependencies**.

Create the API Controller class

We need a controller to handle our API-specific requests.

1. In the **Projects** window, expand your bookstore project.
2. Right-click the **Source Packages** node and select **New → Java Package...**.
3. Enter **com.sharanamvaishali.bookstore.web** as the **Package Name** and click **Finish**.
4. Right-click the **com.sharanamvaishali.bookstore.web** package and select **New → Java Class...**.
5. Enter **BookApiController** as the **Class Name** and click **Finish**.
6. Open the BookApiController.java file and replace its content with the following code. This sets up the class as a REST controller with a base URL for all book-related API endpoints.

```
package com.sharanamvaishali.bookstore.web;
import com.sharanamvaishali.bookstore.domain.Book;
import com.sharanamvaishali.bookstore.repository.BookRepository;
import jakarta.validation.Valid;
import java.util.List;
import java.util.Optional;
import org.springframework.http.HttpStatus;
import org.springframework.http.ResponseEntity;
import org.springframework.web.bind.annotation.DeleteMapping;
import org.springframework.web.bind.annotation.GetMapping;
import org.springframework.web.bind.annotation.PathVariable;
import org.springframework.web.bind.annotation.PostMapping;
import org.springframework.web.bind.annotation.RequestBody;
import org.springframework.web.bind.annotation.RequestMapping;
import org.springframework.web.bind.annotation.RestController;
@RestController
@RequestMapping("/api/v1/books")
public class BookApiController {
    private final BookRepository bookRepository;
    public BookApiController(BookRepository bookRepository) {
        this.bookRepository = bookRepository;
    }
    // Handler methods will go here
    . . .
}
```

Code explanation

- **@RestController:** Marks this class as a controller where every method returns a domain object instead of a view.
- **@RequestMapping("/api/v1/books"):** Defines a base URL for all methods in this controller. All endpoints will be prefixed with **/api/v1/books**.
- **BookRepository bookRepository:** We inject the repository using constructor injection to interact with the database.

Implement the GET Endpoints

Let's add methods to retrieve all books and a single book by its ISBN. Add the following methods inside the BookApiController class:

```
    @GetMapping
    public List<Book> getAllBooks() {
        return bookRepository.findAll();
    }
    @GetMapping("/{isbn}")
    public ResponseEntity<Book> getBookByIsbn(@PathVariable String isbn) {
        Optional<Book> bookOptional = bookRepository.findByIsbn(isbn);
        return bookOptional
                .map(ResponseEntity::ok)
                .orElse(ResponseEntity.notFound().build());
    }
```

Code explanation

- **@GetMapping:** Maps HTTP GET requests to **/api/v1/books** to the getAllBooks method. It returns a List<Book>, which Spring will automatically serialize to a JSON array.
- **@GetMapping("/{isbn}"):** Maps HTTP GET requests like **/api/v1/books/978-0321765723** to the getBookByIsbn method.
- **@PathVariable String isbn:** Extracts the ISBN from the URL path.
- **ResponseEntity<Book>:** This gives us full control over the HTTP response. We can return the Book object with a **200 OK** status if it's found, or an empty body with a **404 Not Found** status if it's not.

Implement the POST Endpoint

Now, let's create an endpoint to add a new book to our catalogue. Add the following method to the BookApiController class:

```
    @PostMapping
    public ResponseEntity<Book> createBook(@Valid @RequestBody Book book) {
        Book savedBook = bookRepository.save(book);
```

```
        return new ResponseEntity<>(savedBook, HttpStatus.CREATED);
    }
```

Code explanation

- **@PostMapping:** Maps HTTP POST requests to **/api/v1/books**.
- **@RequestBody Book book:** Tells Spring to deserialize the JSON body of the incoming request into a Book object.
- **@Valid:** Triggers bean validation on the Book object, ensuring it meets the constraints (e.g., @NotEmpty) defined on the entity. If validation fails, Spring automatically returns a **400 Bad Request**.
- **new ResponseEntity<>(savedBook, HttpStatus.CREATED):** After saving the book, we return the saved book object (which now includes the generated ID) in the response body along with a **201 Created** status code, which is the standard for successful resource creation.

Implement the DELETE Endpoint (Optional)

Finally, let's add an endpoint to remove a book. This demonstrates the use of the DELETE HTTP method. Add the following method to the BookApiController class:

```
    @DeleteMapping("/{id}")
    public ResponseEntity<Void> deleteBook(@PathVariable Long id) {
        if (!bookRepository.existsById(id)) {
            return ResponseEntity.notFound().build();
        }
        bookRepository.deleteById(id);
        return ResponseEntity.noContent().build();
    }
```

Code explanation

- **@DeleteMapping("/{id}"):** Maps HTTP DELETE requests like **/api/v1/books/1**.
- **@PathVariable Long id:** Extracts the book's ID from the URL.
- **ResponseEntity.noContent().build():** For successful DELETE operations, it's common practice to return an HTTP **204 No Content** status code, indicating success without needing a response body. We also explicitly check if the book exists to return a **404** if the client tries to delete a non-existent resource.

Add REST Client Plugin

You can't test a REST API easily with just a browser (especially for POST and DELETE).You need a tool that can craft and send HTTP requests. **cURL** (a command-line tool) or graphical clients like **Postman** or the **HTTP Client** built into NetBeans are excellent choices.

1. In **NetBeans**, select **Tools → Plugins**.
2. In the **Plugins** dialog box, go to **Available Plugins** tab and search for **REST Client**.
3. Select **REST Client** and click **Install**.
4. Now the REST Client is available in NetBeans's **Tools** menu.

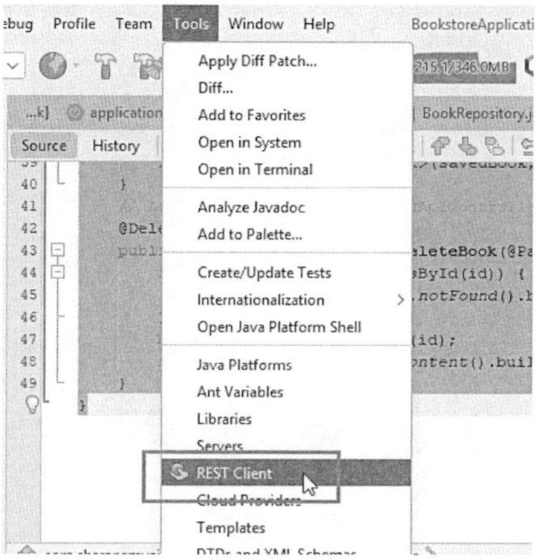

Running and testing

1. Run your Spring Boot application's main class from NetBeans.
2. Open REST Client to test the endpoints.

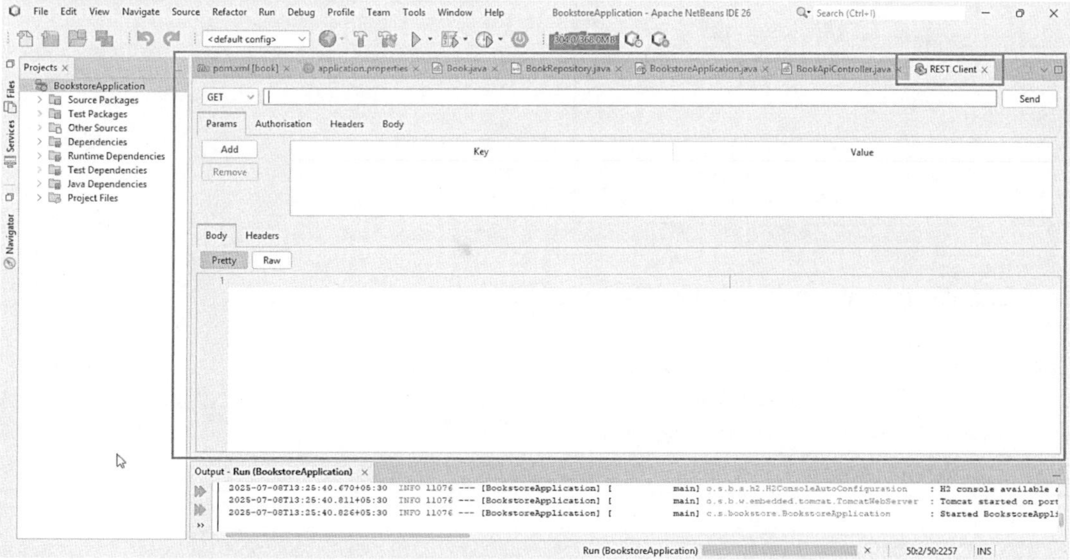

Test 1: Get all books

Send a GET request:

1. Select **GET** from the dropdown.
2. Type the following URL in the adjoining textbox:

```
http://localhost:8080/api/v1/books
```

3. Click **Send**.

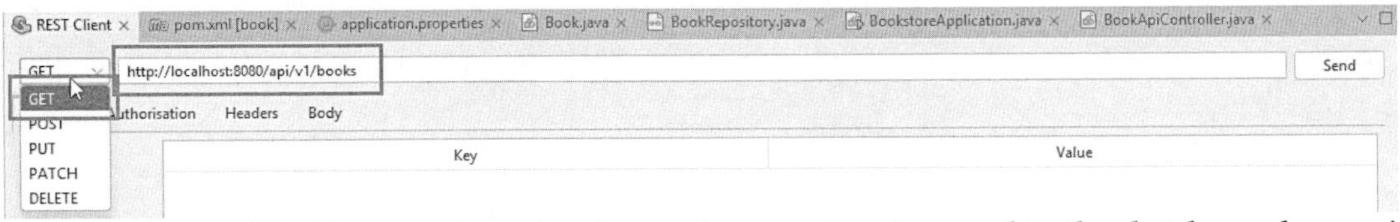

4. You can see a JSON array of any books you've previously saved to the database along with the HTTP status code.

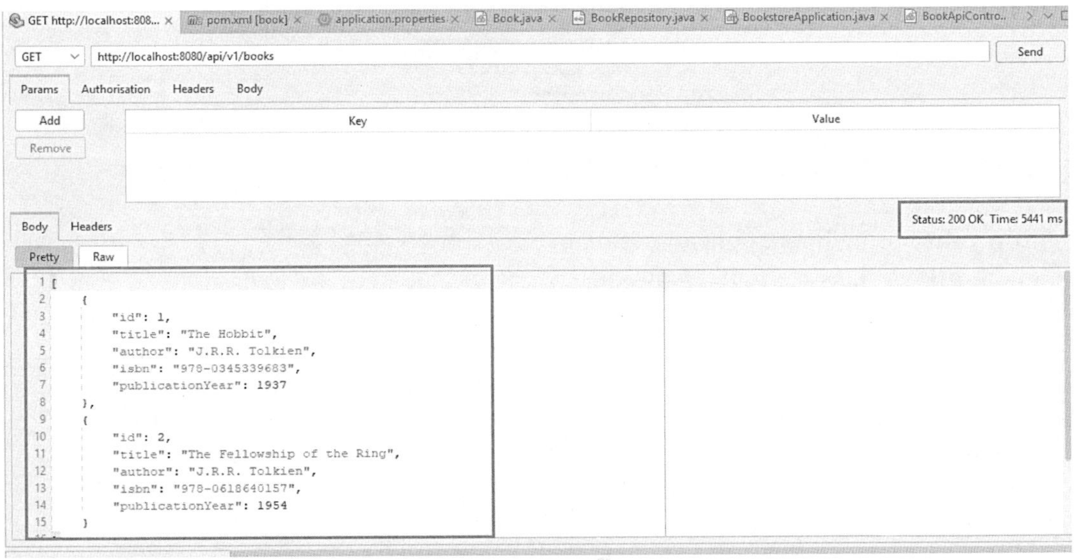

Test 2: Create a new book (with invalid data)

Send a POST request with an empty JSON object:

1. Select **POST** from the dropdown.
2. Type the following URL in the adjoining textbox:

```
http://localhost:8080/api/v1/books
```

3. Select **Body** tab → **JSON** from dropdown and type the following text in the adjoining textbox:

```
Content-Type: application/json -d {}
```

4. Click **Send**.

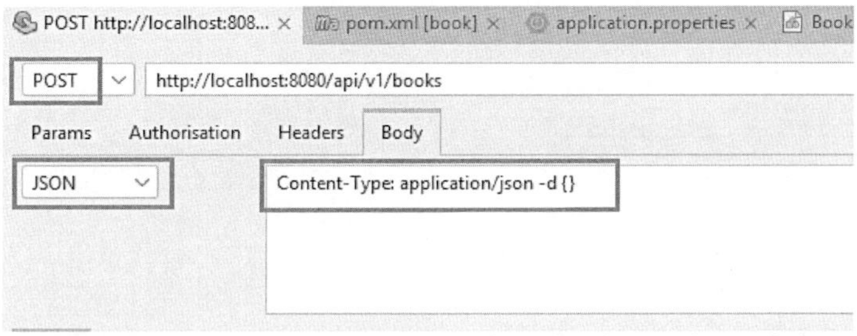

5. You receive a **400 Bad Request** response with details about the validation errors.

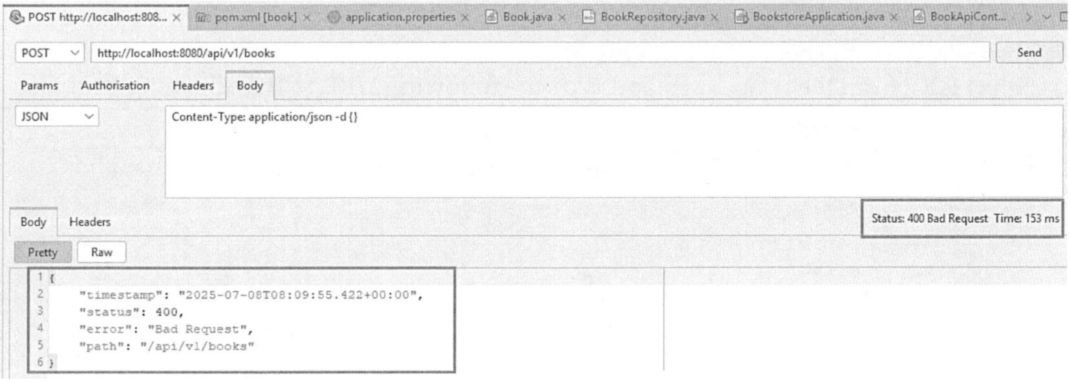

Test 3: Create a new book (with valid data)

Send a POST request with a valid book:

1. Select **POST** from the dropdown.
2. Type the following URL in the adjoining textbox:

```
http://localhost:8080/api/v1/books
```

3. Select **Body** tab → **JSON** from dropdown and type the following text in the adjoining textbox:

```
{"title":"The Pragmatic Programmer","author":"Andrew Hunt, David Thomas","isbn":"978-0135957059","publicationYear":1999}"
```

4. Click **Send**.
5. You receive a **201 Created** status and the created book object (with its new ID) in the response body.

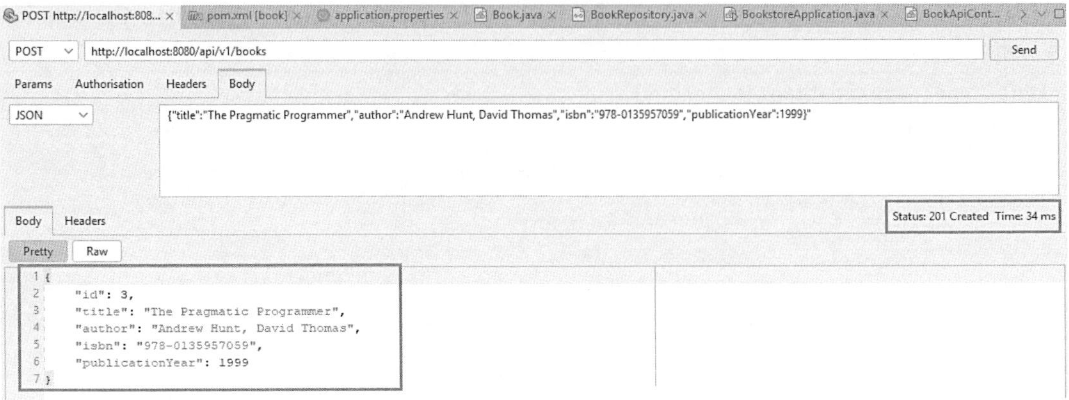

Test 4: Get a book by its ISBN

Use the ISBN from the book you just created:

1. Select **GET** from the dropdown and type the following URL in the adjoining textbox:

```
http://localhost:8080/api/v1/books/978-0135957059
```

2. Click **Send**. You get a **200 OK** response with the JSON representation of that book.

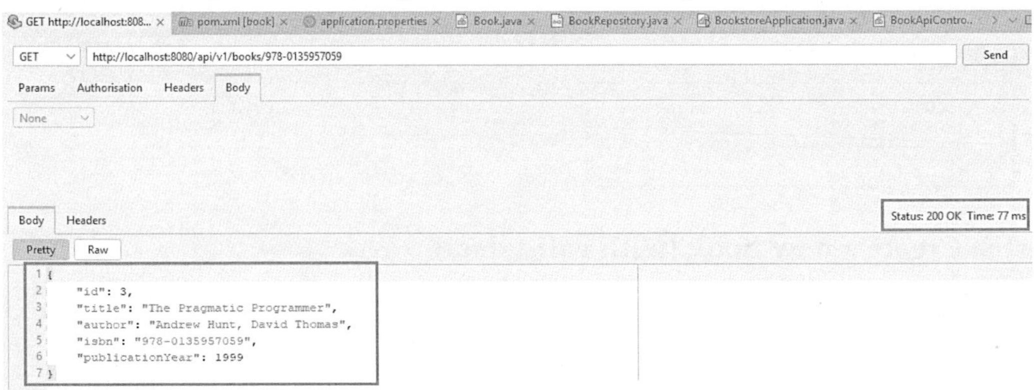

Test 5: Delete a book

Use the ID of the book you created (you can find it from the GET all books response, let's assume it's **1**):

1. Select **DELETE** from the dropdown and type the following URL in the adjoining textbox:

```
http://localhost:8080/api/v1/books/1
```

2. You do receive a response. If you try to get all books again, the deleted book is gone.

Bridging the gap: Learned concepts and application implementation

This hands-on exercise directly translates the chapter's theory into practice:

- You used @RestController instead of @Controller to signal that this class will write directly to the response body, which is fundamental for APIs.
- You witnessed Spring Boot's automatic JSON conversion powered by the Jackson library. You simply returned Java objects (List<Book>, Book), and they were transformed into JSON responses without any extra code. Similarly, @RequestBody seamlessly converted an incoming JSON string into your Book object.
- You used @PathVariable to create clean, resource-oriented URLs like **/api/v1/books/{isbn}**, a core tenet of RESTful design.
- You leveraged ResponseEntity to gain fine-grained control over the HTTP response, allowing you to return specific status codes like **201 Created**, **204 No Content**, and **404 Not Found**, making your API more robust and explicit.
- You applied @Valid to your @RequestBody to enforce server-side validation rules on incoming data, ensuring data integrity at the API layer.

Exploring application behaviour: A practical run-through

When you send a request like POST /api/v1/books with a JSON body, the flow is as follows:

1. The embedded Tomcat server receives the HTTP request.

2. Spring's DispatcherServlet routes the request to BookApiController based on the URL and HTTP method (/api/v1/books and POST).
3. The @RequestBody annotation triggers the Jackson library to read the JSON string from the request body and construct a Book Java object from it.
4. The @Valid annotation initiates the validation process. If there are errors, the process stops, and a **400** response is sent.
5. If valid, the createBook() method body executes, calling the bookRepository.save() method, which persists the entity to the database.
6. The method then wraps the saved Book object and an HttpStatus.CREATED status code into a ResponseEntity.
7. Jackson is once again invoked, this time to serialize the Book object back into a JSON string.
8. The final HTTP response is sent to the client with a **201** status code and the JSON representation of the newly created book in its body.

Harnessing Simple REST APIs in real-world contexts

The skills you've just learned are foundational to modern software development. REST APIs are the glue that holds many systems together.

- **Backend for Single-Page Applications (SPAs):** Frameworks like React, Angular, and Vue.js build dynamic user interfaces in the browser. They rely on REST APIs to fetch data, submit forms, and update application state without reloading the page.
- **Mobile app backend:** iOS and Android applications need a way to get and store data on a server. A REST API provides the necessary endpoints for user authentication, data synchronization, and other backend services.
- **Microservice communication:** In a microservices architecture, different services often communicate with each other via lightweight REST APIs to perform their specialized functions.
- **System integration:** APIs allow you to integrate your application with third-party services (e.g., payment gateways, shipping providers, social media platforms) or expose your own data for others to consume.

Wrapping up

- **REST** is an architectural style for creating stateless, resource-based APIs.
- REST APIs use standard **HTTP methods** (GET, POST, PUT, DELETE) for operations.
- **HTTP status codes** (200, 201, 404, 400) are crucial for communicating request outcomes.

- **@RestController** is the primary annotation for building JSON-based APIs in Spring Boot.
- **Spring Boot's web starter** includes Jackson for automatic JSON-to-Object conversion.
- **@RequestBody** and **@PathVariable** are used to extract data from incoming requests.
- **ResponseEntity** gives you complete control over the HTTP response, including the status code and body.

Congratulations! You have successfully built a clean, functional REST API and learned how to interact with it. You've moved beyond creating applications that only a human can interact with through a web browser and have now created a service that other programs can consume. This is a massive step in your journey as a developer.

In the next chapter, we'll put all your web development skills together in a fun culmination project: building a complete URL shortener application from scratch.

Chapter 14

Section 03: Building web applications with Spring Boot

Culmination: Building a URL Shortener web app

What you'll learn

- MVC reinforcement
- Form handling
- Dynamic URL processing
- Server-side rendering

In today's digital landscape, sharing information quickly and efficiently is paramount. Whether it's a link to a news article, a product page, or a social media post, long and cumbersome URLs can be a significant hurdle. They are difficult to remember, messy to share, and can break when copied into emails or messages. This is where URL shorteners come in. Services like **bit.ly** or **t.co** transform unwieldy web addresses into neat, shareable links.

This chapter brings together all the web development skills you have acquired so far—controllers, Thymeleaf views, form submissions, and data handling. You will build a fully functional URL shortener application. This project will solidify your understanding of how the different parts of a Spring MVC application work in concert to create a practical and powerful web tool. You'll see firsthand how a request to display a form, the submission of that form, and a subsequent redirect to a dynamic URL are all handled seamlessly by the framework.

PRD: URL shortener

- **Requirement:** The primary goal is to build a web application that allows a user to input a long URL.
- **Functionality:** Upon submission, the application should generate a unique short code, save the mapping between the short code and the original long URL, and then display the newly created short URL to the user.
- **Core feature:** When anyone navigates to the generated short URL, they must be automatically redirected to the original long URL.

Tools and Frameworks

To bring URL shortener to life, you will use the robust stack of technologies you've become familiar with throughout this book. The foundation will be built on everything from Section 1 and 2, and for the web-facing components, we will specifically leverage the **Spring Boot Web Starter** and the **Thymeleaf Starter** for dynamic views.

Hands-on: Developing the URL shortener

In this hands-on section, we will build the URL shortener from the ground up. This exercise is designed to provide a comprehensive review of the entire Model-View-Controller (MVC) flow. You will create controllers to handle user requests, design Thymeleaf templates to render the user interface, process form submissions to get user data, and implement the backend logic to make it all work. For simplicity in this chapter, we will use an in-memory Map to store the URL mappings, allowing us to focus purely on the web layer mechanics without introducing database complexity yet.

Building the application

Create a Spring Boot project

1. In NetBeans, go to **File → New Project...**.
2. In the **Choose Project** dialog, select **Java with Maven** from the **Categories** list and **Spring Boot Initializr project** from the **Projects** list.
3. Click **Next**. In the **Base Properties** step:
    - Set **Group** to **com.sharanamvaishali** and **Artifact** to **shortenurl**.
    - Keep the **Version** as it is (i.e. **0.0.1-SNAPSHOT**).

- Ensure **Packaging** is **Jar**.
- Set **Name** to **ShortyUrlShortener** and **Package Name** to **com.sharanamvaishali.shorty**.
- Select **Java** from the **Language** list and the appropriate **Java Version** (e.g., **24**).

4. Click **Next**. In the **Dependencies** step:
    - Select the appropriate **Spring Boot Version** (e.g., **4.0.0 (SNAPSHOT)**).
    - In the **Available** dependencies list, find and select **Spring Web**.
5. Click **Next**. In the **Name and Location** step:
    - Set **Project Name** to **ShortyUrlShortenerProject**.
    - Choose a suitable **Project Location**.
6. Click **Finish**. NetBeans generates the project structure and downloads dependencies.

Add the Thymeleaf Starter dependency

1. In the **Projects** window, expand your project.
2. Right-click **Dependencies** and select **Add Dependency....**
3. In the **Add Dependency** dialog box, enter **spring-boot-starter-thymeleaf** in the **Query** textbox. NetBeans searches for the dependency. Select the entry under the **org.springframework.boot:spring-boot-starter-thymeleaf** group and click **Add**.
4. The Thymeleaf JAR file now appears under **Dependencies**.

Create a Service to manage URLs

For this application, we will use a simple service class that uses a Map to store the short codes and their corresponding long URLs.

1. In the **Projects** window, expand your **ShortyUrlShortener** project.
2. Right-click the **Source Packages** node and select **New → Java Package....**
3. Enter **com.sharanamvaishali.shorty.service** as the **Package Name** and click **Finish**.
4. Right-click the **com.sharanamvaishali.shorty.service** package and select **New → Java Class....**
5. Enter **UrlShortenerService** as the **Class Name** and click **Finish**.
6. Open the UrlShortenerService.java file and replace its content with the following code:

```
package com.sharanamvaishali.shorty.service;
import java.util.HashMap;
import java.util.Map;
import java.util.concurrent.atomic.AtomicLong;
```

```
import org.springframework.stereotype.Service;
@Service
public class UrlShortenerService {
    private final Map<String, String> urlMap = new HashMap<>();
    private final Map<String, String> shortToLongMap = new HashMap<>();
    private final AtomicLong counter = new AtomicLong(1000);
    public String shortenUrl(String longUrl) {
        if (urlMap.containsKey(longUrl)) {
            return urlMap.get(longUrl);
        }
        long nextId = counter.getAndIncrement();
        String shortCode = Long.toHexString(nextId);
        urlMap.put(longUrl, shortCode);
        shortToLongMap.put(shortCode, longUrl);
        return shortCode;
    }
    public String getLongUrl(String shortCode) {
        return shortToLongMap.get(shortCode);
    }
}
```

Code explanation

This service is annotated with **@Service**, making it a Spring-managed bean. It uses two maps:

- One to ensure we don't create duplicate short codes for the same long URL
- Another to quickly look up a long URL from a short code.

An **AtomicLong** generates a unique, incrementing number that we convert to a hexadecimal string for our short code.

Create the web Controller

The controller will handle all incoming web requests, from displaying the main page to processing the form and handling the final redirect.

1. In the **Projects** window, expand your **ShortyUrlShortener** project.
2. Right-click the **Source Packages** node and select **New → Java Package…**.
3. Enter **com.sharanamvaishali.shorty.web** as the **Package Name** and click **Finish**.
4. Right-click the **com.sharanamvaishali.shorty.web** package and select **New → Java Class…**.
5. Enter **UrlController** as the **Class Name** and click **Finish**.
6. Open the UrlController.java file and replace its contents with the following:

```
package com.sharanamvaishali.shorty.web;
import com.sharanamvaishali.shorty.service.UrlShortenerService;
import org.springframework.stereotype.Controller;
```

```
import org.springframework.ui.Model;
import org.springframework.web.bind.annotation.GetMapping;
import org.springframework.web.bind.annotation.PathVariable;
import org.springframework.web.bind.annotation.PostMapping;
import org.springframework.web.bind.annotation.RequestParam;
@Controller
public class UrlController {
    private final UrlShortenerService urlShortenerService;
    public UrlController(UrlShortenerService urlShortenerService) {
        this.urlShortenerService = urlShortenerService;
    }
    @GetMapping("/")
    public String showForm(Model model) {
        model.addAttribute("shortUrl", null);
        return "index";
    }
    @PostMapping("/shorten")
    public String shortenUrl(@RequestParam("longUrl") String longUrl, Model model) {
        String shortCode = urlShortenerService.shortenUrl(longUrl);
        String fullShortUrl = "http://localhost:8080/" + shortCode;
        model.addAttribute("shortUrl", fullShortUrl);
        return "index";
    }
    @GetMapping("/{shortCode}")
    public String redirectToLongUrl(@PathVariable String shortCode) {
        String longUrl = urlShortenerService.getLongUrl(shortCode);
        if (longUrl != null) {
            return "redirect:" + longUrl;
        }
        return "redirect:/"; // Or a custom error page
    }
}
```

Code explanation

- **@Controller:** Marks this class as a Spring MVC controller.
- **@GetMapping("/"):** This method handles requests to the root URL and displays the main form page by returning the view name **index**.
- **@PostMapping("/shorten"):** This method processes the form submission from our view. It takes the long URL, uses the service to create a short code, and then adds the result back to the model to be displayed on the same **index** page.
- **@GetMapping("/{shortCode}"):** This is the key to our redirect functionality. It captures a path variable from the URL (the short code), finds the corresponding long URL, and issues a redirect. The **redirect:** prefix is crucial; it tells Spring MVC to send an HTTP redirect response to the user's browser.

Create the Thymeleaf View

This HTML file will contain the form for submitting a URL and the area to display the result.

1. In the **Projects** window, navigate to **Source Packages → src/main/resources → templates**.
2. Right-click the **templates** folder and select **New → HTML File...**.
3. Name the file **index** and click **Finish**.
4. Open index.html and replace its content with the following code:

```
<!DOCTYPE html>
<html xmlns:th="http://www.thymeleaf.org">
    <head>
        <title>Shorty URL Shortener</title>
        <meta charset="UTF-8">
        <meta name="viewport" content="width=device-width, initial-scale=1.0">
    </head>
    <body>
        <h1>Shorty: The Simple URL Shortener</h1>
        <form th:action="@{/shorten}" method="post">
            <label for="longUrl">Enter a long URL to shorten:</label><br>
            <input type="url" id="longUrl" name="longUrl" size="50" required>
            <button type="submit">Shorten!</button>
        </form>
        <div th:if="${shortUrl}">
            <h2>Your shortened URL:</h2>
            <p>
                <a th:href="${shortUrl}" th:text="${shortUrl}" target="_blank"></a>
            </p>
        </div>
    </body>
</html>
```

Code explanation:

- **th:action="@{/shorten}":** This Thymeleaf attribute directs the form to submit its data via a POST request to the **/shorten** URL we defined in our controller.
- **th:if="${shortUrl}":** This block will only be rendered if the **shortUrl** attribute exists in the model. This is how we conditionally display the result after a successful form submission.
- **th:href** and **th:text:** These attributes populate the link with the generated short URL, making it clickable.

Running and testing

1. Run the application by right-clicking the **ShortyUrlShortener** project and selecting **Run**. The embedded Tomcat server will start.

2. Open a web browser and navigate to **http://localhost:8080**. You can see the URL submission form.

3. Enter a long URL, for example, **https://www.spring.io/projects/spring-boot**, and click **Shorten!**.
4. The page refreshes, and below the form, you see the newly generated short URL, such as **http://localhost:8080/3e8**.

5. Click on this new short URL. Your browser immediately redirects you to the original Spring Boot project page.

Bridging the gap: Learned concepts and application implementation

This hands-on exercise is a practical demonstration of several key Spring MVC concepts working in unison.

- **MVC with @Controller:** UrlController is the heart of the web layer, orchestrating the entire flow. It receives requests, delegates business logic to UrlShortenerService, and determines which view to render.

- **Form handling:** You implemented a complete form handling cycle. The @GetMapping("/") method prepares the initial view, and the @PostMapping("/shorten") method receives and processes the submitted data. The use of @RequestParam shows a simple way to bind form field data to method parameters.
- **Dynamic URL handling:** The use of @GetMapping("/{shortCode}") with the @PathVariable annotation is a powerful feature for creating clean, REST-ful URLs. It allows the application to respond to a wide range of dynamic URLs (e.g., **/3e8**, **/3e9**) with a single handler method, which is the core of the redirect functionality.
- **Server-side rendering with Thymeleaf:** The index.html template is not static. Thymeleaf processes it on the server, using data from the Model (like the generated **shortUrl**) to render the final HTML that is sent to the browser. This is evident in the conditional rendering of the result block.

Exploring application behaviour: A practical run-through

The user journey you just tested demonstrates the complete request-response cycle of the application:

1. **Initial request:** When you first visit **http://localhost:8080**, DispatcherServlet routes the request to the showForm() method in UrlController. This method adds null to the model and returns the logical view name **index**. Spring, with Thymeleaf's help, renders **index.html** and sends it to your browser.
2. **Form submission:** When you submit the form, the browser sends a POST request to **/shorten**. The shortenUrl() method in the controller is invoked. It calls the service to generate a short code, constructs the full short URL, and adds it to the model. It then returns **index** again.
3. **View re-rendering:** Thymeleaf re-processes **index.html**. This time, the shortUrl attribute in the model is not null, so the th:if condition is true, and the result div is rendered with the new link.
4. **Redirect flow:** Clicking the short link sends a GET request to a URL like **/3e8**. The redirectToLongUrl() method captures **3e8** as a PathVariable. It looks up the original URL in the service and returns the special string **redirect:https://...**. Spring MVC interprets this as an instruction to send a **302 Found** HTTP redirect response to the browser, which then automatically navigates to the long URL.

Harnessing Spring MVC in real-world contexts

The patterns used in this application are fundamental to building a vast majority of interactive websites. The core workflow of displaying forms, processing user input, interacting with a service layer, and rendering dynamic results is the backbone of applications ranging from simple blogs and contact forms to complex e-commerce platforms and social media sites. Mastering this flow is a critical step in becoming a proficient Spring developer.

Wrapping up

This chapter was a significant milestone, integrating many different concepts into a single, functional application. Here's a quick summary of what you accomplished:

- **MVC flow:** You implemented a full Model-View-Controller workflow.
- **Form processing:** You created a web form and handled its submission using @PostMapping.
- **Path Variables:** You used @PathVariable to handle dynamic URLs for the redirect logic.
- **Thymeleaf rendering:** You used Thymeleaf for conditional rendering and to display dynamic data.
- **Redirects:** You learned how to programmatically trigger an HTTP redirect from a controller.

Congratulations! You have successfully built a complete web application that brings together the core components of Spring MVC. You've seen how controllers, services, and views collaborate to create a seamless user experience. This project serves as a strong foundation for building even more complex applications.

In this next chapter, we're taking a significant leap forward. We'll be moving beyond traditional, rule-based programming to explore the revolutionary world of **Generative AI**. For a long time, building applications meant crafting meticulous, explicit instructions for every scenario. But imagine an application that can understand language, create new content, and offer intelligent suggestions on its own. This is no longer the stuff of science fiction; it is the new reality of modern software development.

Chapter 15

Section 04: Integrating AI with Spring applications

The AI revolution: Why every Spring developer needs to pay attention

What you'll learn

- AI integration benefits
- Real-world AI use cases
- Large Language Models (LLMs)
- API-first AI approach

Welcome to the new frontier. For years, developers have focused on writing explicit, rule-based logic to build applications. You write code that tells the application exactly how to handle every situation. But what if your application could move beyond static logic? What if it could understand language, generate creative content, and make intelligent suggestions on its own? This is no longer science fiction; it is the reality of modern software development powered by Generative AI. This chapter explains why Generative AI is not just hype, but a fundamental shift in software development that every Java and Spring professional needs to understand. It is the key to creating the next generation of smarter, more dynamic, and deeply personalized applications.

The importance and benefits of AI integration

Integrating Artificial Intelligence into your Spring applications is about more than just adding a trendy feature; it is about fundamentally enhancing what your software can do. By connecting to powerful AI models, you can unlock capabilities that were previously unimaginable for most developers.

- **Create smarter applications:** Move beyond static, predictable logic. With AI, you can build applications that are more dynamic, intuitive, and offer personalized experiences to your users. Imagine an e-commerce site that does not just show products but helps a user find the perfect gift by understanding natural language descriptions of the person they are shopping for.
- **Automate complex tasks:** Offload demanding tasks like content creation, data analysis, and complex decision-making to AI models that excel at them. This frees up your application's core logic to focus on its primary business purpose while letting the AI handle specialized, creative, or analytical work. You could, for instance, generate detailed product descriptions or summarize thousands of user reviews with a single API call.
- **Boost productivity:** The benefits of AI extend to the development process itself. AI tools can automatically generate boilerplate code, write documentation based on your methods, and even create realistic test data, allowing you to focus on the more creative and strategic aspects of your work.

What is a Large Language Model (LLM)?

At the heart of the current AI revolution is the **Large Language Model**, or **LLM**. Think of an LLM as a very advanced, very large brain that has been trained on a massive amount of text and code from the internet. Through this training, it does not just memorize information; it learns the patterns, structure, grammar, context, and nuances of human language.

This allows it to perform remarkable tasks:

- **Generate text:** It can write original text, from emails and poems to marketing copy and technical articles.
- **Understand and respond:** It can process a user's question or command—a **prompt**—and provide a relevant, coherent answer.
- **Translate and summarize:** It can translate between languages or distill a long document down to its key points.
- **Analyse sentiment:** It can determine if a piece of text is positive, negative, or neutral.

- **Write code:** It can even generate code snippets in various programming languages based on a description of the desired functionality.

Powerful LLMs, such as those from **Cohere** and Google's **Gemini**, are the engines that will power the AI features we build in our Spring applications. You do not need to build or train these massive models yourself. Instead, you can access their capabilities through a simple programming interface.

Harnessing AI in real-world contexts

The applications of LLMs in business are not just theoretical; they are practical, impactful, and being implemented today. You can integrate AI to create both user-facing features and powerful internal tools.

- **Intelligent features for users:**
    - **Smart search:** Go beyond simple keyword matching. Allow users to search your product catalogue by describing what they want, like **find a "laptop for a college student under $500 that is good for coding"**.
    - **E-commerce product descriptions:** Automatically generate compelling and unique descriptions for thousands of products, complete with specifications and marketing highlights.
    - **Review summarization:** Condense hundreds of user reviews for a product or service into a short, easy-to-read summary of the main pros and cons.
- **Internal tools for your business:**
    - **Customer support chatbots:** Create intelligent chatbots that can answer common customer questions, freeing up human agents for more complex issues.
    - **Feedback analysis:** Feed customer emails, support tickets, and survey responses into an AI model to categorize issues, identify trends, and analyse sentiment.
    - **Automated reporting:** Generate daily, weekly, or monthly business reports by having an AI analyse raw data and write up the summary and key findings.

The API-first approach to AI

The most powerful aspect of this technology for a Spring developer is that you do not need a Ph.D. in machine learning to use it. The companies that build these massive LLMs provide an **Application Programming Interface (API)**. This is the same API-based approach you already know.

Just as you might call a third-party API for payment processing or sending emails, you can now make an API call to an AI model. The workflow is straightforward:

1. Your Spring application gathers some data or user input.
2. You construct a clear **prompt** that tells the AI what you want it to do.
3. You send this prompt to the AI provider's API endpoint.
4. The AI model processes your request.
5. The model sends back a response, typically in a simple format like **JSON**, containing the generated text or analysis.
6. Your application uses this response to display information to a user, save data to your database, or perform another action.

This API-first approach means you can harness the power of a multi-billion-dollar AI model from within your Spring service or controller with just a few lines of code, making it incredibly accessible and manageable.

Wrapping up

- **AI is practical:** Integrating AI moves applications from static logic to dynamic, intelligent experiences.
- **Key benefits**: AI integration helps create smarter apps, automates complex tasks, and boosts developer productivity.
- **LLMs are the engine**: Large Language Models understand and generate human-like text, powering modern AI features.
- **APIs are the bridge**: You can access massive AI models easily through simple API calls within your Spring application.

Congratulations on taking your first step into the world of AI-powered Java development! You now understand the immense potential that AI holds and the practical, API-driven approach we can use to harness it.

In the next chapter, we will put this theory into practice. You will take the simple command-line quote generator from ***Chapter 4 - Culmination: Building a Command-Line Quote Generator*** and transform it, using the Cohere API to generate unique, thematic quotes on demand, making your first direct connection to a powerful LLM.

Chapter 16

Section 04: Integrating AI with Spring applications

Building an AI-powered Content Generator with Cohere

What you'll learn

- API Providers
- Managing API keys
- Calling REST APIs
- Our choice: Cohere
- Using Spring profiles
- Implementing service interfaces

Welcome to the new frontier of software development. In ***Chapter 4 - Culmination: Building a Command-Line Quote Generator***, you built a solid command-line application that printed quotes from a predefined, hardcoded list. While functional, it's static and limited. What if you could break free from these limitations? Imagine an application that generates unique, thematic content on demand, providing an endless stream of creative output.

This chapter introduces you to the transformative power of Generative AI by integrating a Large Language Model (LLM) directly into your Spring application. You will replace the static quote list with live calls to the Cohere API, turning your simple application into a dynamic content generator. This is the first step in building truly intelligent applications that can create, analyse, and communicate in ways that were previously impossible.

Exploring AI API providers

The power of modern AI, especially large language models, often comes packaged as a service. Companies invest heavily in training massive models and then provide access to their capabilities through Application Programming Interfaces (APIs). This means you don't need to build these complex models yourself; you can simply send requests to the provider's API and receive intelligent responses.

Some prominent players in this space include:

- **OpenAI:** Widely known for its GPT series of models (like GPT-3.5 and GPT-4), excelling in text generation, conversation, and code generation.
- **Google AI (Gemini):** Offers a suite of powerful models under the Gemini family, capable of handling multimodal inputs (text, images, audio, video) and providing strong performance across various tasks.
- **Cohere:** Focuses significantly on Natural Language Processing (NLP) for enterprise applications, offering models for generation, summarization, classification, embeddings, and more, often with an emphasis on data privacy and business use cases.

These providers differ in their specific model strengths, areas of focus, API design, ease of use for developers, documentation quality, and, importantly, pricing models.

Our choice: Cohere

For this chapter, we focus on **Cohere**. This choice is based on several factors relevant to learners:

- **Beginner-friendly:** Cohere offers clear documentation and aims for ease of integration.
- **NLP focus:** Its strong suit in natural language processing aligns well with common web application enhancements like text generation, summarization, and analysis.
- **Feature balance:** It provides a good mix of powerful capabilities without being overly complex for initial integration.
- **Free tier:** Cohere typically offers a free tier suitable for experimentation and learning, allowing you to build and test applications without immediate financial commitment.

While we use Cohere for demonstration, the principles of interacting with AI APIs learned here are transferable to other providers as well.

Getting started with Cohere

Before you can ask an AI to generate content, you need a way to communicate with it. This is done through an Application Programming Interface (API), and to use it, you need an API key. This key is a unique secret token that identifies your application and authorizes it to make requests.

Follow these steps to get your free developer key from Cohere:

1. Visit **Cohere's website** (www.cohere.ai). Look for a "Sign Up" or "Get Started" button. Cohere typically offers a free trial.

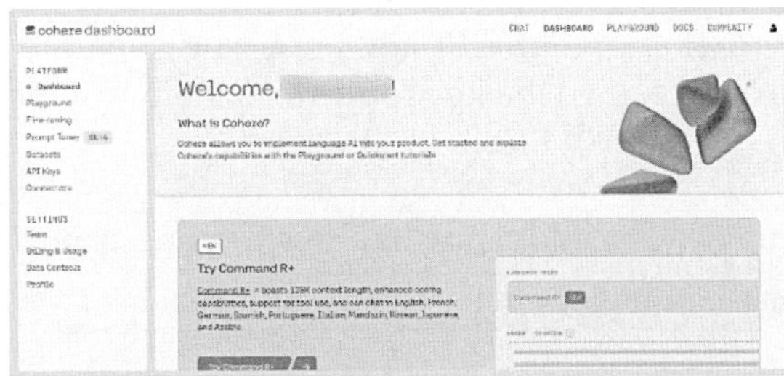

2. Provide the required information and create a **Cohere account**.
3. Once logged in, locate your API key (often found in the **Trial keys** or a similar section). This key is crucial for connecting to Cohere's services. Keep it secure!

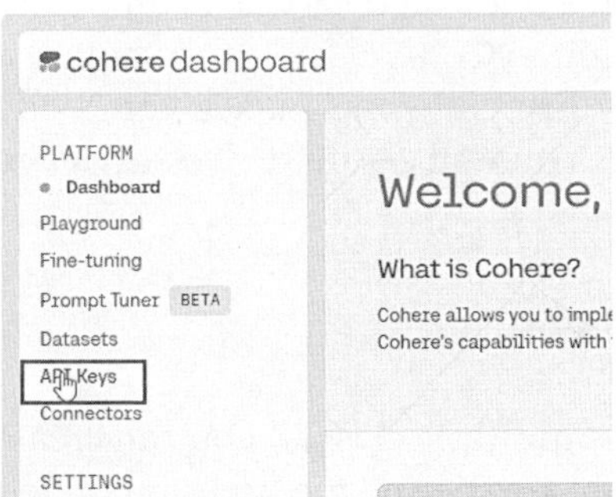

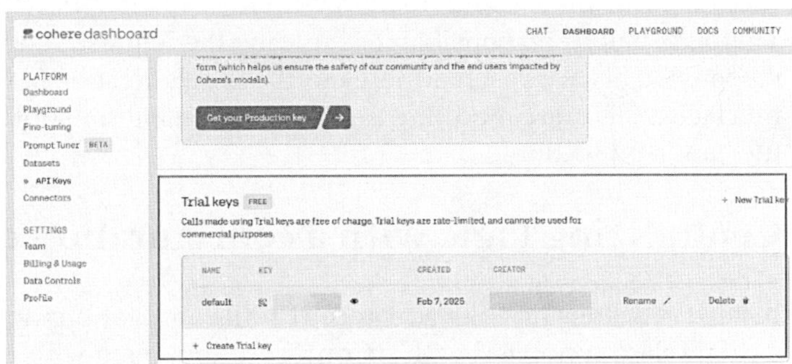

TIP Treat your API key like a sensitive password!

Integrating an AI client with Spring Boot

Interacting with an external API involves securely managing your credentials (the API key) and writing clean, organized code to handle the communication.

A highly effective pattern in Spring is to centralize the creation of service beans in a dedicated configuration class.

Securely managing API keys

A common mistake is to hardcode secret keys directly into the Java source code. This is a significant security risk, as the key becomes part of your version control history and is difficult to change without recompiling the application. The best practice is to externalize this configuration.

Spring Boot's application.properties file is the perfect place to store this kind of information. By defining your API key here, you separate the configuration from the code. This makes it easy to change the key for different environments (development, production) and keeps it out of your source files.

You need to add a line like this to your application.properties file:

```
cohere.api.key=<YOUR_COHERE_API_KEY>
```

Creating a dedicated AI service

To avoid cluttering your application logic with the details of making HTTP requests, you should encapsulate all interaction with the Cohere API within a dedicated service component. This class will be responsible for building the request, sending it to Cohere, and processing the response. This approach adheres to the Single Responsibility Principle and makes your code much cleaner, more modular, and easier to test and maintain. You will create such a service in the hands-on section.

Centralizing logic with a configuration class

Instead of scattering @Service and @Profile annotations across multiple classes, you can create a single class annotated with **@Configuration**. Inside this class, you define methods annotated with **@Bean**. Each method is a factory that produces an object (a bean) for Spring to manage.

This approach gives you precise control over how your beans are created. You can attach **@Profile** annotations to these @Bean methods, allowing the configuration class to act as a central switchboard. Based on the active profile, it will execute the correct method to provide the appropriate implementation of an interface, like our QuoteService. This keeps your business logic classes clean of configuration annotations and consolidates environment-specific logic in one place.

Hands-on: The dynamic quote generator

In this hands-on lab, you will modify the command-line quote generator project from ***Chapter 4 - Culmination: Building a Command-Line Quote Generator***. You will create a new service that calls the Cohere API to generate quotes instead of using the hardcoded list. You will also implement a powerful Spring feature, Profiles, to let you easily switch between the original local service and your new AI-powered service without changing a single line of application logic.

Building the application

First, open the command-line quote generator project from ***Chapter 4 - Culmination: Building a Command-Line Quote Generator*** in the NetBeans IDE.

Configure your API key

1. In the **Projects** window, expand your project.
2. Navigate to **Other Sources** → **src/main/resources** → **<default package>**.
3. Double-click application.properties to open it.
4. Add the following lines to the file. This sets the default behaviour to use the original, non-AI service:

```
# Cohere API Configuration
cohere.api.key=<YOUR_COHERE_API_KEY>
# Set the default active profile
spring.profiles.active=local
```

Code explanation

- **cohere.api.key=<YOUR_COHERE_API_KEY>**
  - This line defines a custom property named cohere.api.key.
  - <YOUR_COHERE_API_KEY> is a placeholder that you are instructed to replace with your actual API key obtained from Cohere.
  - Spring's @Value annotation can later be used in your Java code to inject the value of this property into a field or constructor parameter. This keeps sensitive information out of the code itself and makes it easy to change.
- **spring.profiles.active=local**
  - This is a crucial Spring Boot property that sets the **default active profile(s)** for your application.

- **Spring Profiles** are a powerful feature that allows you to register different beans (components) or apply different configurations based on the environment your application is running in.
- By setting spring.profiles.active=local, you're telling Spring that, by default, it should activate the "local" profile. This means that any @Profile("local") annotated beans or configurations will be enabled, while others will be ignored unless their respective profiles are also active. In this context, it ensures the original InspirationalQuoteService (which will be associated with the "local" profile) is used by default.

Add the WebClient dependency

To make HTTP calls to the Cohere API, you need an HTTP client. Spring's modern, non-blocking client is called WebClient, and it's included in the spring-boot-starter-webflux dependency.

1. In the **Projects** window, right-click **Dependencies** and select **Add Dependency....**
2. In the **Add Dependency** dialog, enter **spring-boot-starter-webflux** in the **Query** textbox. Select the entry **org.springframework.boot:spring-boot-starter-webflux**. Click **Add**.
3. The WebClient JAR file appears under **Dependencies** and the dependency is added to your pom.xml file.

Update the original Service implementation

You will now modify the service classes to be simple Java objects without Spring annotations.

Open InspirationalQuoteService.java and ensure it looks like this (remove @Service):

```
package com.sharanamvaishali.quoteapp;
import java.util.List;
import java.util.Random;
public class InspirationalQuoteService implements QuoteService {
    private static final List<String> QUOTES = List.of(
        "The only way to do great work is to love what you do. - Steve Jobs",
        "Success is not final, failure is not fatal: it is the courage to continue
            that counts. - Winston Churchill",
        "Believe you can and you're halfway there. - Theodore Roosevelt",
        "The future belongs to those who believe in the beauty of their
            dreams. - Eleanor Roosevelt"
    );
    private final Random random = new Random();
    @Override
    public String getQuote() {
        return QUOTES.get(random.nextInt(QUOTES.size()));
    }
```

```
}
```

Create the AI-powered Service implementation

Now, create the new service class that generates quotes using Cohere.

1. In the **Projects** window, find the package containing your QuoteService interface (e.g., **com.sharanamvaishali.quoteapp**).
2. Right-click the package and select **New → Java Class....**
3. Enter **AiQuoteService** as the **Class Name** and click **Finish**.
4. Open the AiQuoteService.java file and replace its content with the following code:

```
package com.sharanamvaishali.quoteapp;
import com.fasterxml.jackson.databind.JsonNode;
import org.springframework.beans.factory.annotation.Value;
import org.springframework.web.reactive.function.client.WebClient;
public class AiQuoteService implements QuoteService {
    private record CohereRequest(String prompt, int max_tokens) {}
    private final WebClient webClient;
    @Value("${cohere.api.key}")
    private String cohereApiKey;
    public AiQuoteService(WebClient.Builder webClientBuilder, String apiKey) {
        this.cohereApiKey = apiKey;
        this.webClient = webClientBuilder.baseUrl("https://api.cohere.ai/v1")
                                         .build();
    }
    @Override
    public String getQuote() {
        String prompt = "Provide a single, short, inspirational quote.";
        CohereRequest requestBody = new CohereRequest(prompt, 100);
        try {
            JsonNode response = webClient.post().uri("/generate")
                    .header("Authorization", "Bearer " + cohereApiKey)
                    .bodyValue(requestBody).retrieve()
                    .bodyToMono(JsonNode.class).block();
            if (response != null && response.has("generations")) {
                return response.get("generations").get(0).get("text").asText()
                            .trim();
            }
        } catch (Exception e) {
            // In a real app, you'd have more robust error handling
            return "The AI is pondering... Please try again later.";
        }
        return "Could not generate an AI quote at this time.";
    }
}
```

Code explanation

- **implements QuoteService {:** The AiQuoteService class implements QuoteService, making it interchangeable with InspirationalQuoteService through the QuoteService interface.
- **private record CohereRequest(String prompt, int max_tokens) {}:** This is a **Java Record** (introduced in Java 16). Records are concise classes for holding immutable data. Here, it models the structure of the JSON request body that will be sent to the Cohere /generate endpoint. It automatically generates a constructor, getters, equals(), hashCode(), and toString().
- **private final WebClient webClient;:** Declares a final WebClient instance, used for making HTTP calls.
- **@Value("${cohere.api.key}") private String cohereApiKey;:** This attempts to inject the value of the cohere.api.key property from application.properties. However, in this specific code, the cohereApiKey field is also initialized via the constructor, which is generally the preferred method for injecting dependencies. The @Value annotation here might be a leftover or intended for a different injection strategy if the constructor were not present. When both are used, the constructor injection usually takes precedence for the initial value.
- **public AiQuoteService(WebClient.Builder webClientBuilder, String apiKey) { ... }:** This is the constructor for AiQuoteService. It takes two parameters:
    - **WebClient.Builder webClientBuilder**: Spring will automatically inject a WebClient.Builder instance. This builder is used to configure and build WebClient instances. It's common practice to inject the builder rather than WebClient directly, as it allows for specific configurations (like base URL, headers) for different API calls.
    - **String apiKey:** This apiKey parameter will be injected with the value from the cohere.api.key property (this injection will happen at the @Bean method level in AppConfig).
- **this.webClient = webClientBuilder.baseUrl("https://api.cohere.ai/v1").build();:** Configures the WebClient instance. baseUrl() sets the base URI for all requests made by this webClient instance, so you only need to specify the path (/generate) later. build() creates the actual WebClient instance.
- **public String getQuote() { ... }:** This method contains the logic for calling the Cohere API.
    - **String prompt = "Provide a single, short, inspirational quote.";:** Defines the text prompt to send to the Cohere API.
    - **CohereRequest requestBody = new CohereRequest(prompt, 100);:** Creates an instance of the CohereRequest record with the prompt and a maximum token limit (number of words/tokens to generate).

- **JsonNode response = webClient.post():** Starts building an HTTP POST request using the configured webClient.
  - **.uri("/generate"):** Appends /generate to the base URL (https://api.cohere.ai/v1/generate).
  - **.header("Authorization", "Bearer " + cohereApiKey):** Sets the Authorization header required for Cohere API authentication. The API key is prefixed with "Bearer ".
  - **.bodyValue(requestBody):** Sets the request body. Spring's WebClient (with Jackson) will automatically serialize the CohereRequest record into a JSON string.
  - **.retrieve():** Executes the request and retrieves the response.
  - **.bodyToMono(JsonNode.class):** Specifies that the response body should be converted into a Mono<JsonNode>. A Mono is a reactive publisher that emits 0 or 1 item (in this case, the JsonNode representing the JSON response).
  - **.block();:** This is a **blocking call**. In a purely reactive application, you would typically avoid .block() and continue with reactive operations (e.g., subscribe(), flatMap()). However, for simple command-line applications or when integrating reactive clients into an otherwise blocking context, .block() is used to wait for the result synchronously.
- **if (response != null && response.has("generations")) { ... }:** Checks if the response is not null and contains a generations field, which is expected from the Cohere API.
- **return response.get("generations").get(0).get("text").asText().trim();:**
  - Navigates the JSON structure to extract the generated text. Cohere's response typically puts the generated text inside generations (an array), then the first element (get(0)), then a text field.
  - **.asText():** Converts the JsonNode content to a String.
  - **.trim():** Removes leading/trailing whitespace.

- **catch (Exception e) { ... }:** Basic error handling. If the API call fails, it returns a generic error message. In a real application, you'd log the exception (e) and potentially provide more specific feedback.
- **return "Could not generate an AI quote at this time.";:** A fallback message if the if condition fails or if no specific exception is caught, meaning the response structure wasn't as expected.

Create the Configuration Class

This class will act as the factory for your QuoteService beans.

1. In the **Projects** window, right-click the main application package (e.g., **com.sharanamvaishali.quoteapp**) and select **New → Java Class....**
2. Enter **AppConfig** as the **Class Name** and click **Finish**.
3. Open the AppConfig.java file and replace its content with the following code:

```
package com.sharanamvaishali.quoteapp;
import org.springframework.beans.factory.annotation.Value;
import org.springframework.context.annotation.Bean;
import org.springframework.context.annotation.Configuration;
import org.springframework.context.annotation.Profile;
import org.springframework.web.reactive.function.client.WebClient;
@Configuration
public class AppConfig {
    @Bean
    public WebClient.Builder webClientBuilder() {
        return WebClient.builder();
    }
    @Bean
    @Profile("local")
    public QuoteService localQuoteService() {
        return new InspirationalQuoteService();
    }
    @Bean
    @Profile("ai")
    public QuoteService aiQuoteService(WebClient.Builder webClientBuilder,
                                       @Value("${cohere.api.key}") String apiKey) {
        return new AiQuoteService(webClientBuilder, apiKey);
    }
}
```

Code explanation

- **@Configuration:** This annotation tells Spring that this class contains @Bean methods that define Spring beans.
- **@Bean public WebClient.Builder webClientBuilder() { ... }:**
    - This method creates and exposes a WebClient.Builder as a Spring bean.
    - By making WebClient.Builder a bean, other beans (like AiQuoteService) can easily depend on it, and Spring will inject an instance of it when needed. This allows for consistent configuration of WebClient instances throughout your application.
- **@Bean @Profile("local") public QuoteService localQuoteService() { ... }:**
    - **@Bean:** This method will produce a QuoteService bean.
    - **@Profile("local"):** This is the key annotation for conditional bean creation. This localQuoteService bean will **only be created and registered by Spring if the "local" profile is active**.

- o **return new InspirationalQuoteService();:** If the "local" profile is active, an instance of InspirationalQuoteService (your original hardcoded quote service) is created and returned as the QuoteService bean.

❑ **@Bean @Profile("ai") public QuoteService aiQuoteService(WebClient.Builder webClientBuilder, @Value("${cohere.api.key}") String apiKey) { ... }:**

- o **@Bean:** This method will produce another QuoteService bean.
- o **@Profile("ai"):** This aiQuoteService bean will only be created and registered by Spring if the "ai" profile is active.
- o **WebClient.Builder webClientBuilder:** Spring will automatically inject the WebClient.Builder bean into this method's parameter.
- o **@Value("${cohere.api.key}") String apiKey:** Spring will inject the value of the cohere.api.key property (from application.properties) into this apiKey parameter.
- o **return new AiQuoteService(webClientBuilder, apiKey);:** If the "ai" profile is active, an instance of AiQuoteService is created using the injected WebClient.Builder and apiKey, and this instance is returned as the QuoteService bean.

Running and testing

Now run the application twice to see how a simple profile change completely alters its behaviour.

Run using the 'local' profile

1. Ensure your application.properties file contains the line

```
spring.profiles.active=local
```

2. Run the application by right-clicking the project and selecting **Run**.
3. Observe the console output. You see one of the original, hardcoded quotes from the InspirationalQuoteService.

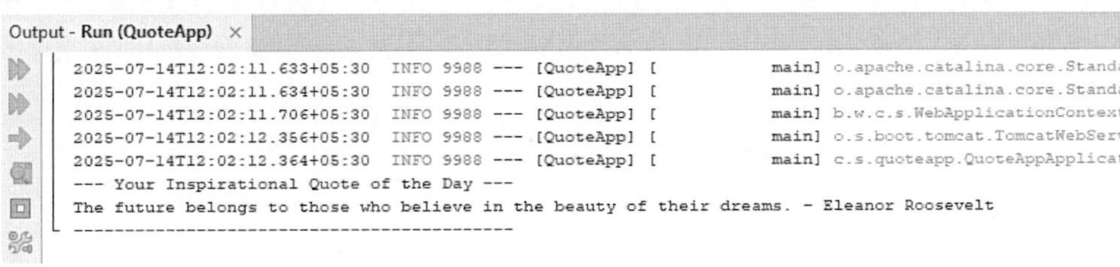

Run using the 'ai' profile

1. Open your application.properties file.
2. Change the active profile line to:

```
spring.profiles.active=ai
```

3. Save the file and run the application's main method again.
4. Observe the console output. After a brief moment (while the API call is made), you see a brand new, unique quote generated by Cohere.

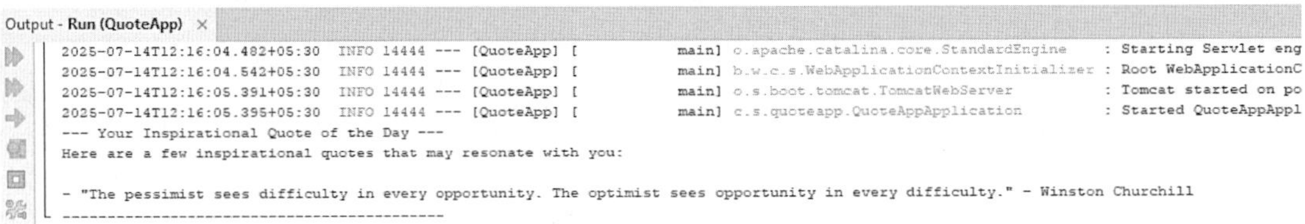

5. Run it again, and you'll get another different quote!

Bridging the gap: Learned concepts and application implementation

This architecture demonstrates a more advanced and flexible way to manage Spring beans:

- **@Configuration:** This annotation marks AppConfig as a source of bean definitions. Spring will process this class to find beans to add to the application context.
- **@Bean:** Each method annotated with @Bean produces a bean that Spring will manage. The method name (localQuoteService, aiQuoteService) becomes the default bean ID.
- **@Profile on @Bean methods:** By placing the @Profile annotation on the @Bean method instead of the class, you centralize the decision-making. The AppConfig class now decides which implementation of QuoteService to create based on the active Spring profile.
- **Programmatic dependency injection:** Notice the aiQuoteService() bean method takes parameters: WebClient.Builder and the apiKey. Spring automatically finds the required WebClient.Builder bean and injects the API key from application.properties (using @Value) into the method, which you then pass to the AiQuoteService constructor. This is a very clean way to construct your objects with their required dependencies.

Exploring application behaviour: A practical run-through

1. When you run the application, Spring Boot starts and reads application.properties to determine the active profile.

2. It discovers the AppConfig class because it's annotated with @Configuration.
3. Spring then inspects the @Bean methods inside.
    a. If the **local** profile is active, it sees the @Profile("local") annotation on the localQuoteService() method, executes it, and registers the returned InspirationalQuoteService object as the QuoteService bean.
    b. If the **ai** profile is active, it instead executes the aiQuoteService() method, creating and registering the AiQuoteService instance.
4. CommandLineRunner simply asks for a QuoteService bean, and Spring provides the one that was created based on the active profile.

Harnessing Cohere in a real-world context

This pattern of creating a dedicated service to call an AI API is a fundamental blueprint for building a vast array of intelligent features. Imagine extending this simple quote generator. You could change the prompt to ask for a "three-paragraph blog post introduction about the benefits of remote work" or "five social media post ideas for a new coffee shop." This same mechanism can be used to:

- Draft marketing copy and product descriptions.
- Generate boilerplate email responses.
- Create summaries of long documents.
- Brainstorm ideas for any creative endeavour.

By simply changing the prompt sent to the Cohere API, you can repurpose your Spring application to automate countless content creation tasks, saving time and boosting creativity.

Wrapping up

In this chapter, you took a massive leap from writing static applications to building dynamic, AI-powered ones.

- You learned to securely manage API keys in application.properties.
- You centralized bean creation logic in a @Configuration class.
- You mastered using @Profile on @Bean methods to switch implementations.
- You successfully used WebClient to call an external REST API.
- You transformed a basic app into an endless content generator.

Congratulations on integrating your first AI model! You've learned one of the most valuable and forward-looking skills in modern software development.

In the next chapter (which also happens to be the culmination project of this section), we'll take this knowledge and apply it to a web application, using the Google Gemini API to build an AI assistant that drafts professional emails, demonstrating a true full-stack AI feature.

Chapter 17

Section 04: Integrating AI with Spring applications

Culmination: Supercharging a web app with Gemini

What you'll learn

- Gemini API setup
- Full-stack AI integration
- Connecting UI to AI
- Building an AI service
- Writing effective prompts

This is an exciting moment in your journey as a developer. You have mastered the fundamentals of building robust, database-driven applications with Spring Boot. Now, it's time to elevate your creations from merely functional to truly intelligent. In today's software landscape, Artificial Intelligence is not a futuristic concept; it's a practical tool that can create dynamic, responsive, and highly personalized user experiences. By integrating a powerful Large Language Model (LLM) like Google's Gemini, you can add features that once seemed like science fiction, such as automatically drafting communications, summarizing complex information, or providing intelligent suggestions.

This chapter shows you how to take a standard web application and infuse it with AI, transforming a simple tool into a smart assistant. You will learn to connect the solid backend you've built with the creative power of generative AI, unlocking a new dimension of possibilities for your projects.

In the previous chapter, you saw how to enhance a simple command-line tool with AI-generated content from Cohere. Now, we take a significant leap forward by integrating one of the world's most powerful AI models, Google Gemini, into the full-stack Contact Manager web application you built in ***Chapter 9 - Culmination: Building a simple Contact Manager***.

This isn't just about replacing a list of quotes; it's about adding a "smart feature" that provides genuine value to the user. We will build an AI-powered assistant that can draft a professional follow-up email tailored to a specific contact, demonstrating a seamless integration between a user-facing web interface, your Spring Boot backend, and a cutting-edge AI service.

Getting started with the Gemini API

Before we can write any code, you need to get access to the Gemini API. Google provides a straightforward process for developers to get started, often including a generous free tier perfect for learning and experimentation.

1. Visit the Google AI for Developers website. Register your details and Google AI Studio's page appears.

2. Select **Dashboard** or click **Get API Key**. The **API Keys** page appears.

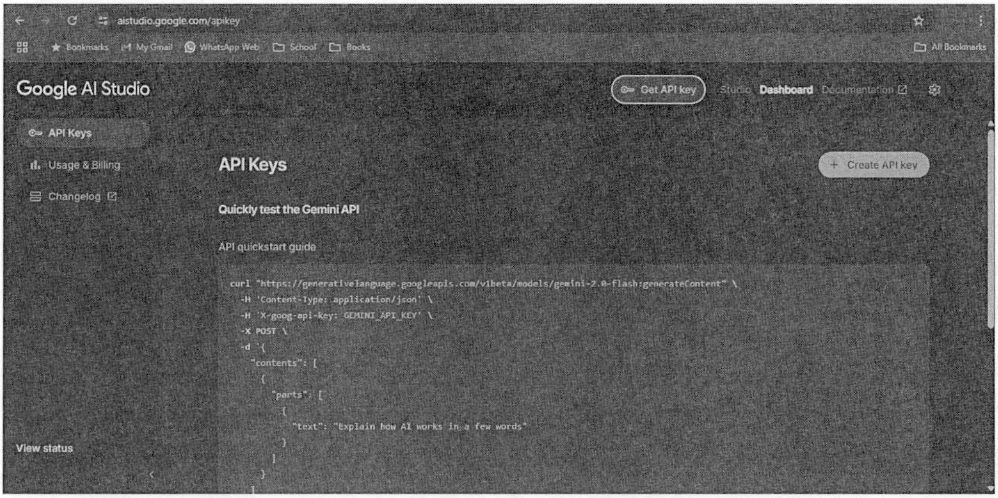

3. Click on **Create API Key**. This will generate and enable your Gemini API Key. The key piece of information you will receive is an **API Key**.

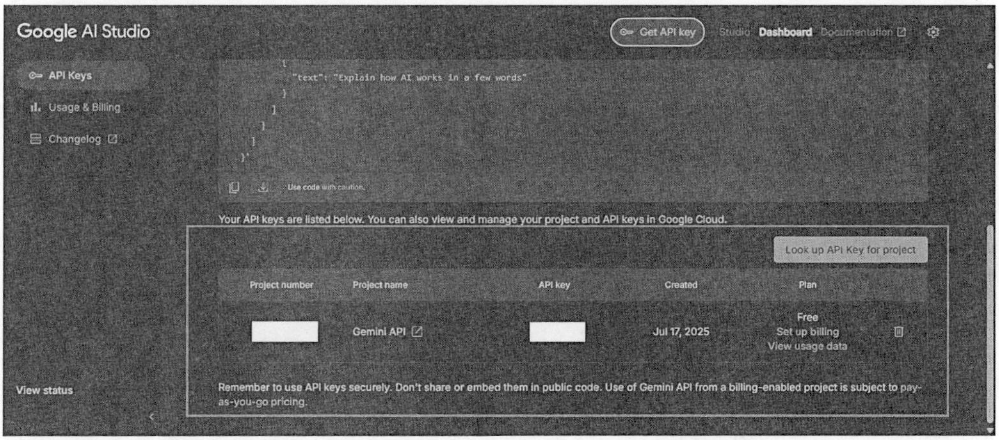

Treat your API Key like a password. It is your secret credential for accessing the service. Never share it publicly or commit it to a version control system like Git. As we learned in previous chapters, the best practice is to store it securely in your **application.properties** file.

PRD: The AI email assistant

- **Feature:** AI Email Assistant.
- **Requirement:** On the contact list page, each contact should have a button labeled **Draft Follow-up**.

- **User story:** When a user clicks the **Draft Follow-up** button, the system must make a call to an AI service (Gemini) to generate a professional and contextually appropriate follow-up email draft addressed to that specific contact. The draft should then be displayed to the user on the screen.

This feature adds a layer of intelligence that helps the user be more productive, transforming the application from a simple data store into a proactive tool.

Hands-on: The AI email assistant

In this hands-on section, we will recreate the Contact Manager project of ***Chapter 9 - Culmination: Building a simple Contact Manager***. The goal is to implement the AI Email Assistant feature. You will create a dedicated service to communicate with the Gemini API, expose this functionality through a new REST endpoint, and use JavaScript in the Thymeleaf front end to call this endpoint and display the AI-generated email draft to the user. This exercise demonstrates a true full-stack AI integration.

Building the application

Create a Spring Boot project

1. In NetBeans, go to **File → New Project...**.
2. In the **Choose Project** dialog, select **Java with Maven** from the **Categories** list and **Spring Boot Initializr project** from the **Projects** list.
3. Click **Next**. In the **Base Properties** step:
    - Set **Group** to **com.sharanamvaishali** and **Artifact** to **contactproject**.
    - Keep the **Version** as it is (i.e. **0.0.1-SNAPSHOT**).
    - Ensure **Packaging** is **Jar**.
    - Set **Name** to **ContactManager** and **Package Name** to **com.sharanamvaishali.contactmanager**.
    - Select **Java** from the **Language** list and the appropriate **Java Version** (e.g., **24**).
4. Click **Next**. In the **Dependencies** step:
    - Select the appropriate **Spring Boot Version** (e.g., **4.0.0 (SNAPSHOT)**).
    - In the **Available** dependencies list, find and select:
        - **Spring Web:** For building web applications with Spring MVC.
        - **Spring Data JPA:** For database interaction.

- **H2 database:** An in-memory database, great for development / testing.
- **Thymeleaf:** For server-side rendering of HTML.
- **Lombok:** Optional, but highly recommended for reducing boilerplate code like getters / setters.

5. Click **Next**. In the **Name and Location** step:
   - Set **Project Name** to **ContactManagerProject**.
   - Choose a suitable **Project Location**.
6. Click **Finish**. NetBeans generates the project structure and downloads dependencies.

Project structure and initial code

Your project structure looks something like this (key folders highlighted):

```
ContactManager
├── pom.xml
└── src
    ├── main
    │   ├── java
    │   │   └── com
    │   │       └── sharanamvaishali
    │   │           └── contactmanager
    │   │               ├── ContactManagerApplication.java
    │   │               └── (Other Java files will go here)
    │   ├── resources
    │   │   ├── application.properties
    │   │   ├── static  (For CSS, JS, images)
    │   │   └── templates (For Thymeleaf HTML files)
    │   └── webapp (Exists sometimes, but for Spring Boot, static and templates are preferred)
    └── test
        └── java
            └── com
                └── sharanamvaishali
                    └── contactmanager
                        └── ContactManagerApplicationTests.java
```

Configure H2 database and console

Open application.properties and add the following lines for H2 database and console:

```
# H2 Database Configuration
spring.h2.console.enabled=true
```

```
spring.h2.console.path=/h2-console
spring.datasource.url=jdbc:h2:mem:contactdb;DB_CLOSE_DELAY=-1;DB_CLOSE_ON_EXIT=FALSE
spring.datasource.driverClassName=org.h2.Driver
spring.datasource.username=sa
spring.datasource.password=
spring.jpa.database-platform=org.hibernate.dialect.H2Dialect
# Creates/updates schema on startup
spring.jpa.hibernate.ddl-auto=update
# Show SQL queries in console
spring.jpa.show-sql=true
# Thymeleaf configuration (optional, defaults are usually fine)
spring.thymeleaf.prefix=classpath:/templates/
spring.thymeleaf.suffix=.html
spring.thymeleaf.mode=HTML5
spring.thymeleaf.encoding=UTF-8
# Set to true in production for performance
spring.thymeleaf.cache=false
# Server Port (optional, default is 8080)
server.port=8080
```

Code explanation

This file configures your Spring Boot application's behaviour.

- **spring.h2.console.enabled=true:** Enables the H2 database web console. The H2 console is a simple web interface that allows you to interact with your H2 database, run SQL queries, and inspect data. It's incredibly useful for development and debugging.
- **spring.h2.console.path=/h2-console:** Defines the URL path under which the H2 console will be accessible in your application. So, if your application runs on http://localhost:8080, you can access the H2 console at http://localhost:8080/h2-console.
- **spring.datasource.url=jdbc:h2:mem:contactdb;DB_CLOSE_DELAY=-1;DB_CLOSE_ON_EXIT=FALSE:** This is the JDBC URL for connecting to the H2 database.
    - **jdbc:h2:mem:contactdb**: Specifies that it's an H2 database and mem: indicates it's an **in-memory database** named contactdb. This means the data will reside in your application's RAM and will be lost when the application stops. This is ideal for development, testing, and learning.
    - **DB_CLOSE_DELAY=-1:** Keeps the database alive as long as the JVM (your application) is running, even if there are no active connections. Without this, the in-memory database might close prematurely.
    - **DB_CLOSE_ON_EXIT=FALSE:** Ensures the database doesn't close automatically when the last connection is closed.
- **spring.datasource.driverClassName=org.h2.Driver:** Specifies the JDBC driver class for H2 database. This tells Spring how to connect to the database.
- **spring.datasource.username=sa:** Sets the username for connecting to the H2 database. sa (system administrator) is the default username for H2.

- **spring.datasource.password=:** Sets the password for connecting to the H2 database. In a real application, you'd use a stronger, ideally environment-specific, password.
- **spring.jpa.database-platform=org.hibernate.dialect.H2Dialect:** This tells Spring Data JPA (which uses Hibernate internally) which specific SQL dialect to use for H2. Hibernate uses dialects to generate database-specific SQL queries.
- **spring.jpa.hibernate.ddl-auto=update:** This is a crucial Hibernate property for DDL (Data Definition Language) generation.
    - **update:** When the application starts, Hibernate will compare the defined JPA entities (like Contact.java) with the actual database schema. If there are differences, it will attempt to ***update*** the schema (add new tables, add new columns, etc.) to match the entities. It will ***not*** drop existing tables or columns, which makes it relatively safe for development but can lead to issues in production if not managed carefully.
    - Other common values include none (no DDL operations), create (drops and recreates the schema on every startup), and create-drop (creates on startup, drops on shutdown).
- **spring.jpa.show-sql=true:** If set to true, Hibernate will log all the SQL queries it executes to the console. This is extremely helpful for debugging and understanding what database operations are being performed by your application.
- **spring.thymeleaf.prefix=classpath:/templates/:** This property configures Thymeleaf, a server-side Java template engine. It tells Thymeleaf where to find your HTML template files. classpath:/templates/ means it will look for templates in the src/main/resources/templates directory of your project.
- **spring.thymeleaf.suffix=.html:** Specifies the file extension for your Thymeleaf template files. So, if you refer to a template named "contacts", Thymeleaf will look for contacts.html.
- **spring.thymeleaf.mode=HTML5:** Sets the template mode to HTML5, which influences how Thymeleaf parses and processes your HTML files.
- **spring.thymeleaf.encoding=UTF-8:** Specifies the character encoding for your Thymeleaf templates, ensuring proper display of various characters.
- **spring.thymeleaf.cache=false:** Disables caching for Thymeleaf templates. This is highly recommended during development, as it means any changes you make to your HTML templates will be immediately reflected without needing to restart the application. For production, you would typically set this to true for performance.
- **server.port=8080:** Defines the port on which your Spring Boot application will run. The default is 8080, so this line is optional if you're happy with the default.

Define the Model (Entity)

Create a new Java class for your Contact entity.

1. In the **Projects** window, right-click the **com.sharanamvaishali.contactmanager** package and select **New → Java Package...**.
2. Enter **com.sharanamvaishali.contactmanager.model** as the **Package Name** and click **Finish**.
3. Right-click the **com.sharanamvaishali.contactmanager.model** package and select **New → Java Class...**.
4. Enter **Contact** as the **Class Name** and click **Finish**.
5. Replace the content of the Contact.java file with the following code:

```
package com.sharanamvaishali.contactmanager.model;
import jakarta.persistence.Entity;
import jakarta.persistence.GeneratedValue;
import jakarta.persistence.GenerationType;
import jakarta.persistence.Id;
import lombok.Data; // From Lombok dependency
import lombok.NoArgsConstructor;
import lombok.AllArgsConstructor;
@Entity // Marks this class as a JPA entity
@Data // Generates getters, setters, toString, equals, hashCode
@NoArgsConstructor // Generates no-argument constructor
@AllArgsConstructor // Generates constructor with all fields
public class Contact {
    @Id // Marks this field as the primary key
    @GeneratedValue(strategy = GenerationType.IDENTITY) // Auto-incrementing ID
    private Long id;
    private String name;
    private String email;
    private String phone;
    // You can add more fields as needed
}
```

Code explanation

This class represents the Contact entity that will be stored in your H2 database.

- **@Entity:** This annotation tells Spring Data JPA (and Hibernate) that Contact is a persistent entity and should be mapped to a table in the database. By default, the table name will be "contact".
- **@Data, @NoArgsConstructor, @AllArgsConstructor:** These Lombok annotations simplify the code by automatically generating methods and constructors.
    - **@Data:** Generates getters for all fields, setters for all non-final fields, and equals(), hashCode(), and toString() methods.
    - **@NoArgsConstructor:** Generates a constructor with no arguments. JPA often requires a no-argument constructor for entity instantiation.
    - **@AllArgsConstructor:** Generates a constructor with all fields as arguments.

- **@Id:** Marks the id field as the **primary key** of the Contact entity. This means it uniquely identifies each contact record in the database table.
- **@GeneratedValue(strategy = GenerationType.IDENTITY):** Specifies how the primary key value will be generated. GenerationType.IDENTITY indicates that the database will automatically assign a unique, auto-incrementing value to the primary key. This is a common strategy for primary keys in many databases (like H2, MySQL).
- **private Long id;, private String name;, private String email;, private String phone;:** These are the fields (properties) of the Contact entity. Each of these will typically correspond to a column in the contact table in your database.
    - **id:** Long is suitable for auto-incrementing primary keys.
    - **name, email, phone:** String for text-based data.

Data access (Repository)

Create a Spring Data JPA repository for Contact.

1. In the **Projects** window, expand your **Contact Manager** project.
2. Right-click the main package (e.g., **com.sharanamvaishali.contactmanager**) and select **New → Java Package....** Enter **repository** as the **Package Name** and click **Finish**.
3. Right-click the **com.sharanamvaishali.contactmanager.repository** package and select **New → Java Interface....**
4. Enter **ContactRepository** as the **Interface Name** and click **Finish**.
5. Replace the content of the ContactRepository.java file with the following code:

```
package com.sharanamvaishali.contactmanager.repository;
import com.sharanamvaishali.contactmanager.model.Contact;
import org.springframework.data.jpa.repository.JpaRepository;
import org.springframework.stereotype.Repository;
@Repository // Optional, but good practice to indicate it's a repository component
public interface ContactRepository extends JpaRepository<Contact, Long> {
    // Spring Data JPA automatically provides CRUD methods (save, findById, findAll,
    // delete, etc.) You can add custom query methods here if needed, e.g.,
    // List<Contact> findByNameContaining(String name);
}
```

Code explanation

This is the interface responsible for interacting with the Contact data in the database.

- **@Repository:** This annotation is a specialization of @Component and is used to indicate that the class provides the mechanism for storage, retrieval, search, update, and delete operation on objects. Spring uses this to detect and register the bean. It also enables Spring's exception translation mechanism, converting data access exceptions into a consistent hierarchy.

- **public interface ContactRepository extends JpaRepository<Contact, Long> { ... }:** This is the heart of the repository.
  - **extends JpaRepository<Contact, Long>:** This is where the magic of Spring Data JPA happens. By extending JpaRepository, your ContactRepository interface automatically inherits a vast array of methods to interact with the Contact entity.
    - **Contact:** The first generic type argument specifies the **entity type** that this repository will manage (i.e., Contact objects).
    - **Long:** The second generic type argument specifies the **data type of the entity's primary key** (i.e., id is a Long).
  - **Automatic methods:** Because of this extension, you immediately get methods like:
    - **save(Contact contact):** Inserts or updates a contact.
    - **findById(Long id):** Retrieves a contact by its ID.
    - **findAll():** Retrieves all contacts.
    - **delete(Contact contact):** Deletes a contact.
    - **deleteById(Long id):** Deletes a contact by ID.
    - And many more!

Business logic (Service)

Create a service layer for business operations.

1. In the **Projects** window, expand your **Contact Manager** project.
2. Right-click the main package (e.g., **com.sharanamvaishali.contactmanager**) and select **New → Java Package...**.
3. Enter **service** as the **Package Name** and click **Finish**.
4. Right-click the **com.sharanamvaishali.contactmanager.service** package and select **New → Java Class...**.
5. Enter **ContactService** as the **Class Name** and click **Finish**.
6. Replace the content of the ContactService.java file with the following code:

```
package com.sharanamvaishali.contactmanager.service;
import com.sharanamvaishali.contactmanager.model.Contact;
import com.sharanamvaishali.contactmanager.repository.ContactRepository;
import org.springframework.beans.factory.annotation.Autowired;
import org.springframework.stereotype.Service;
import java.util.List;
import java.util.Optional;
@Service // Marks this class as a Spring service component
public class ContactService {
```

```
    @Autowired // Injects the ContactRepository
    private ContactRepository contactRepository;
    public List<Contact> getAllContacts() {
        return contactRepository.findAll();
    }
    public Optional<Contact> getContactById(Long id) {
        return contactRepository.findById(id);
    }
    public Contact saveContact(Contact contact) {
        return contactRepository.save(contact);
    }
    public void deleteContact(Long id) {
        contactRepository.deleteById(id);
    }
}
```

Code explanation

This class acts as an intermediary between the web layer (controller) and the data access layer (repository). It encapsulates the business logic.

- **@Service:** Marks this class as a Spring service component. Like @Repository, it's a specialization of @Component. Service classes typically contain the core business logic and coordinate calls to multiple repositories if needed.
- **@Autowired:** This annotation performs **dependency injection**. Spring will automatically find and inject an instance of ContactRepository into the contactRepository field. This means you don't have to manually create new ContactRepository().
- **private ContactRepository contactRepository;:** Declares the ContactRepository dependency.
- **public List<Contact> getAllContacts() { ... }:** Retrieves all contacts from the database by simply delegating the call to the contactRepository.findAll() method.
- **public Optional<Contact> getContactById(Long id) { ... }:** Retrieves a single contact by its ID. findById returns an Optional<Contact>, which is a Java 8 feature to handle cases where the contact might not be found (to avoid NullPointerExceptions).
- **public Contact saveContact(Contact contact) { ... }:** Saves a new contact or updates an existing one. If the contact object has a non-null ID that exists in the database, save() will perform an update; otherwise, it will perform an insert.
- **public void deleteContact(Long id) { ... }:** Deletes a contact by its ID.

Web interface (Controller)

Create a Spring MVC controller to handle web requests and render Thymeleaf templates.

1. In the **Projects** window, expand your **Contact Manager** project.

2. Right-click the main package (e.g., **com.sharanamvaishali.contactmanager**) and select **New → Java Package...**.
3. Enter **controller** as the **Package Name** and click **Finish**.
4. Right-click the **com.sharanamvaishali.contactmanager.controller** package and select **New → Java Class...**.
5. Enter **ContactController** as the **Class Name** and click **Finish**.
6. Replace the content of the ContactController.java file with the following code:

```
package com.sharanamvaishali.contactmanager.controller;
import com.sharanamvaishali.contactmanager.model.Contact;
import com.sharanamvaishali.contactmanager.service.ContactService;
import org.springframework.beans.factory.annotation.Autowired;
import org.springframework.stereotype.Controller;
import org.springframework.ui.Model;
import org.springframework.web.bind.annotation.*;
import org.springframework.web.servlet.mvc.support.RedirectAttributes;
@Controller // Marks this as a Spring MVC controller
@RequestMapping("/contacts") // Base path for all methods in this controller
public class ContactController {
    @Autowired
    private ContactService contactService;
    // Display list of contacts
    @GetMapping
    public String listContacts(Model model) {
        model.addAttribute("contacts", contactService.getAllContacts());
        // Refers to src/main/resources/templates/contacts.html
        return "contacts";
    }
    // Show form for adding new contact
    @GetMapping("/new")
    public String showAddContactForm(Model model) {
        // Empty contact object for the form
        model.addAttribute("contact", new Contact());
        model.addAttribute("formAction", "/contacts/save"); // Set form action
        // Refers to src/main/resources/templates/contact-form.html
        return "contact-form";
    }
    // Save a new contact
    @PostMapping("/save")
    public String saveContact(@ModelAttribute("contact") Contact contact,
                              RedirectAttributes redirectAttributes) {
        contactService.saveContact(contact);
        redirectAttributes.addFlashAttribute("message", "Contact saved
                                             successfully!");
        return "redirect:/contacts";
    }
    // Show form for editing existing contact
    @GetMapping("/edit/{id}")
    public String showEditContactForm(@PathVariable Long id,
```

```
                              Model model, RedirectAttributes redirectAttributes) {
        return contactService.getContactById(id).map(contact -> {
            model.addAttribute("contact", contact);
            // Set form action
            model.addAttribute("formAction", "/contacts/update");
            return "contact-form";
        }).orElseGet(() -> {
            redirectAttributes.addFlashAttribute("error", "Contact not found!");
            return "redirect:/contacts";
        });
    }
    // Update an existing contact
    @PostMapping("/update")
    public String updateContact(@ModelAttribute("contact") Contact contact,
                                RedirectAttributes redirectAttributes) {
        // Ensure the ID exists before updating
        if (contactService.getContactById(contact.getId()).isPresent()) {
            // save() also handles updates if ID is present
            contactService.saveContact(contact);
            redirectAttributes.addFlashAttribute("message", "Contact updated
                                                  successfully!");
        } else {
            redirectAttributes.addFlashAttribute("error", "Contact not found for
                                                  update!");
        }
        return "redirect:/contacts";
    }
    // Delete a contact
    @GetMapping("/delete/{id}")
    public String deleteContact(@PathVariable Long id,
                                RedirectAttributes redirectAttributes) {
        contactService.deleteContact(id);
        redirectAttributes.addFlashAttribute("message", "Contact deleted
                                              successfully!");
        return "redirect:/contacts";
    }
}
```

Code explanation

This class acts as the **web interface** for your application. It receives incoming HTTP requests from the browser, processes them, interacts with the ContactService to perform business logic,

- **@Controller:** This annotation marks a class as a Spring MVC controller. Spring's component scanning will detect it and register it as a bean. Controllers are responsible for handling HTTP requests and returning views (HTML pages, JSON, etc.).
- **@RequestMapping("/contacts"):** This annotation specifies the base path for all request mappings within this controller. So, any @GetMapping or @PostMapping in this class will be prefixed with /contacts.

- **@GetMapping** on a method (e.g., listContacts()) is a shortcut for @RequestMapping(method = RequestMethod.GET).
- **@PostMapping** on a method (e.g., saveContact()) is a shortcut for @RequestMapping(method = RequestMethod.POST).

❑ **@Autowired:** This is a core Spring annotation for **dependency injection**. When Spring initializes ContactController, it sees @Autowired on private ContactService contactService; and automatically finds a ContactService bean (which we've annotated with @Service) and injects it into this controller. This means you don't manually instantiate ContactService using new ContactService().

❑ **Model:** This is an interface provided by Spring MVC. It's used to pass data from your controller to the view (Thymeleaf template). You add attributes to the Model object, and these attributes become accessible in your HTML using Thymeleaf's syntax (th:text="${attributeName}", th:each="item : ${list}", etc.).

❑ **@PathVariable Long id:** This annotation is used to extract a variable from the URL path. For example, in /contacts/edit/123, 123 would be extracted as the id and converted to a Long.

❑ **@ModelAttribute("contact") Contact contact:** This annotation is crucial for form binding.

- When a form is submitted (e.g., contact-form.html), Spring looks at the name attributes of the form fields (e.g., name="name", name="email").
- It then creates a Contact object and tries to set its properties (name, email, phone, id) using the values from the form.
- The ("contact") part specifies the name under which this object will be accessible in the Thymeleaf template if the form is rendered again (e.g., for error messages, though not implemented here, or for pre-filling the form in an edit scenario).

❑ **RedirectAttributes redirectAttributes:** This is used when you want to redirect the user to a different URL after a form submission (e.g., after saving or deleting a contact).

- **redirectAttributes.addFlashAttribute("message", "..."):** "Flash attributes" are temporary attributes that are stored in the session and are available only for the ***next*** request after the redirect. This is perfect for displaying one-time success or error messages after an action.
- **return "redirect:/contacts";:** This tells Spring MVC to issue an HTTP redirect to the /contacts URL. The browser will then make a new GET request to /contacts, and the listContacts method will be invoked.

❑ **Return type String:** When a controller method returns a String, Spring MVC interprets it as the **logical view name**. In a Thymeleaf setup, this means it will look for an HTML file with that name in src/main/resources/templates/. So, return "contacts"; means contacts.html.

This controller provides the full set of CRUD (Create, Read, Update, Delete) operations for your contacts via a web interface, driven by Spring MVC and rendered using Thymeleaf.

AI Integration

Securely configure your API key

Again, open your application.properties file located in src/main/resources and add your Gemini API key. This keeps your key safe and separate from your source code.

```
# Gemini API Configuration
gemini.api.key=<YOUR_API_KEY_HERE>
```

Create the GeminiEmailService Service

For this hands-on, we'll create an AI service. This service will contain the logic for interacting with the Gemini API.

1. In the **Projects** window, expand your **Contact Manager** project.
2. Right-click the main package (e.g., **com.sharanamvaishali.contactmanager**) and select **New → Java Package...**.
3. Enter **ai** as the new package name and click **Finish**.
4. Right-click the **com.sharanamvaishali.contactmanager.ai** package and select **New → Java Class...**.
5. Enter **GeminiEmailService** as the **Class Name** and click **Finish**.
6. Open the GeminiEmailService.java file and replace its content with the following code:

```
package com.sharanamvaishali.contactmanager.ai;
import com.fasterxml.jackson.databind.JsonNode;
import com.fasterxml.jackson.databind.ObjectMapper;
import org.springframework.beans.factory.annotation.Value;
import org.springframework.http.HttpEntity;
import org.springframework.http.HttpHeaders;
import org.springframework.http.MediaType;
import org.springframework.stereotype.Service;
import org.springframework.web.client.RestTemplate;
@Service
public class GeminiEmailService {
  @Value("${gemini.api.key}") private String apiKey;
  private static final String MODEL_NAME = "gemini-2.5-flash";
  private static final String BASE_API_URL =
      "https://generativelanguage.googleapis.com/v1beta/models/";
  private final RestTemplate restTemplate = new RestTemplate();
  private final ObjectMapper objectMapper = new ObjectMapper();
  public String draftFollowUpEmail(String contactName) {
```

```
    String prompt = "Write a short, professional follow-up email to "
        + contactName + ". " + ("The email should be friendly and inquire
         about the next steps for " + "a recent project discussion. ")
        + "Sign off as 'Best regards, Your Name'.";
    System.out.println("----PROMPT SENT TO GEMINI (draftFollowUpEmail)----");
    System.out.println(prompt);
    System.out.println("------------------------------------------------------");
    // Construct the full API URL
    String geminiApiUrl =
        BASE_API_URL + MODEL_NAME + ":generateContent?key=" + apiKey;
    HttpHeaders headers = new HttpHeaders();
    headers.setContentType(MediaType.APPLICATION_JSON);
    // Construct the request body as a JSON string, escaping the prompt text
    String requestBody = "{\"contents\":[{\"parts\":[{\"text\":\""
        + escapeJson(prompt) + "\"}]}]}";
    HttpEntity<String> entity = new HttpEntity<>(requestBody, headers);
    try {
      // Send the POST request
      String response =
          restTemplate.postForObject(geminiApiUrl, entity, String.class);
      System.out.println(
          "----RAW RESPONSE FROM GEMINI (draftFollowUpEmail)----\n" + response);
      // Parse the JSON response
      JsonNode root = objectMapper.readTree(response);
      // Navigate the JSON path to extract the generated text
      String geminiResponseText = root.path("candidates")
                                     .get(0).path("content").path("parts")
                                     .get(0).path("text").asText();
      System.out.println(
          "----PARSED RESPONSE FROM GEMINI (draftFollowUpEmail)----\n"
          + geminiResponseText);
      return geminiResponseText;
    } catch (Exception e) {
      System.err.println(
          "Error calling Gemini API for draftFollowUpEmail: " + e.getMessage());
      e.printStackTrace(); // Print stack trace for debugging
      // Fallback: Return a generic error message or a dummy email
      return "Subject: [Error] Follow Up Email\n\n"
          + "Hi " + contactName + ",\n\n"
          + "There was an error drafting your email: "
          + (e.getMessage() != null && e.getMessage().length() > 100
                 ? e.getMessage().substring(0, 100) + "...": e.getMessage())
          + "\n\n"
          + "Best regards,\n"
          + "Your Name";
    }
  }
  // Helper method to escape special characters for JSON
  private String escapeJson(String text) {
    return text
        .replace("\\", "\\\\") // Escape backslashes first
```

```
            .replace("\"", "\\\"") // Escape double quotes
            .replace("\n", "\\n") // Escape newlines
            .replace("\r", "\\r") // Escape carriage returns
            .replace("\t", "\\t"); // Escape tabs
    }
}
```

Code explanation

GeminiEmailService provides a robust way to integrate with Gemini AI to automate the process of drafting follow-up emails. It handles API communication, request/response formatting, and error handling, making it a reusable component within a Spring Boot application.

- **@Service:** Marks GeminiEmailService as a service component. In Spring applications, service layers typically encapsulate business logic and are often used to call external APIs or interact with databases. This allows Spring to automatically detect and manage this class as a Spring bean, meaning you can easily inject it into other parts of your application.
- **@Value("${gemini.api.key}") private String apiKey;:** Uses Spring's @Value annotation to inject the value of the gemini.api.key property from your application's configuration (e.g., application.properties) into the apiKey field. This is a secure and flexible way to manage sensitive credentials like API keys, keeping them out of the source code.
- **private static final String MODEL_NAME = "gemini-2.5-flash";:** Defines a specific **Gemini AI model** to be used for generating email content. "gemini-2.5-flash" indicates a particular version or type of the Gemini model known for its speed.
- **private static final String BASE_API_URL = "https://....";:** The base URL for **Gemini API endpoint**. The full API call will be constructed by appending the MODEL_NAME and the apiKey to this base.
- **private final RestTemplate restTemplate = new RestTemplate();:** RestTemplate is a synchronous HTTP client provided by Spring that simplifies making RESTful API calls. It's used here to send HTTP requests (specifically, a POST request) to the Gemini API.
- **private final ObjectMapper objectMapper = new ObjectMapper();:** ObjectMapper is part of the Jackson library, a popular Java library for serializing and deserializing JSON. It's used here to parse the JSON response received from the Gemini API.
- **draftFollowUpEmail(String contactName):** The main method responsible for generating a follow-up email.
  - **Constructing the prompt:**
    - A prompt string is created dynamically, incorporating contactName provided as input. This prompt instructs Gemini AI to "Write a short, professional follow-up email" that is "friendly and inquire about the next steps for a recent project discussion," and to "Sign off as 'Best regards, Your Name'."

    - The System.out.println statements are for **logging purposes**, showing the prompt that's being sent to Gemini for debugging and monitoring.

- **Building the API URL:** geminiApiUrl is assembled using BASE_API_URL, MODEL_NAME, and the injected apiKey. This forms the complete endpoint URL for the Gemini API call.
- **Setting up HTTP headers:** HttpHeaders are created, and the Content-Type header is set to MediaType.APPLICATION_JSON. This tells Gemini API that the request body will be in JSON format.
- **Creating the Request body:**
    - requestBody is constructed as a JSON string. Gemini API expects the prompt text within a specific JSON structure: {"contents":[{"parts":[{"text":"YOUR_PROMPT_HERE"}]}]}.
    - The escapeJson(prompt) helper method is crucial here to ensure that any special characters in the prompt (like double quotes or newlines) are properly escaped so that the JSON remains valid.
- **Sending the HTTP request:**
    - HttpEntity<String> entity = new HttpEntity<>(requestBody, headers); wraps the JSON request body and headers into a single entity.
    - restTemplate.postForObject(geminiApiUrl, entity, String.class); sends a **POST request** to geminiApiUrl with the entity (containing the prompt and headers). String.class indicates that the expected response from the API is a plain string (which will be a JSON string).
    - System.out.println logs the raw JSON response received from Gemini.
- **Parsing the Gemini response:**
    - The try-catch block handles potential errors during the API call or response parsing.
    - JsonNode root = objectMapper.readTree(response); parses the raw JSON response string into a JsonNode object, which allows for easy navigation through the JSON structure.
    - root.path("candidates").get(0).path("content").path("parts").get(0).path("text").asText(); demonstrates **JSON path traversal**. This line navigates through the JSON response hierarchy (e.g., candidates array, content object, parts array, etc.) to extract the actual generated email text, which is typically found within the "text" field.
    - The extracted text is then logged and returned by the method.

- **Error handling:**
    - If any Exception occurs during the API call or JSON parsing, the catch block is executed.
    - An error message is printed to System.err, and a stack trace is printed for detailed debugging.
    - As a fallback, a generic error email message is returned to the caller, indicating that there was an issue. This prevents the application from crashing and provides a user-friendly error response.

- **Helper method: escapeJson(String text):** This private utility method is essential for **JSON safety**. It takes a raw string (text) and replaces special characters (like backslashes, double quotes, newlines, carriage returns, and tabs) with their JSON-escaped equivalents. This is crucial because if the prompt text contains these characters directly, it would break the JSON structure of the request body, leading to API errors.

Create a REST Controller for the AI Service

To allow our frontend to access the GeminiEmailService, we need to expose it through a controller.

1. Right-click the **com.sharanamvaishali.contactmanager.controller** package and select **New → Java Class....**
2. Enter **AiController** in the **Class Name** and click **Finish**.
3. Open the AiController.java file and replace its content with the following code:

```java
package com.sharanamvaishali.contactmanager.controller;
import com.sharanamvaishali.contactmanager.ai.GeminiEmailService;
import java.util.Map;
import org.springframework.web.bind.annotation.PostMapping;
import org.springframework.web.bind.annotation.RequestMapping;
import org.springframework.http.ResponseEntity;
import org.springframework.web.bind.annotation.RequestBody;
import org.springframework.web.bind.annotation.RestController;
@RestController
@RequestMapping("/api/v1/ai")
public class AiController {
    private final GeminiEmailService geminiEmailService;
    public AiController(GeminiEmailService geminiEmailService) {
        this.geminiEmailService = geminiEmailService;
    }
    @PostMapping("/draft-email")
    public ResponseEntity<Map<String, String>> getEmailDraft(@RequestBody
                                Map<String, String> payload) {
        String contactName = payload.get("contactName");
        if (contactName == null || contactName.trim().isEmpty()) {
            return ResponseEntity.badRequest().body(Map.of("error",
```

```
                        "contactName is required."));
            }
            String draft = geminiEmailService.draftFollowUpEmail(contactName);
            return ResponseEntity.ok(Map.of("draft", draft));
        }
}
```

Code explanation:

- **@RestController:** Designates this as a REST controller where every method returns a domain object instead of a view.
- **@RequestMapping("/api/v1/ai"):** Sets the base path for all endpoints in this controller.
- **Constructor injection:** We inject our GeminiEmailService to make its methods available.
- **@PostMapping("/draft-email"):** Maps HTTP POST requests to this method. We use POST because the request will contain a body with the contact's name.
- **@RequestBody:** Tells Spring to convert the incoming JSON request body into a Map.
- **ResponseEntity:** This allows us to return the AI-generated draft along with an HTTP status code (e.g., 200 OK).

Create Thymeleaf HTML templates

Create the necessary HTML files in **Other Sources → src/main/resources → templates** by right-clicking **templates** and selecting **New → HTML Files...**:

- contacts.html
- contact-form.html

contacts.html

Open the contacts.html file and replace its content with the following code:

```
<!DOCTYPE html>
<html lang="en" xmlns:th="http://www.thymeleaf.org">
    <head>
        <meta charset="UTF-8">
        <title>Contact Manager</title>
        <link href="https://stackpath.bootstrapcdn.com/bootstrap/4.5.2
                    /css/bootstrap.min.css" rel="stylesheet">
        <style>
            body { padding: 20px; }
            .table th, .table td { vertical-align: middle; }
        </style>
    </head>
    <body>
        <div class="container">
```

```
            <h2 class="mb-4">Contact List</h2>
            <div th:if="${message}" class="alert alert-success" role="alert">
                <p th:text="${message}"></p>
            </div>
            <div th:if="${error}" class="alert alert-danger" role="alert">
                <p th:text="${error}"></p>
            </div>
            <a th:href="@{/contacts/new}" class="btn btn-primary mb-3">
               Add New Contact</a>
            <table class="table table-bordered table-striped">
                <thead class="thead-dark">
                    <tr>
                        <th>ID</th>
                        <th>Name</th>
                        <th>Email</th>
                        <th>Phone</th>
                        <th>Actions</th>
                    </tr>
                </thead>
                <tbody>
                    <tr th:each="contact : ${contacts}">
                        <td th:text="${contact.id}"></td>
                        <td th:text="${contact.name}"></td>
                        <td th:text="${contact.email}"></td>
                        <td th:text="${contact.phone}"></td>
                        <td>
                            <a th:href="@{/contacts/edit/{id}(id=${contact.id})}"
                               class="btn btn-info btn-sm">Edit</a>
                            <a th:href="@{/contacts/delete/{id}(id=${contact.id})}"
                               class="btn btn-danger btn-sm" onclick="return
                               confirm('Are you sure you want to delete this
                               contact?');">Delete</a>
                            <button type="button" class="btn btn-info btn-sm"
                                    th:attr="data-contact-name=${contact.name}"
                                    onclick="draftEmail(this.getAttribute
                                            ('data-contact-name'))">
                                Draft Follow-up
                            </button>
                        </td>
                    </tr>
                    <tr th:if="${contacts.empty}">
                        <td colspan="5" class="text-center">No contacts found.</td>
                    </tr>
                </tbody>
            </table>
        </div>
        <script src="https://code.jquery.com/jquery-3.5.1.slim.min.js"></script>
        <script src="https://cdn.jsdelivr.net/npm/@popperjs/core@2.5.4/dist/umd/
                popper.min.js"></script>
        <script src="https://stackpath.bootstrapcdn.com/bootstrap/4.5.2/js/
                bootstrap.min.js"></script>
```

```
        <script>
            async function draftEmail(contactName) {
                try {
                    const response = await fetch('/api/v1/ai/draft-email', {
                        method: 'POST',
                        headers: {
                            'Content-Type': 'application/json',
                            'Accept': 'application/json'
                        },
                        body: JSON.stringify({ contactName: contactName })
                    });
                    if (!response.ok) {
                        throw new Error('Network response was not ok. Status: '
                                        + response.status);
                    }
                    const result = await response.json();
                    // For simplicity, we use a browser alert.
                    // A more sophisticated UI would show this in a modal dialog.
                    alert('AI-Generated Draft:\n\n' + result.draft);
                } catch (error) {
                    console.error('There was a problem drafting the email:', error);
                    alert('Could not generate email draft. Please check the console
                          for errors.');
                }
            }
        </script>
    </body>
</html>
```

Code explanation

This is the HTML file, which is responsible for displaying the list of contacts.

- **Bootstrap CSS link:** Links an external CSS stylesheet from a Content Delivery Network (CDN). This line imports **Bootstrap**, a popular front-end framework that provides pre-designed components and styles (tables, buttons, forms, layout grids) to make your web page look good and be responsive without writing much custom CSS.
- **Success message display (<div th:if="${message}" ...>):** This is a **Thymeleaf conditional attribute**. It means this <div> element (and its content) will **only be rendered** if a model attribute named message exists and has a non-null value from the Spring controller. This is typically used to display success messages passed via RedirectAttributes after an operation (like saving a contact).
- **Error message display (<div th:if="${error}" ...>):** Similar to the success message, this div will **only be rendered** if an error model attribute exists.
- **Add New Contact button (<a th:href="@{/contacts/new}" ...>):** An anchor tag, creating a hyperlink. This is a **Thymeleaf URL expression**. It generates a URL dynamically. Here, it creates a link to the /contacts/new endpoint, which corresponds to the showAddContactForm() method in your ContactController.

- **Contacts table (<table class="table table-bordered table-striped">):** This is the HTML structure for displaying tabular data.
- **Iterating through contacts (<tr th:each="contact : ${contacts}">):** This is a Thymeleaf iteration attribute. It works like a for-each loop in Java. For every contact object in the contacts list (which is passed from the controller via the Model), Thymeleaf will create a new <tr> (table row) and populate its cells.
- **Displaying contact data (<td th:text="${contact.id}">):** This is a **Thymeleaf text expression**. It replaces the content of the <td> tag with the value of the id property of the current contact object. Similar expressions are used for name, email, and phone.
- **Action buttons for each contact (<td>):**
    - **Edit button (<a th:href="@{/contacts/edit/{id}(id=${contact.id})}" ...>):** This creates a link to the /contacts/edit/{id} endpoint. {id}(id=${contact.id}) dynamically inserts the current contact.id into the {id} placeholder in the URL.
    - **Delete button (<a th:href="@{/contacts/delete/{id}(id=${contact.id})}" ... onclick="return confirm(...)">):** Similar URL generation for the delete endpoint.
        - **onclick="return confirm('Are you sure you want to delete this contact?');":** This is a client-side JavaScript confirmation dialog. If the user clicks "Cancel", the return false prevents the link from being followed.
    - **Draft Follow-up button (AI Integration): <button type="button" ... onclick="draftEmail(...)">**
        - **type="button":** Specifies it's a button, not a form submission button.
        - **th:attr="data-contact-name=${contact.name}":** This **Thymeleaf attribute processor** sets a custom HTML data-contact-name attribute on the button. The value of this attribute is dynamically set to the contact.name from the current loop iteration. This allows JavaScript to easily access the contact's name when the button is clicked.
        - **onclick="draftEmail(this.getAttribute('data-contact-name'))":** When the button is clicked, this JavaScript function draftEmail is called, passing the value of the data-contact-name attribute (i.e., the contact's name).
- **"No Contacts Found" row (<tr th:if="${contacts.empty}">):** This row will **only be rendered** if the contacts list (passed from the controller) is empty.
- **Bootstrap JavaScript Dependencies:** These <script> tags load necessary JavaScript files from CDNs.
    - **jquery-3.5.1.slim.min.js:** A lightweight version of jQuery, a popular JavaScript library, used by Bootstrap.
    - **popper.min.js:** A positioning engine for tooltips and popovers, also required by Bootstrap.

- **bootstrap.min.js:** The main Bootstrap JavaScript file, providing interactive components like dropdowns, modals, etc.

- **Custom JavaScript for AI draft (<script>):**
  - **async function draftEmail(contactName):** Defines an asynchronous function to handle our API call without freezing the browser.
  - **fetch('/api/v1/ai/draft-email', { ... }):** This is the core of the AJAX call.
    - **fetch():** The modern JavaScript API for making network (HTTP) requests.
    - **'/api/v1/ai/draft-email':** The URL endpoint to which the request is sent. This implies that you would need a ***separate*** REST Controller (e.g., AiRestController) with a @PostMapping("/api/v1/ai/draft-email") that accepts JSON and returns JSON. This is different from the AiController provided in the earlier steps which returns a Thymeleaf view.
    - **method: 'POST':** Specifies that it's a POST request.
    - **headers:** Sets HTTP headers, indicating that the request body will be JSON ('Content-Type': 'application/json') and that the client expects a JSON response ('Accept': 'application/json').
    - **body: JSON.stringify({ contactName: contactName }):** Converts a JavaScript object { contactName: contactName } into a JSON string and sends it as the request body.
  - **alert(...):** For simplicity, we use a standard browser alert box to display the AI's response. In a real application, you would use a more elegant modal or text area.

contact-form.html

Open the contact-form.html file and replace its content with the following code:

```
<!DOCTYPE html>
<html lang="en" xmlns:th="http://www.thymeleaf.org">
    <head>
        <meta charset="UTF-8">
        <title th:text="${contact.id == null ? 'Add New Contact' :
                       'Edit Contact'}"></title>
        <link href="https://stackpath.bootstrapcdn.com/bootstrap/4.5.2/css/
                   bootstrap.min.css" rel="stylesheet">
        <style>
            body { padding: 20px; }
            .form-group { margin-bottom: 15px; }
        </style>
    </head>
    <body>
        <div class="container">
            <h2 th:text="${contact.id == null ? 'Add New Contact' :
```

```
                        'Edit Contact'}" class="mb-4"></h2>
            <form th:action="${formAction}" th:object="${contact}" method="post">
                <input type="hidden" th:field="*{id}" />
                <div class="form-group">
                    <label for="name">Name:</label>
                    <input type="text" id="name" th:field="*{name}"
                           class="form-control" required />
                </div>
                <div class="form-group">
                    <label for="email">Email:</label>
                    <input type="email" id="email" th:field="*{email}"
                           class="form-control" required />
                </div>
                <div class="form-group">
                    <label for="phone">Phone:</label>
                    <input type="text" id="phone" th:field="*{phone}"
                           class="form-control" />
                </div>
                <button type="submit" class="btn btn-success">Save Contact</button>
                <a th:href="@{/contacts}" class="btn btn-secondary">Cancel</a>
            </form>
        </div>
        <script src="https://code.jquery.com/jquery-3.5.1.slim.min.js"></script>
        <script src="https://cdn.jsdelivr.net/npm/@popperjs/core@2.5.4/dist/umd/
                    popper.min.js"></script>
        <script src="https://stackpath.bootstrapcdn.com/bootstrap/4.5.2/js/
                    bootstrap.min.js"></script>
    </body>
</html>
```

Code explanation

contact-form.html file is a Thymeleaf template used for both **adding new contacts** and **editing existing contacts**. This file is designed to be versatile. The Spring controller decides whether to show it for adding or editing based on whether a Contact object with an ID (for editing) or an empty Contact object (for adding) is passed to it.

Running and testing

1. Right-click **ContactManagerProject** in NetBeans and select **Run**.
2. Open your web browser and navigate to the contact list page (e.g., **http://localhost:8080/contacts**).
3. You see an empty contact list.

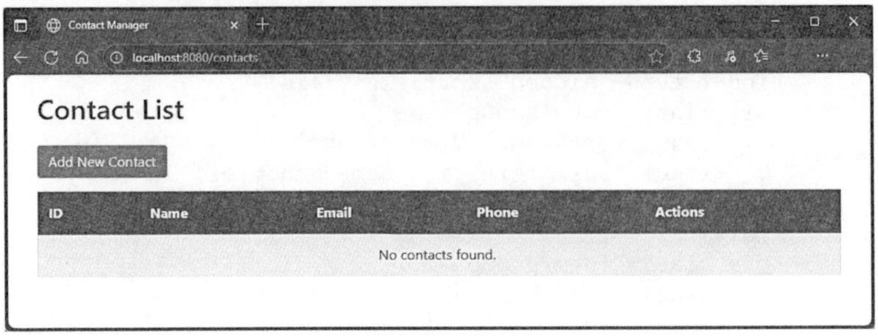

Add contacts

1. To add contact, click **Add New Contact**.
2. You see a page with an empty **Add New Contact** form.

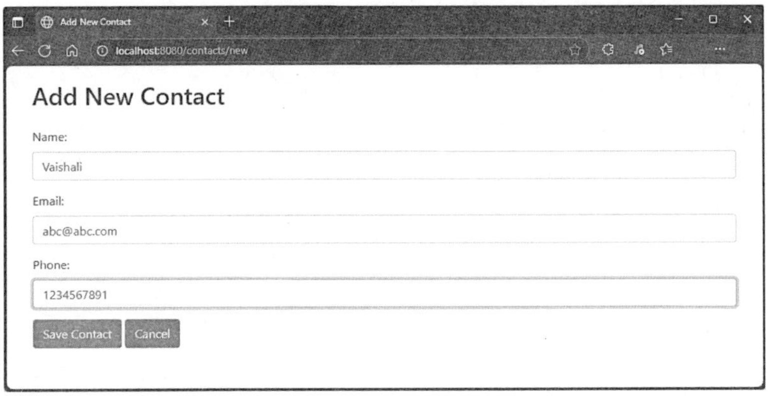

3. Fill in the details like Name, Email and Phone. Click **Save Contact**.
4. You see the contact list with one record of contact along with buttons like Edit, Delete and Draft Follow-up. You also see a successful message displayed above the Add New Contact.

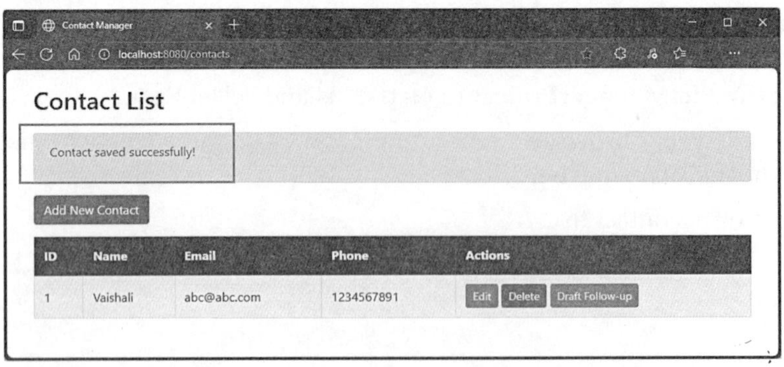

Edit contact

1. To edit a contact, click **Edit** available on that particular contact you want to edit.
2. You see **Edit Contact** page filled with the details of that particular contact.

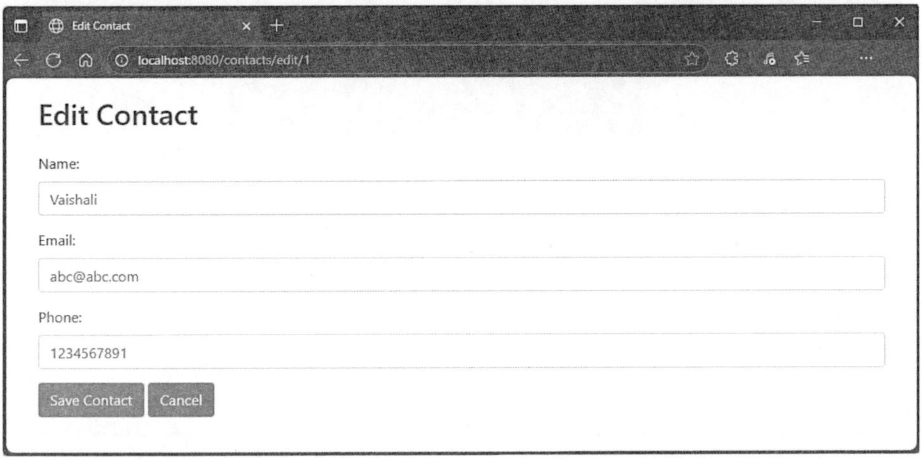

3. Modify the details. Click **Save Contact**.
4. You see the updated contact list. You also see a successful message displayed above the Add New Contact.

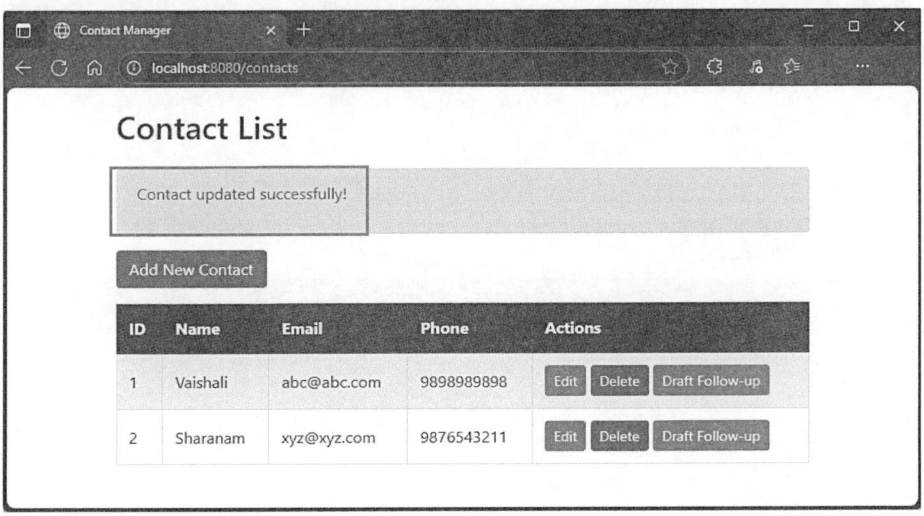

Delete contact

1. To delete a contact, click **Delete** available on that particular contact you want to delete.

2. You see an alert message to confirm whether you want to delete that particular contact. Click **OK** on the alert message.

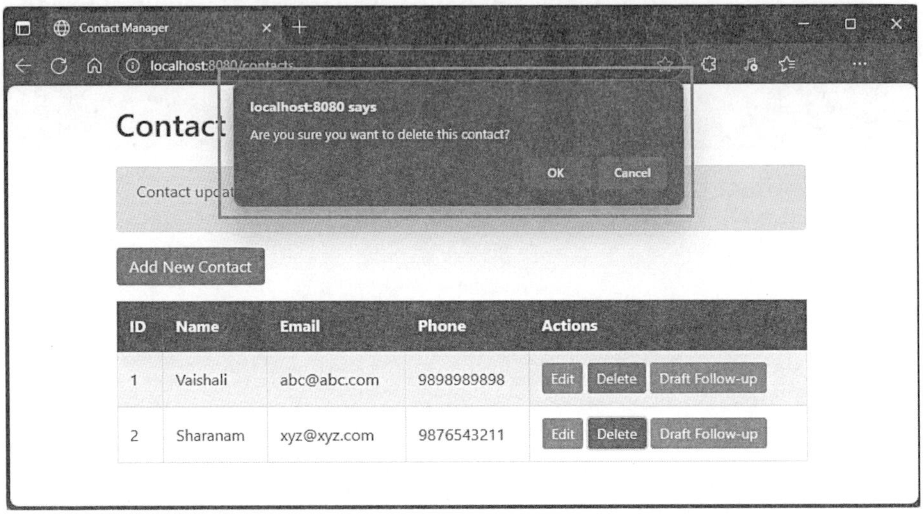

3. You see the record is deleted. You also see a successful message displayed above the Add New Contact.

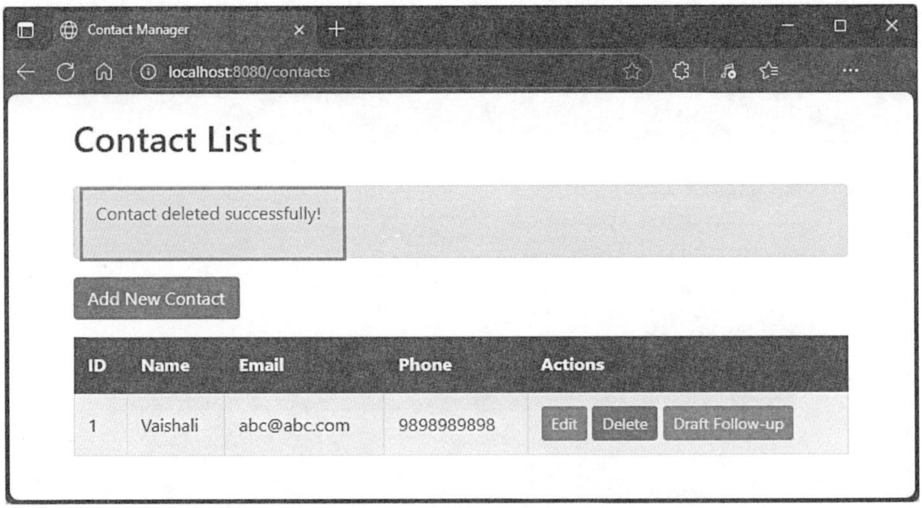

Draft email follow-up

1. Click **Draft Follow-up** available for a contact.

2. An alert box appears, displaying the AI-generated (currently simulated) email draft, personalized with the contact's name. Click **OK** on the alert message.

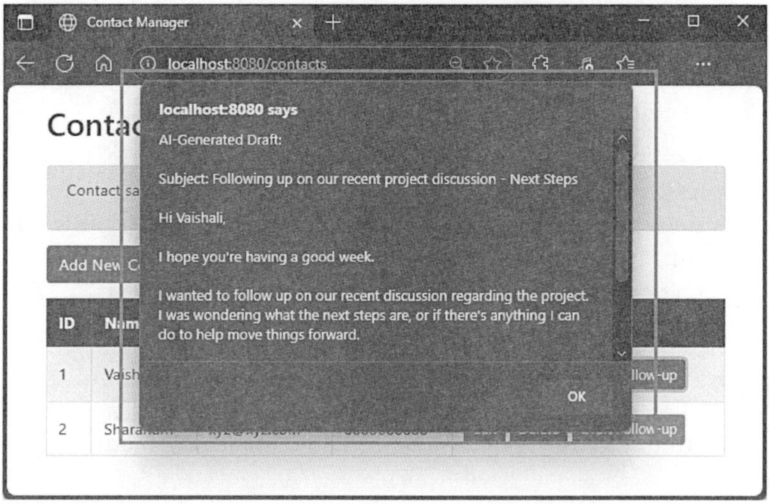

Bridging the gap: Learned concepts and application implementation

This comprehensive hands-on exercise demonstrates how to build a full-stack application from the ground up, connecting all the layers we've discussed.

- **Full-stack development:** A complete, layered application is constructed. The Contact class serves as the JPA **Model** (@Entity), ContactRepository is the **Data Access Layer** (Spring Data JPA), ContactService holds the **Business Logic** (@Service), and ContactController and AiController manage the **Web/API Layer** (@Controller and @RestController).
- **CRUD operations:** ContactController perfectly illustrates how Spring MVC handles web interactions for data management. @GetMapping is used to display forms and lists, while @PostMapping processes form submissions for creating and updating contacts.
- **AI service abstraction:** By creating GeminiEmailService, we've neatly encapsulated the logic for interacting with the AI. This is a core principle of good software design: it isolates the AI functionality, making it easy to manage, update, or even swap out for a different AI provider in the future without changing the rest of the application.

- **Dynamic frontend with a REST API:** This is the most advanced concept we implemented. Instead of having the "Draft Follow-up" button lead to a new page, you used client-side JavaScript's fetch API. This script calls a dedicated REST endpoint (/api/v1/ai/draft-email) that you created in AiController. This is a powerful, modern pattern that enhances a server-side rendered application with dynamic, API-driven features without requiring a full page reload, leading to a much smoother user experience.
- **Effective prompts:** In GeminiEmailService, we created a prompt that was specific and gave clear instructions to the AI: "Write a short, professional follow-up email to [Contact Name]...". This demonstrates the art of prompt engineering—guiding the AI to produce the desired output.
- **Connecting web UI to backend:** The JavaScript fetch call in the Thymeleaf template is the bridge between the user's action in the browser and our Spring Boot backend.
- **Seamless user experience:** When the user clicks the button, the entire chain—JavaScript call, REST controller, service logic, and AI interaction—executes in the background, finally presenting a result to the user, creating an intelligent and interactive experience.

Exploring application behaviour: A practical run-through

Let's trace the flow of data and execution when you use the AI feature:

1. **User action:** The user is on the contacts list page and clicks the **Draft Follow-up** button for a contact.
2. **Client-side JavaScript:** The **onclick** attribute on that button immediately calls the draftEmail('Jane Doe') JavaScript function embedded in the contacts.html file.
3. **API request:** The **fetch()** function sends an asynchronous POST request to your running Spring Boot application. The target URL is /api/v1/ai/draft-email, and the body of the request is a JSON object: {"contactName": "Jane Doe"}.
4. **Backend routing:** Spring's DispatcherServlet receives the request and, based on the URL and HTTP method, routes it to the getEmailDraft() method inside your AiController.
5. **Controller logic:** The @RequestBody annotation tells Spring to automatically convert the incoming JSON into a Java Map. The controller extracts the contact name and passes it to GeminiEmailService.
6. **Service execution:** The draftFollowUpEmail() method in the service constructs a detailed prompt using the contact's name, simulates a call to Gemini API, and returns a fully drafted email as a String.
7. **API response:** AiController takes the returned String, wraps it in a new JSON object {"draft": "..."}, and sends this back to the browser with an HTTP 200 OK status.

8. **Displaying the result:** Back in the browser, the fetch call's promise resolves. The JavaScript code parses the response JSON and uses a simple alert() to display the AI-generated draft to the user. The key here is that the main contacts page never reloaded.

Harnessing Gemini in a real-world context

The pattern you just implemented—a UI trigger, a backend API endpoint, and an AI service call—is incredibly powerful and versatile. This is the foundational blueprint for an enormous range of intelligent features. Imagine using this exact same architecture to build:

- **Customer email auto-responders:** Analyse an incoming customer support email and automatically draft a reply that addresses their likely issue.
- **Support ticket summarizers:** Read a long thread of support messages and generate a concise summary for a human agent to review quickly.
- **Internal communication assistants:** Create a tool for managers that can draft project update announcements or welcome emails for new team members.

By simply changing the prompt and the context you provide to Gemini API, you can adapt this system to automate and enhance countless business processes.

Wrapping up

This chapter was a deep dive into building a complete, intelligent web application. You've successfully integrated multiple technologies to create a functional and modern project.

- **Full-stack CRUD application:** You built an entire database-driven application from scratch, implementing all Create, Read, Update, and Delete operations with Spring Boot, Spring Data JPA, and Thymeleaf.
- **Secure API key management:** You learned the importance of storing credentials like API keys in application.properties and accessing them with @Value.
- **Dedicated AI service:** You learned to abstract AI logic into a separate @Service component and expose it securely and efficiently through a dedicated @RestController.
- **Dynamic UI with JavaScript:** You enhanced a server-side rendered Thymeleaf page with client-side JavaScript, using the fetch API to call the backend and dynamically display data without a page refresh.
- **Practical application structure:** You now understand the complete workflow: from a user clicking a button in the browser, through the controller and service layers on the backend, to interacting with an external service, and finally returning data to the UI.

- **The power of prompting:** You saw how crafting a detailed prompt is the key to directing the AI to generate useful, context-aware content.

Congratulations! You have successfully supercharged a standard CRUD application with the power of Google's Gemini API. You've bridged the gap between the frontend and the backend, creating a seamless, intelligent user experience. This full-stack integration pattern is a cornerstone of modern application development and a highly valuable skill.

In the next chapter, we will embark on our first grand culmination project: building the AI-powered "TaskMaster" application. This project will bring together every single concept from this book—Spring Core, Data JPA, MVC, Thymeleaf, and AI integration—into one complete, polished, and powerful portfolio piece. Get ready to build something truly impressive!

Chapter 18

Section 05: Grand Culmination

Building the AI-powered TaskManager application

What you'll learn

- Full-stack application development
- Database-backed persistence
- Handling user input
- Integrating AI services
- Dynamic web views
- Transactional service layers

Welcome to the first grand culmination of your learning journey so far. This chapter is where the core principles of Spring, the power of data persistence, the interactivity of web development, and the intelligence of AI all come together. We move beyond isolated examples to build a complete, cohesive, and modern application from the ground up. You will construct TaskMaster, a dynamic, single-page, AI-enhanced task management application. This project is a comprehensive demonstration of integrating a database-backed backend with a styled frontend and powerful AI capabilities, using all the technologies covered in this book. It's a project that not only solidifies your understanding but also serves as a definitive portfolio piece, proving your ability to work across the full stack—from database to AI-powered UI.

PRD (Project requirements)

Before we start coding, let's review the product requirements for TaskMaster:

- **Manual and AI task creation:** Users can add tasks manually or provide a high-level goal (e.g., plan a birthday party) and use Gemini AI to automatically generate a list of detailed sub-tasks.
- **Centralized display:** All tasks are displayed in a single, styled table on the main page.
- **Task lifecycle management:** Tasks can be marked as **Completed**, which updates their status and records a completion date. Tasks can also be deleted entirely.
- **AI-powered summaries:** A **Summarise my tasks** feature uses Gemini AI to provide an overview of progress and offer guidance on what to tackle next.
- **Data persistence:** All task data is saved in an H2 in-memory database, ensuring data integrity.
- **Technology stack:** The application uses Spring Boot Web, Spring Data JPA, H2, Thymeleaf for the view, and the Gemini AI API for its intelligent features.

Hands-on: Developing the TaskMaster application

We will construct this application from the ground up, following a logical progression from the data model to the AI services, culminating in a fully interactive web interface. This systematic approach mirrors how real-world applications are built, ensuring a solid foundation at each stage.

Building the application

Create a Spring Boot project

1. In NetBeans, go to **File → New Project...**.
2. In the **Choose Project** dialog, select **Java with Maven** from the **Categories** list and **Spring Boot Initializr project** from the **Projects** list.
3. Click **Next**. In the **Base Properties** step:
   - Set **Group** to **com.sharanamvaishali** and **Artifact** to **taskmaster**.
   - Keep the **Version** as it is (i.e. **0.0.1-SNAPSHOT**).
   - Ensure **Packaging** is **Jar**.
   - Set **Name** to **TaskMaster** and **Package Name** to **com.sharanamvaishali.taskmaster**.
   - Select **Java** from the **Language** list and the appropriate **Java Version** (e.g., **24**).

4. Click **Next**. In the **Dependencies** step:
    - Select the appropriate **Spring Boot Version** (e.g., **4.0.0 (SNAPSHOT)**).
    - In the **Available** dependencies list, find and select:
        - **Spring Web:** For building web applications with Spring MVC.

          This dependency brings in all the necessary components for developing web applications, including Spring MVC (Model-View-Controller) framework, which is fundamental for handling HTTP requests and rendering web pages.
        - **Spring Data JPA:** For database interaction.

          JPA (Jakarta Persistence API) is a specification for managing relational data in Java applications. Spring Data JPA provides a higher-level abstraction, dramatically simplifying data access by automatically generating repository implementations based on interface definitions.
        - **H2 database:** An in-memory database, great for development / testing.

          H2 is a lightweight, embeddable, and in-memory relational database. It's excellent for development and testing environments because it's fast, doesn't require separate installation, and clears its data when the application stops, ensuring a clean slate for each run.
        - **Thymeleaf:** For server-side rendering of HTML.

          Thymeleaf is a modern server-side Java template engine. It integrates seamlessly with Spring MVC, allowing you to create dynamic HTML pages that are both developer-friendly and browser-friendly (they can be opened directly in a browser even before being served by the application).
5. Click **Next**. In the **Name and Location** step:
    - Set **Project Name** to **TaskMasterProject**.
    - Choose a suitable **Project Location**.
6. Click **Finish**. NetBeans generates the project structure and downloads dependencies.

Configure the application

We need to configure the H2 database and store our Gemini API key securely.

1. In the NetBeans **Projects** window, navigate to **Other Source → src/main/resources → <default package>**.
2. Open the application.properties file and add the following lines to configure the H2 database, enable its web console, and add a placeholder for your Gemini API key:

```
# H2 Database Configuration
spring.h2.console.enabled=true
```

```
spring.datasource.url=jdbc:h2:mem:taskmasterdb
spring.datasource.driverClassName=org.h2.Driver
spring.datasource.username=sa
spring.datasource.password=
spring.jpa.database-platform=org.hibernate.dialect.H2Dialect
# Gemini API Key
gemini.api.key=<YOUR GEMINI API KEY>
```

Code explanation

- **spring.datasource.url=jdbc:h2:mem:taskmasterdb:** This specifies the JDBC URL for connecting to the H2 database. jdbc:h2:mem: indicates an in-memory database, and taskmasterdb is the name of our database instance.
- **gemini.api.key=<YOUR GEMINI API KEY>:** This is a custom property where you'll store your Gemini API key. Spring's @Value annotation can inject this value into your Java code. **Remember to replace <YOUR GEMINI API KEY> with your actual key from Google AI Studio.**

Create the Domain model

The Task entity is the core of our application. It represents a single to-do item.

1. Right-click the **com.sharanamvaishali.taskmaster** package and select **New → Java Package...**.
2. Enter the **Package Name** as **domain** and click **Finish**.
3. Right-click the **com.sharanamvaishali.taskmaster.domain** package and select **New → Other...**.
4. In the **New File** dialog box, select **Java** from the **Categories** list and **Java Enum** from the **File Types** list. Click **Next**.
5. Enter **TaskStatus** in the **Class Name** and click **Finish**.
6. Open the TaskStatus.java file and replace the contents with the following code:

```
package com.sharanamvaishali.taskmaster.domain;
public enum TaskStatus {
    PENDING,
    COMPLETED
}
```

Code explanation

This is a simple Java **enum (enumeration)**. It defines a fixed set of named constants that represent the possible statuses of a task: PENDING (the task is not yet done) and COMPLETED (the task is finished). Using an enum ensures type safety and prevents invalid status values.

1. Right-click the **com.sharanamvaishali.taskmaster.domain** package and select **New → Java Class...**.
2. Enter **Task** in the **Class Name** and click **Finish**.
3. Open the Task.java file and replace the contents with the following code:

```
package com.sharanamvaishali.taskmaster.domain;
import jakarta.persistence.Entity;
import jakarta.persistence.EnumType;
import jakarta.persistence.Enumerated;
import jakarta.persistence.GeneratedValue;
import jakarta.persistence.GenerationType;
import jakarta.persistence.Id;
import java.time.LocalDateTime;
@Entity
public class Task {
    @Id
    @GeneratedValue(strategy = GenerationType.IDENTITY)
    private Long id;
    private String description;
    @Enumerated(EnumType.STRING)
    private TaskStatus status;
    private LocalDateTime creationDate;
    private LocalDateTime completionDate;
    // Getters and Setters
    public Long getId() {
        return id;
    }
    public void setId(Long id) {
        this.id = id;
    }
    public String getDescription() {
        return description;
    }
    public void setDescription(String description) {
        this.description = description;
    }
    public TaskStatus getStatus() {
        return status;
    }
    public void setStatus(TaskStatus status) {
        this.status = status;
    }
    public LocalDateTime getCreationDate() {
        return creationDate;
    }
    public void setCreationDate(LocalDateTime creationDate) {
        this.creationDate = creationDate;
    }
    public LocalDateTime getCompletionDate() {
        return completionDate;
```

```
    }
    public void setCompletionDate(LocalDateTime completionDate) {
        this.completionDate = completionDate;
    }
}
```

Code explanation

- **@Enumerated(EnumType.STRING):** This annotation is crucial for persisting the TaskStatus enum. EnumType.STRING tells JPA to store the enum's name (e.g., "PENDING", "COMPLETED") as a VARCHAR string in the database, rather than its ordinal value (0, 1), which makes the database more readable and robust to changes in enum order.
- **private TaskStatus status;:** The current status of the task.
- **private LocalDateTime creationDate;:** Records when the task was created. LocalDateTime is a modern Java 8 date/time API class, good for storing date and time without timezone information.
- **private LocalDateTime completionDate;:** Records when the task was completed.

Create the Repository

The TaskRepository interface will handle all database operations for our Task entity.

1. Right-click the **com.sharanamvaishali.taskmaster** package and select **New → Java Package...**.
2. Enter **repository** as the **Package Name** and click **Finish**.
3. Right-click the **com.sharanamvaishali.taskmaster.repository** package and select **New → Java Interface...**.
4. Enter **TaskRepository** in the **Interface Name** and click **Finish**.
5. Open the TaskRepository.java file to modify its contents to extend JpaRepository:

```
package com.sharanamvaishali.taskmaster.repository;
import com.sharanamvaishali.taskmaster.domain.Task;
import org.springframework.data.jpa.repository.JpaRepository;
import org.springframework.stereotype.Repository;
@Repository
public interface TaskRepository extends JpaRepository<Task, Long> {
}
```

Code explanation

- **@Repository:** Indicates that this interface is a "repository", a mechanism for encapsulating storage, retrieval, and search behaviour that emulates a collection of objects. Spring's component scanning will find and manage this bean.

- **extends JpaRepository<Task, Long>:** The core of Spring Data JPA's power. By extending JpaRepository, our TaskRepository automatically inherits a rich set of pre-defined methods for common CRUD (Create, Read, Update, Delete) operations on Task entities.
    - **Task:** The first type parameter specifies the entity type that this repository will manage.
    - **Long:** The second type parameter specifies the data type of the entity's primary key (id in our Task class).

Create the AI Service

This service will contain all the logic for interacting with the Gemini API.

1. Right-click the **com.sharanamvaishali.taskmaster** package and select **New → Java Package...**.
2. Enter the **Package Name** as **service** and click **Finish**.

1. Right-click the **com.sharanamvaishali.taskmaster.service** package and select **New → Java Class...**.
2. Enter **GeminiTaskService** in the **Class Name** and click **Finish**.
3. Open the GeminiTaskService.java file and replace the contents with the following code:

```
package com.sharanamvaishali.taskmaster.service;
import com.fasterxml.jackson.databind.JsonNode;
import com.fasterxml.jackson.databind.ObjectMapper;
import com.sharanamvaishali.taskmaster.domain.Task;
import java.util.Arrays;
import java.util.List;
import java.util.stream.Collectors;
import org.springframework.beans.factory.annotation.Value;
import org.springframework.http.HttpEntity;
import org.springframework.http.HttpHeaders;
import org.springframework.http.MediaType;
import org.springframework.stereotype.Service;
import org.springframework.web.client.RestTemplate;
@Service
public class GeminiTaskService {
  @Value("${gemini.api.key}") private String geminiApiKey;
  private static final String MODEL_NAME = "gemini-2.5-flash";
  private static final String BASE_API_URL =
      "https://generativelanguage.googleapis.com/v1beta/models/";
  private final RestTemplate restTemplate = new RestTemplate();
  private final ObjectMapper objectMapper = new ObjectMapper();
  public List<String> generateSubTasks(String descriptiveGoal) {
    String prompt = "Based on the goal '" + descriptiveGoal
        + ("', generate a short, actionable list of sub-tasks. Return ONLY the "
           + "sub-tasks, one per line. Ensure each sub-task is concise and "
           + "directly related to the goal.");
```

```
    System.out.println(
        "----PROMPT FOR GEMINI (generateSubTasks)----\n" + prompt);
    String geminiApiUrl =
        BASE_API_URL + MODEL_NAME + ":generateContent?key=" + geminiApiKey;
    HttpHeaders headers = new HttpHeaders();
    headers.setContentType(MediaType.APPLICATION_JSON);
    String requestBody = "{\"contents\":[{\"parts\":[{\"text\":\""
        + escapeJson(prompt) + "\"}]}]}";
    HttpEntity<String> entity = new HttpEntity<>(requestBody, headers);
    try {
      String response =
          restTemplate.postForObject(geminiApiUrl, entity, String.class);
      System.out.println(
          "----RAW RESPONSE FROM GEMINI (generateSubTasks)----\n" + response);
      JsonNode root = objectMapper.readTree(response);
      String geminiResponseText = root.path("candidates")
                                     .get(0).path("content").path("parts")
                                     .get(0).path("text").asText();
      System.out.println(
          "----PARSED RESPONSE FROM GEMINI (generateSubTasks)----\n"
          + geminiResponseText);
      return Arrays.stream(geminiResponseText.split("\n"))
          .map(String::trim).filter(s -> !s.isEmpty())
          .collect(Collectors.toList());
    } catch (Exception e) {
      System.err.println(
          "Error calling Gemini API for generateSubTasks: " + e.getMessage());
      e.printStackTrace();
      return Arrays.asList("Failed to generate sub-tasks: "
          + (e.getMessage() != null && e.getMessage().length() > 100
                  ? e.getMessage().substring(0, 100) + "..."
                  : e.getMessage()));
    }
  }
  public String summarizeTaskList(List<Task> tasks) {
    String taskListString = tasks.stream()
            .map(task -> "- " + task.getDescription()
                    + " (Status: " + task.getStatus() + ")")
            .collect(Collectors.joining("\n"));
    String prompt = "Here is my current task list:\n" + taskListString
        + ("\n\nPlease provide a brief, encouraging summary of my progress and "
           + "suggest what I should focus on next. Be a friendly assistant. "
           + "Keep the response concise.");
    System.out.println(
        "----PROMPT FOR GEMINI (summarizeTaskList)----\n" + prompt);
    String geminiApiUrl =
        BASE_API_URL + MODEL_NAME + ":generateContent?key=" + geminiApiKey;
    HttpHeaders headers = new HttpHeaders();
    headers.setContentType(MediaType.APPLICATION_JSON);
    String requestBody = "{\"contents\":[{\"parts\":[{\"text\":\""
        + escapeJson(prompt) + "\"}]}]}";
```

```
    HttpEntity<String> entity = new HttpEntity<>(requestBody, headers);
    try {
      String response =
          restTemplate.postForObject(geminiApiUrl, entity, String.class);
      System.out.println(
          "----RAW RESPONSE FROM GEMINI (summarizeTaskList)----\n" + response);
      JsonNode root = objectMapper.readTree(response);
      String geminiResponseText = root.path("candidates")
                                      .get(0).path("content").path("parts")
                                      .get(0).path("text").asText();
      System.out.println(
          "----PARSED RESPONSE FROM GEMINI (summarizeTaskList)----\n"
          + geminiResponseText);
      return geminiResponseText;
    } catch (Exception e) {
      System.err.println(
          "Error calling Gemini API for summarizeTaskList: " + e.getMessage());
      e.printStackTrace();
      return "Error summarizing tasks: "
          + (e.getMessage() != null && e.getMessage().length() > 100
                  ? e.getMessage().substring(0, 100) + "..."
                  : e.getMessage()) + ". You're doing great, keep going!";
    }
  }
  private String escapeJson(String text) {
    return text.replace("\\", "\\\\")
        .replace("\"", "\\\"").replace("\n", "\\n")
        .replace("\r", "\\r").replace("\t", "\\t");
  }
}
```

Code explanation

- **public List<String> generateSubTasks(String descriptiveGoal):**
  - This method takes a descriptiveGoal (e.g., "Plan a weekend trip") as input.
  - It constructs a prompt string specifically designed to instruct the Gemini model to generate a list of actionable sub-tasks, one per line, and to return ***only*** the sub-tasks.
  - **geminiApiUrl:** Formulates the complete API endpoint URL, including the model name and your API key.
  - **HttpHeaders headers = new HttpHeaders(); headers.setContentType(MediaType.APPLICATION_JSON);:** Sets the Content-Type header to application/json, indicating that the request body will be JSON.
  - **String requestBody = "{\"contents\":[{\"...+ "\"}]}]}";:** This creates the JSON request body that the Gemini API expects. It embeds the prompt within a JSON structure. The escapeJson helper method ensures that special characters in the prompt are correctly escaped for JSON.

- **HttpEntity<String> entity = new HttpEntity<>(requestBody, headers);:** Wraps the request body and headers into an HttpEntity object.
- **String response = restTemplate.postForObject(geminiApiUrl, entity, String.class);:** This is the actual call to Gemini API. It sends a POST request with the constructed entity and expects a String response.
- **JSON Parsing:**
  - **JsonNode root = objectMapper.readTree(response);:** Parses the raw JSON response string into a JsonNode tree, allowing easy navigation and extraction of specific values.
  - **String geminiResponseText = root.path("....asText();:** This chained series of path() and get() calls navigates the JSON response structure to extract the actual text generated by the Gemini model. Gemini's API response typically contains the generated text nested deep within candidates, content, parts, and text fields.
- **return Arrays.stream(geminiResponseText.....toList());:** The extracted text is split by newlines, trimmed of whitespace, and empty lines are filtered out, resulting in a List<String> where each string is a sub-task.
- **try-catch block:** Handles potential exceptions (e.g., network issues, invalid API key, malformed JSON response) during the API call. It logs the error and returns a user-friendly error message.

- **public String summarizeTaskList(List<Task> tasks):**
  - This method takes a List<Task> as input.
  - **String taskListString = tasks.stream().....joining("\n"));:** It transforms the list of Task objects into a human-readable string representation, suitable for sending to the AI model.
  - It then constructs another prompt to ask Gemini to provide a brief, encouraging summary of the task list and suggest next steps.
  - The rest of the method follows a similar pattern to generateSubTasks for calling the Gemini API and parsing the response.
- **private String escapeJson(String text):** A helper method to properly escape special characters (like backslashes, double quotes, newlines, carriage returns, and tabs) within a string so it can be safely embedded as a JSON string value. This prevents JSON parsing errors.

Create the core Business Service

The TaskService orchestrates the application's business logic, using the repository for data and the AI service for intelligent features.

1. In the same **service** package, create a new class named **TaskService**.
2. Add the following code:

```
package com.sharanamvaishali.taskmaster.service;
import com.sharanamvaishali.taskmaster.domain.Task;
import com.sharanamvaishali.taskmaster.domain.TaskStatus;
import com.sharanamvaishali.taskmaster.repository.TaskRepository;
import java.time.LocalDateTime;
import java.util.List;
import org.springframework.stereotype.Service;
import org.springframework.transaction.annotation.Transactional;
@Service
public class TaskService {
    private final TaskRepository taskRepository;
    private final GeminiTaskService geminiTaskService;
    public TaskService(TaskRepository taskRepository, GeminiTaskService
                       geminiTaskService) {
        this.taskRepository = taskRepository;
        this.geminiTaskService = geminiTaskService;
    }
    public List<Task> getAllTasks() {
        return taskRepository.findAll();
    }
    public void addTask(String description) {
        Task task = new Task();
        task.setDescription(description);
        task.setStatus(TaskStatus.PENDING);
        task.setCreationDate(LocalDateTime.now());
        taskRepository.save(task);
    }
    public void deleteTask(Long id) {
        taskRepository.deleteById(id);
    }
    @Transactional
    public void markTaskAsCompleted(Long id) {
        Task task = taskRepository.findById(id)
          .orElseThrow(() -> new IllegalArgumentException("Invalid task Id:" + id));
        task.setStatus(TaskStatus.COMPLETED);
        task.setCompletionDate(LocalDateTime.now());
        taskRepository.save(task);
    }
    @Transactional
    public void generateAndAddSubTasks(String descriptiveGoal) {
        List<String> subTaskDescriptions = geminiTaskService
                                 .generateSubTasks(descriptiveGoal);
        for (String desc : subTaskDescriptions) {
            addTask(desc);
        }
    }
    public String getTaskSummary() {
        List<Task> tasks = taskRepository.findAll();
```

```
        return geminiTaskService.summarizeTaskList(tasks);
    }
}
```

Code explanation

- **private final TaskRepository taskRepository; and private final GeminiTaskService geminiTaskService;:** These fields declare dependencies on our TaskRepository and GeminiTaskService. The final keyword indicates that these fields will be initialized once during construction.
- **public TaskService(TaskRepository taskRepository, GeminiTaskService geminiTaskService):** This is the preferred way to inject dependencies in Spring (constructor injection). Spring's IoC container automatically detects this constructor and provides instances of TaskRepository and GeminiTaskService when creating a TaskService bean.
- **public List<Task> getAllTasks():** Retrieves all tasks from the database using the findAll() method provided by JpaRepository.
- **public void addTask(String description):**
    - Creates a new Task object.
    - Sets its description, sets the status to PENDING, and records creationDate as the current time.
    - Saves the new task to the database using taskRepository.save().
- **public void deleteTask(Long id):** Deletes a task by its ID using taskRepository.deleteById().
- **@Transactional public void markTaskAsCompleted(Long id):**
    - **@Transactional:** This annotation ensures that the entire method executes within a database transaction. If any part of the method fails (e.g., database connection issue), the entire operation is rolled back, maintaining data consistency.
    - **Task task = taskRepository.findById(id)....+ id));:** Retrieves a Task by its ID. findById() returns an Optional, and orElseThrow() is used to throw an IllegalArgumentException if the task with the given ID is not found.
    - **task.setStatus(TaskStatus.COMPLETED);:** Updates the task's status to COMPLETED.
    - **task.setCompletionDate(LocalDateTime.now());:** Records the completion time.
    - **taskRepository.save(task);:** Saves the updated task back to the database. Since the task object is already managed by JPA, this will perform an UPDATE operation.

- **@Transactional public void generateAndAddSubTasks(String descriptiveGoal):**
    - Calls geminiTaskService.generateSubTasks(descriptiveGoal) to get a list of sub-task descriptions from the AI.
    - Iterates through the generated descriptions and calls addTask() for each, effectively adding multiple new tasks to the database based on the AI's output.
- **public String getTaskSummary():**
    - Fetches all tasks from the database.
    - Passes the list of tasks to geminiTaskService.summarizeTaskList() to get an AI-generated summary.
    - Returns the summary string.

Create the Web Controller

The TaskController handles incoming web requests, calls the appropriate service methods, and directs Spring MVC to render the correct view.

1. Right-click the **com.sharanamvaishali.taskmaster** package and select **New → Java Package...**.
2. Enter the **Package Name** as **web** and click **Finish**.
3. Right-click the **com.sharanamvaishali.taskmaster.web** package and select **New → Java Class...**.
4. Enter **TaskController** in the **Class Name** and click **Finish**.
5. Add the following code.

```
package com.sharanamvaishali.taskmaster.web;
import com.sharanamvaishali.taskmaster.service.TaskService;
import org.springframework.stereotype.Controller;
import org.springframework.ui.Model;
import org.springframework.web.bind.annotation.GetMapping;
import org.springframework.web.bind.annotation.PathVariable;
import org.springframework.web.bind.annotation.PostMapping;
import org.springframework.web.bind.annotation.RequestParam;
import org.springframework.web.servlet.mvc.support.RedirectAttributes;
@Controller
public class TaskController {
    private final TaskService taskService;
    public TaskController(TaskService taskService) {
        this.taskService = taskService;
    }
    @GetMapping("/")
    public String displayHomePage(Model model) {
        model.addAttribute("tasks", taskService.getAllTasks());
        return "index";
```

```
    }
    @PostMapping("/add")
    public String handleAddTask(@RequestParam String description) {
        if (description != null && !description.trim().isEmpty()) {
            taskService.addTask(description);
        }
        return "redirect:/";
    }
    @PostMapping("/auto-create")
    public String handleAutoCreateSubTasks(@RequestParam String descriptiveGoal) {
        if (descriptiveGoal != null && !descriptiveGoal.trim().isEmpty()) {
            taskService.generateAndAddSubTasks(descriptiveGoal);
        }
        return "redirect:/";
    }
    @PostMapping("/delete/{id}")
    public String handleDeleteTask(@PathVariable Long id) {
        taskService.deleteTask(id);
        return "redirect:/";
    }
    @PostMapping("/complete/{id}")
    public String handleMarkTaskCompleted(@PathVariable Long id) {
        taskService.markTaskAsCompleted(id);
        return "redirect:/";
    }
    @GetMapping("/summarize")
    public String handleGetSummary(RedirectAttributes redirectAttributes) {
        String summary = taskService.getTaskSummary();
        redirectAttributes.addFlashAttribute("summary", summary);
        return "redirect:/";
    }
}
```

Code explanation

- **@Controller:** Marks this class as a web controller, responsible for handling incoming HTTP requests.
- **private final TaskService taskService;:** The controller has a dependency on TaskService, which handles the business logic. This dependency is injected via constructor injection.
- **@GetMapping("/") public String displayHomePage(Model model):**
  - **@GetMapping("/"):** Maps HTTP GET requests to the root URL (/) of the application to this method.
  - **Model model:** The Model object is provided by Spring MVC. It's used to pass data from the controller to the view (Thymeleaf template).
  - **model.addAttribute("tasks", taskService.getAllTasks());:** Retrieves all tasks from taskService and adds them to the Model under the attribute name "tasks." The Thymeleaf template will then be able to access this tasks list.

  - **return "index";:** Returns the logical view name "index." Spring Boot, with Thymeleaf configured, will resolve this to src/main/resources/templates/index.html.

- **@PostMapping("/add") public String handleAddTask(@RequestParam String description):**
  - **@PostMapping("/add"):** Maps HTTP POST requests to the /add URL to this method. This method is typically called when a form is submitted to add a new task.
  - **@RequestParam String description:** Binds the value of the request parameter named description (from the form input field) to the description method parameter.
  - **if (description != null && !description.trim().isEmpty()):** Basic validation to ensure the description is not empty.
  - **taskService.addTask(description);:** Calls the service layer to add the new task.
  - **return "redirect:/";:** This is a crucial part of the **Post-Redirect-Get (PRG) pattern**. After a successful POST operation (adding a task), the server sends a redirect response to the client (302 Found), telling the browser to make a new GET request to the root URL (/). This prevents duplicate form submissions if the user refreshes the page after adding a task.

- **@PostMapping("/auto-create") public String handleAutoCreateSubTasks(@RequestParam String descriptiveGoal):** Similar to /add, but for AI-driven task generation. It takes a descriptiveGoal and delegates to taskService.generateAndAddSubTasks(). Also uses PRG.

- **@PostMapping("/delete/{id}") public String handleDeleteTask(@PathVariable Long id):**
  - **@PathVariable Long id:** Extracts the id from the URL path (e.g., /delete/123). The {id} is a placeholder that matches the path variable.
  - Calls taskService.deleteTask() with the extracted ID.
  - Uses PRG to redirect to the home page.

- **@PostMapping("/complete/{id}") public String handleMarkTaskCompleted(@PathVariable Long id):** Similar to /delete, but for marking a task as completed. Extracts the id and calls taskService.markTaskAsCompleted(). Uses PRG.

- **@GetMapping("/summarize") public String handleGetSummary(RedirectAttributes redirectAttributes):**
  - **@GetMapping("/summarize"):** Maps GET requests to /summarize.
  - **RedirectAttributes redirectAttributes:** This object is specifically used with redirects to pass attributes to the target URL's model. Flash attributes are stored temporarily in the session and are available only for the subsequent request, then removed. This is ideal for displaying messages or data after a redirect.

- **String summary = taskService.getTaskSummary();:** Retrieves the AI-generated summary from the service.
- **redirectAttributes.addFlashAttribute("summary", summary);:** Adds the summary as a flash attribute. This means that after the redirect to /, the index.html template will have access to a summary variable in its model. **return "redirect:/";:** Redirects to the home page.

Create the Styling

Add some simple CSS for styling.

1. Right-click **Other Sources → src/main/resources → static** and select **New → Folder…**.
2. Enter **css** as the **Folder Name** and click **Finish**.
3. Right-click **css** folder and select **New → Other…**.
4. In the **New File** dialog box, select **Other** from the **Categories** list and **Empty File** from the **File Types** list.
5. Enter **style.css** in the **File Name** and click **Finish**.
6. Add the following CSS content:

```
body {
    font-family: -apple-system, BlinkMacSystemFont, "Segoe UI", Roboto,
                 Helvetica, Arial, sans-serif;
    margin: 40px auto;
    max-width: 800px;
    line-height: 1.6;
    font-size: 18px;
    color: #333;
    padding: 0 20px;
}
h1, h2 { line-height: 1.2; }
table {
    width: 100%;
    border-collapse: collapse;
    margin-top: 20px;
}
th, td {
    padding: 12px;
    border: 1px solid #ddd;
    text-align: left;
}
th { background-color: #f2f2f2; }
.form-container {
    padding: 20px;
    border: 1px solid #ddd;
    background-color: #f9f9f9;
    margin-bottom: 20px;
```

```
    border-radius: 5px;
}
input[type=text] {
    width: calc(100% - 110px);
    padding: 10px;
    margin-right: 10px;
    border: 1px solid #ccc;
    border-radius: 4px;
}
button {
    padding: 10px 15px;
    background-color: #007bff;
    color: white;
    border: none;
    border-radius: 4px;
    cursor: pointer;
}
button:hover { background-color: #0056b3; }
.delete-button { background-color: #dc3545; }
.delete-button:hover { background-color: #c82333; }
.summary-button { background-color: #28a745; margin-top: 10px; }
.summary-button:hover { background-color: #218838; }
.summary-box {
    background-color: #e6f7ff;
    border-left: 5px solid #007bff;
    padding: 15px;
    margin: 20px 0;
    border-radius: 5px;
}
.completed-task { text-decoration: line-through; color: #888; }
```

Code explanation

This CSS file provides basic styling for the HTML elements, making the web application visually appealing and user-friendly. It defines styles for the body, headings, tables, form containers, input fields, and buttons, including hover effects. It also includes a completed-task class to visually strike through completed tasks and a summary-box for the AI summary.

Create the View

Finally, we create the user interface with Thymeleaf.

1. Right-click **Other Sources → src/main/resources → templates** and select **New → HTML File…**.
2. Enter **index** in the **File Name** and click **Finish**.
3. Open the index.html file and replace its contents with the following Thymeleaf template:

```
<!DOCTYPE html>
<html xmlns:th="http://www.thymeleaf.org">
```

```
    <head>
        <title>AI-Powered TaskMaster</title>
        <meta charset="UTF-8">
        <link rel="stylesheet" th:href="@{/css/style.css}"/>
    </head>
    <body>
        <h1>AI-Powered TaskMaster</h1>
        <div th:if="${summary}" class="summary-box">
            <h2>AI Summary & Guidance</h2>
            <p th:text="${summary}"></p>
        </div>
        <div class="form-container">
            <h2>Generate Tasks with AI</h2>
            <form th:action="@{/auto-create}" method="post">
                <input type="text" name="descriptiveGoal" placeholder="Enter a goal,
                       e.g., 'Plan a weekend trip'" required/>
                <button type="submit">Generate Sub-Tasks</button>
            </form>
        </div>
        <div class="form-container">
            <h2>Add a Task Manually</h2>
            <form th:action="@{/add}" method="post">
                <input type="text" name="description" placeholder="Enter a new
                       task description" required/>
                <button type="submit">Add Task</button>
            </form>
        </div>
        <a th:href="@{/summarize}">
            <button class="summary-button">Summarise my tasks</button>
        </a>
        <h2>My Tasks</h2>
        <table>
            <thead>
                <tr>
                    <th>Description</th>
                    <th>Created</th>
                    <th>Status</th>
                    <th>Actions</th>
                </tr>
            </thead>
            <tbody>
                <tr th:each="task : ${tasks}" th:classappend="${task.status.name()
                            == 'COMPLETED'} ? 'completed-task' : ''">
                    <td th:text="${task.description}">Task Description</td>
                    <td th:text="${#temporals.format(task.creationDate,
                                'MMM dd, yyyy HH:mm')}">Creation Date</td>
                    <td th:text="${task.status.name()}">PENDING</td>
                    <td>
                        <form th:action="@{/complete/{id}(id=${task.id})}"
                              method="post" style="display:inline;"
                              th:if="${task.status.name() == 'PENDING'}">
```

```
                            <button type="submit">Complete</button>
                        </form>
                        <form th:action="@{/delete/{id}(id=${task.id})}"
                              method="post" style="display:inline;">
                            <button type="submit" class="delete-button">Delete
                            </button>
                        </form>
                    </td>
                </tr>
            </tbody>
        </table>
    </body>
</html>
```

Code explanation

- **<html xmlns:th="http://www.thymeleaf.org">:** Declares the Thymeleaf namespace, enabling the use of Thymeleaf attributes (prefixed with th:).
- **<link rel="stylesheet" th:href="@{/css/style.css}"/>:** This links the CSS file. th:href="@{/css/style.css}" is a Thymeleaf URL expression that ensures the correct path to the static CSS file is generated, regardless of the application's context path.
- **<div th:if="${summary}" class="summary-box">:**
  - **th:if="${summary}":** This is a conditional attribute. The <div> (and its content) will only be rendered if a summary attribute exists and is not null in the Model (which is populated by TaskController.handleGetSummary() via RedirectAttributes).
  - **<p th:text="${summary}"></p>:** Displays the text content of the summary attribute.
- **<form th:action="@{/auto-create}" method="post"> and <form th:action="@{/add}" method="post">:**
  - **th:action="@{/auto-create}" and th:action="@{/add}":** Thymeleaf URL expressions that generate the correct action URLs for the forms, pointing to the respective controller methods.
  - **method="post":** Specifies that these forms will submit data using the HTTP POST method.
  - **<input type="text" name="descriptiveGoal" and <input type="text" name="description":** These are input fields whose values will be sent as request parameters (descriptiveGoal and description) to the controller.
- **<a th:href="@{/summarize}">:** A link that, when clicked, will trigger a GET request to /summarize, which will fetch the AI summary.

- **<table> ... <tr th:each="task : ${tasks}" ...>:**
  - **th:each="task : ${tasks}":** This is Thymeleaf's iteration attribute. It loops through the tasks list (which comes from the Model in displayHomePage() method of TaskController). For each Task object in the list, a new <tr> (table row) is rendered, and the current Task object is available as the task variable within the loop.
  - **th:classappend="${task.status.name() == 'COMPLETED'} ? 'completed-task' : '"':** This conditional attribute dynamically adds the completed-task CSS class to a table row if the task's status is COMPLETED. This results in the strikethrough effect defined in style.css.
  - **<td th:text="${task.description}">:** Displays the description of the current task.
  - **<td th:text="${#temporals.format(task.creationDate, 'MMM dd, yyyy HH:mm')}">:** Formats and displays creationDate using Thymeleaf's built-in #temporals utility object for java.time types.
  - **<td th:text="${task.status.name()}">:** Displays the name of the task's status (e.g., "PENDING", "COMPLETED").
  - **Action Forms (Complete/Delete Buttons):**
    - Each task row includes mini-forms for "Complete" and "Delete" actions.
    - **th:action="@{/complete/{id}(id=${task.id})}":** Generates the action URL for completing a task, embedding the task.id as a path variable.
    - **th:if="${task.status.name() == 'PENDING'}":** The "Complete" button is only displayed if the task's status is "PENDING".
    - **th:action="@{/delete/{id}(id=${task.id})}":** Generates the action URL for deleting a task, embedding the task.id.
    - Both buttons submit POST requests, which are then handled by the respective TaskController methods.

Running and testing

Now it's time to see our full-stack application in action.

1. In the NetBeans **Projects** window, right-click the **TaskMaster** project and select **Run**.
2. Open your web browser and navigate to **http://localhost:8080**. You should see the styled interface with the input forms and an empty task list.

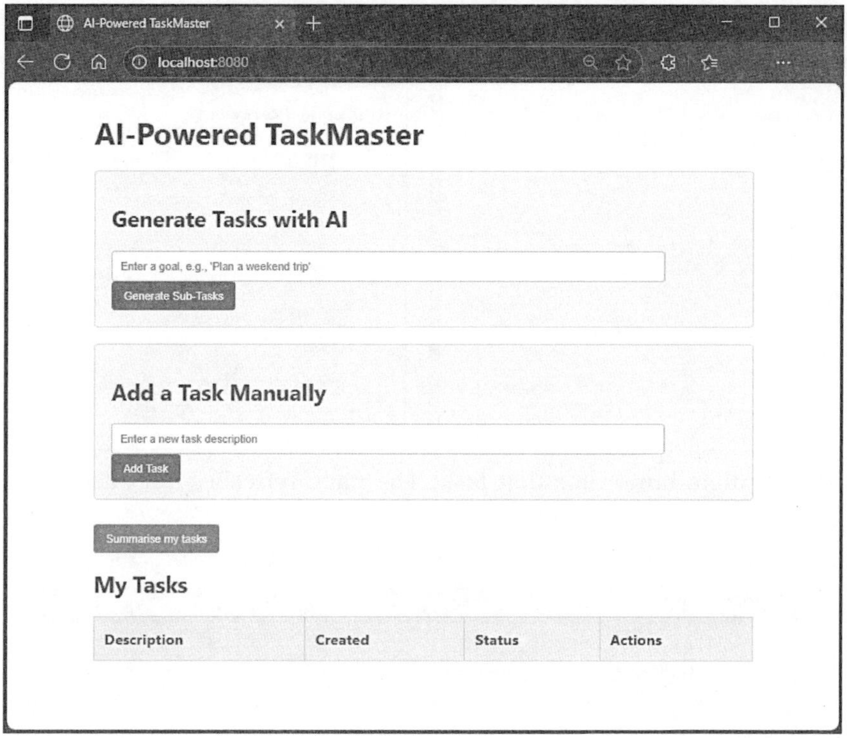

Test manual CRUD

1. In the **Add a Task Manually** form, type **Learn Spring Boot**.

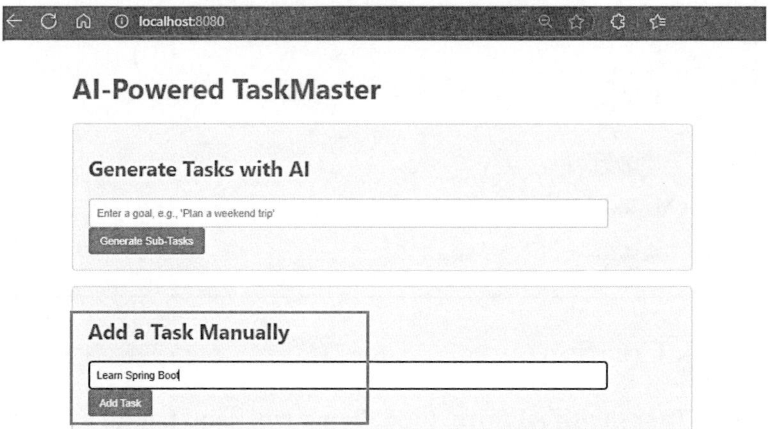

2. Click **Add Task**. The page refreshes, and the task appears in the list.

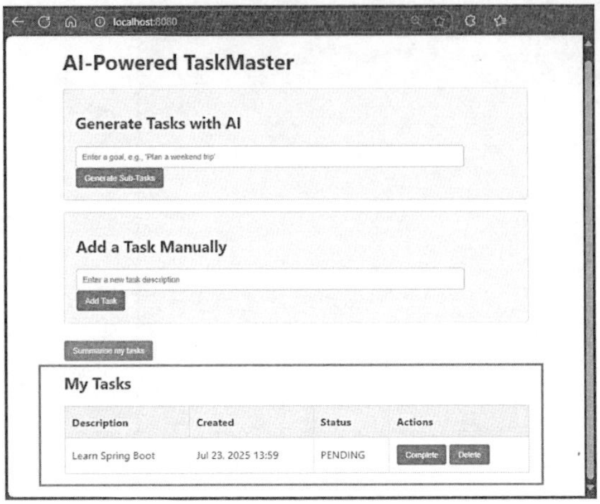

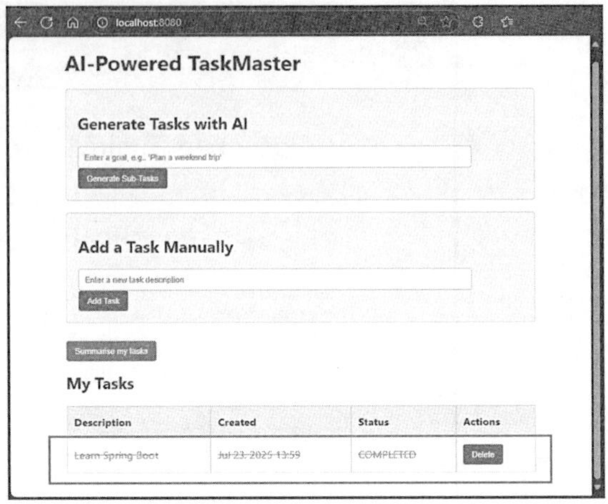

3. Click the **Complete** button for that task. The page refreshes, and its text is now struck through.
4. Click the **Delete** button. The task is removed from the list.

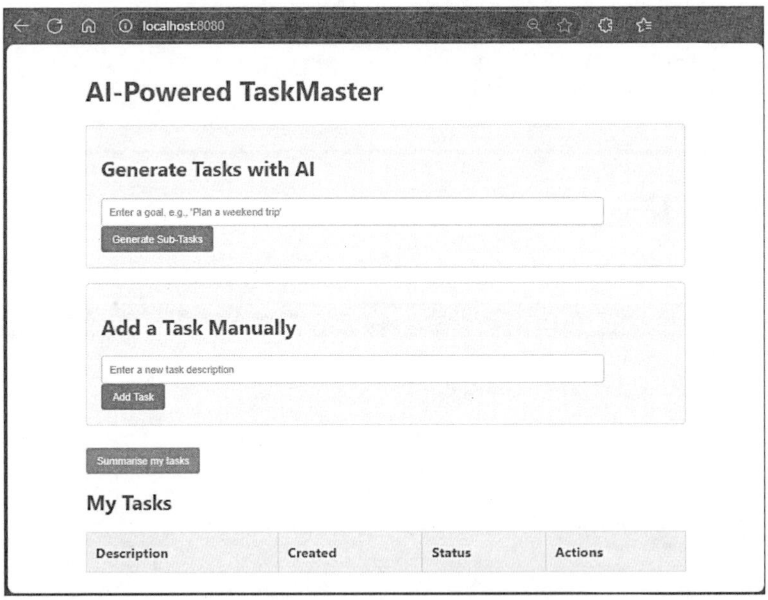

Test AI Sub-Task Creation

1. In the **Generate Tasks with AI** form, type **Plan a weekend trip to a nearby city**.

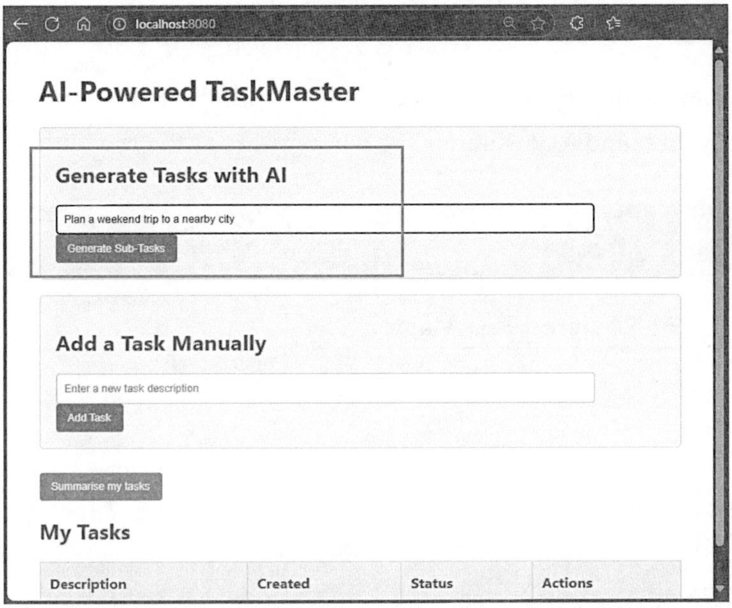

2. Click **Generate Sub-Tasks**. The page refreshes, and several relevant tasks (like "Book a venue", "Plan the menu") are now in your list.

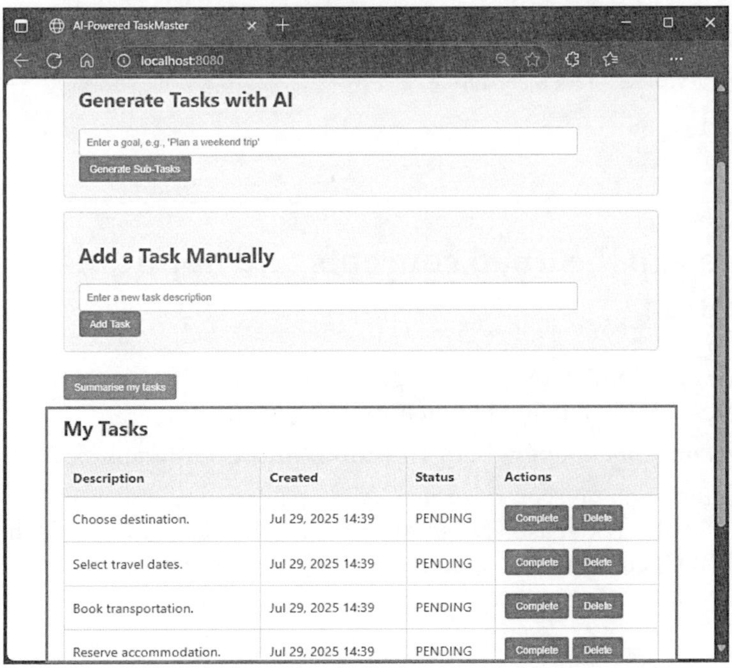

Test AI Summary

1. After adding and completing a few tasks, click the **Summarise my tasks** button.
2. The page refreshes, and a new summary box appears at the top with a helpful overview from the AI.

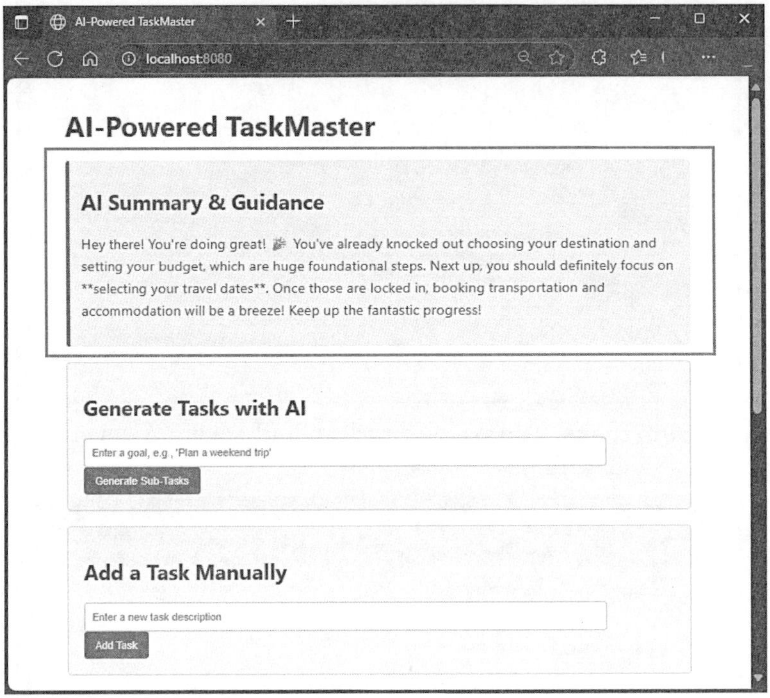

Bridging the gap: Learned concepts and application implementation

This project is the culmination of everything you've learned. It seamlessly synthesizes various core concepts into a functional, intelligent application:

- **Core Spring concepts (Dependency Injection, IoC, Component Scanning):**
  - **Application:** You've seen @Service, @Repository, and @Controller annotations used throughout the codebase. These are not just labels; they tell Spring's **Inversion of Control (IoC) container** to manage these classes as **beans**.

  - **Implementation:** Spring's **component scanning** automatically discovers these annotated classes. When, for instance, TaskService needs a TaskRepository or GeminiTaskService, Spring uses **dependency injection (specifically, constructor injection)** to provide instances of these beans. This means you don't manually create new TaskRepository() or new GeminiTaskService(); Spring handles the wiring for you, making your code modular and easier to test.

- **Persistence with Spring Data JPA:**
  - **Application:** The Task class is annotated with @Entity, mapping it directly to a database table. The TaskRepository interface extends JpaRepository, instantly giving you powerful CRUD operations without writing any SQL or boilerplate code.
  - **Implementation:** JPA and Hibernate (Spring's default JPA provider) automatically generate the necessary SQL to interact with the H2 in-memory database based on your Task entity definition. The @Transactional annotation on service methods like markTaskAsCompleted() ensures **data integrity** by treating a sequence of database operations as a single, atomic unit. If any part fails, the entire transaction is rolled back, preventing corrupted data.

- **Web development with Spring MVC and Thymeleaf:**
  - **Application:** TaskController uses @GetMapping and @PostMapping to define how specific URL paths and HTTP methods map to Java methods. This is the heart of **Spring MVC**, handling incoming web requests.
  - **Implementation:** @RequestParam and @PathVariable annotations efficiently extract data from incoming web requests (like form submissions or URL segments). **Thymeleaf**, as your server-side rendering engine, takes the data prepared by the controller (via the Model object) and dynamically generates the HTML (index.html). It handles loops (th:each), conditionals (th:if), and data formatting (#temporals), providing a rich and interactive user interface without complex client-side JavaScript. The **Post-Redirect-Get (PRG) pattern**, implemented by return "redirect:/" after POST requests, is a crucial web development best practice that prevents duplicate form submissions upon browser refresh.

- **AI Integration and Service layer architecture:**
  - **Application:** GeminiTaskService is dedicated to interacting with the external Gemini API. TaskService then ***uses*** GeminiTaskService for its AI-powered features (like generating sub-tasks or summarizing tasks), without needing to know the low-level details of API calls.

- **Implementation:** This layered approach epitomizes good **service layer architecture**. It clearly separates concerns: TaskController handles web requests, TaskService orchestrates business logic (using repositories for data and AI services for intelligence), and GeminiTaskService encapsulates external AI interactions. This modular design makes the application more maintainable, scalable, and easier to debug, as each layer has a distinct responsibility.

Exploring application behaviour: A practical run-through

When you interact with the TaskMaster application, a complete request-response cycle occurs.

1. Submitting the Add Task form sends a POST request to TaskController.
2. The controller calls TaskService, which creates a Task object and uses TaskRepository to save it to the H2 database.
3. The controller then returns a redirect instruction, causing the browser to make a new GET request to the root URL.
4. The controller fetches the updated task list from the service and passes it to the Thymeleaf view, which renders the final HTML you see on the screen.
5. The AI features follow a similar flow but with an added call from TaskService to GeminiTaskService to generate intelligent content before persisting the results.

Harnessing full-stack Intelligent Development in real-world contexts

The TaskMaster application is a microcosm of modern software development. It demonstrates the standard pattern for building robust, database-driven applications and then enhancing them with a layer of artificial intelligence. This approach is rapidly becoming the new benchmark for creating competitive, engaging, and genuinely useful software products, from internal business tools to feature-rich consumer applications.

Wrapping up

- **Full-stack integration:** You successfully built a complete application from the database layer to the UI.
- **AI enhancement:** You integrated a third-party AI service to provide intelligent, value-added features.

- **Service layer architecture:** You used a service layer to encapsulate business logic and manage transactions.
- **Spring MVC and Thymeleaf**: You created a dynamic web interface using modern Spring web technologies.
- **Data persistence:** You defined a data model and used Spring Data JPA for all database interactions.

Congratulations! You have just built a complex, feature-rich, and intelligent web application. This project proves you have the skills to tackle real-world development challenges.

Let's move to the second grand culmination project of this book now!

Chapter 19

Section 05: Grand Culmination

Building an AI-enhanced E-Commerce website

What you'll learn

- E-commerce application development
- REST API creation
- Jakarta Bean Validation
- Spring Boot, Data JPA, Thymeleaf
- Gemini AI integration

Welcome to the second grand culmination of your journey through Spring Boot & Data Persistence. This chapter presents a hands-on opportunity to synthesize all the knowledge acquired throughout this book by building a comprehensive, AI-enhanced e-commerce website. In today's dynamic digital landscape, e-commerce applications are ubiquitous, ranging from small businesses selling handmade goods to massive online retail giants. They serve as critical platforms for connecting buyers and sellers, facilitating transactions, and offering personalized experiences. This project simulates a real-world development scenario, guiding you from product requirements to a fully functional application, incorporating core Spring principles, robust data persistence, dynamic web interfaces, secure validation, and intelligent features powered by AI.

PRD: E-Commerce web application

This document outlines the features for our e-commerce application, serving as the blueprint for development.

Product requirements (What to build)

Product discovery

- As a user, a list of all available products is displayed, showing their name, an image placeholder with a common dummy image, description, and price.
- As a user, a detailed page for a specific product is viewable.

Shopping Cart management

- As a user, products are added to a shopping cart.
- As a user, all items in the cart are viewable, including their name, quantity, price, and a total price.
- As a user, the quantity of items in the cart is changeable, and items are removable.
- As a user, AI-powered recommendations for similar products appear based on the items currently in the cart. At least 100 sample products are included in the database so that AI-powered recommendations can show similar products from the database. These AI-powered recommendations are shown on the cart page, from where users can add those items to the cart.

Checkout and Ordering

- As a user, there is an option to proceed to a checkout page from the cart.
- As a user, name and shipping information must be provided to place an order.
- As a user, after placing an order, a confirmation page with the order number and details is displayed.

REST API for Products

- As a developer, an API is needed to retrieve all products to potentially power a mobile app or other clients.
- As a developer, an API is needed to retrieve a single product by its ID.

Tools and Frameworks

- Spring Boot (Web, Data JPA)
- CSS for beautification
- Hibernate & Jakarta Persistence
- H2 Database
- Thymeleaf
- Lombok (Optional)
- Bean Validation
- Java 17+, Maven, NetBeans IDE
- Gemini AI (Http client and Flash 2.5)

Hands-on: Developing the E-Commerce application

This hands-on section guides you through building the AI-enhanced e-commerce application layer by layer. We begin with establishing the data model, progress to developing the backend services and REST APIs, and conclude by implementing the user-facing web interface. Each step is designed to reinforce concepts learned previously and integrate them into a cohesive, functional application.

Building the application

Project generation

1. In NetBeans, go to **File → New Project…**.
2. In the **Choose Project** dialog, select **Java with Maven** from the **Categories** list and **Spring Boot Initializr project** from the **Projects** list.
3. Click **Next**. In the **Base Properties** step:
    - Set **Group** to **com.sharanamvaishali** and **Artifact** to **ecommerce**.
    - Keep the **Version** as it is (i.e. **0.0.1-SNAPSHOT**).
    - Ensure **Packaging** is **Jar**.
    - Set **Name** to **ECommerceApp** and **Package Name** to **com.sharanamvaishali.ecommerce**.
    - Select **Java** from the **Language** list and the appropriate **Java Version** (e.g., **24**).

4. Click **Next**. In the **Dependencies** step:
   - Select the appropriate **Spring Boot Version** (e.g., **4.0.0 (SNAPSHOT)**).
   - In the **Available** dependencies list, find and select:
     - Spring Web
     - Spring Data JPA
     - H2 database
     - Thymeleaf
     - Bean Validation
     - Lombok
5. Click **Next**. In the **Name and Location** step:
   - Set **Project Name** to **ECommerceAppProject**.
   - Choose a suitable **Project Location**.
6. Click **Finish**. NetBeans generates the project structure and downloads dependencies.

Configuration (application.properties)

1. In the Projects window, expand your **ECommerceApp** project.
2. Navigate to **Source Packages → src/main/resources → application.properties**.
3. Open the application.properties file and add the following configurations for the H2 database and the Gemini API key:

```
# H2 Database Configuration
spring.h2.console.enabled=true
spring.h2.console.path=/h2-console
spring.datasource.url=jdbc:h2:mem:ecommerce;DB_CLOSE_DELAY=-1
spring.datasource.driverClassName=org.h2.Driver
spring.datasource.username=sa
spring.datasource.password=
spring.jpa.hibernate.ddl-auto=update
spring.jpa.show-sql=true
# Gemini AI Configuration
gemini.api.key=<YOUR_GEMINI_API_KEY_HERE>
```

Replace **<YOUR_GEMINI_API_KEY_HERE>** with your actual Gemini API key.

Domain modeling (JPA Entities)

1. In the Projects window, expand your **ECommerceApp** project.

2. Right-click **Source Packages** and select **New → Java Package…**.
3. Enter **model** as the **Package Name** and click **Finish**.
4. Right-click the **com.sharanamvaishali.ecommerce.model** package and select **New → Java Class…**.
5. Enter **Product** as the **Class Name** and click **Finish**.
6. Open the Product.java file and replace its content with the following code:

```
package com.sharanamvaishali.ecommerce.model;
import jakarta.persistence.Entity;
import jakarta.persistence.GeneratedValue;
import jakarta.persistence.GenerationType;
import jakarta.persistence.Id;
import jakarta.validation.constraints.DecimalMin;
import jakarta.validation.constraints.NotEmpty;
import java.math.BigDecimal;
import lombok.Data;
import lombok.NoArgsConstructor;
import lombok.AllArgsConstructor;
@Entity
@Data
@NoArgsConstructor
@AllArgsConstructor
public class Product {
    @Id
    @GeneratedValue(strategy = GenerationType.IDENTITY)
    private Long id;
    @NotEmpty(message = "Product name cannot be empty")
    private String name;
    private String description;
    @DecimalMin(value = "0.01", message = "Price must be greater than 0")
    private BigDecimal price;
    private String imageUrl;
}
```

Code explanation

This class defines the **Product** data model.

- **@Data, @NoArgsConstructor, @AllArgsConstructor:** These are Lombok annotations that automatically generate boilerplate code like getters, setters, toString(), and constructors, keeping your code clean.
- **@NotEmpty and @DecimalMin:** These are Jakarta Bean Validation annotations that enforce rules on the fields, ensuring data integrity (e.g., a product name cannot be empty).

7. Repeat the steps 4-6 to create **CartItem.java** with the following content:

```
package com.sharanamvaishali.ecommerce.model;
import jakarta.persistence.Entity;
import jakarta.persistence.GeneratedValue;
```

```
import jakarta.persistence.GenerationType;
import jakarta.persistence.Id;
import jakarta.persistence.ManyToOne;
import lombok.Data;
import lombok.NoArgsConstructor;
import lombok.AllArgsConstructor;
@Entity
@Data
@NoArgsConstructor
@AllArgsConstructor
public class CartItem {
    @Id
    @GeneratedValue(strategy = GenerationType.IDENTITY)
    private Long id;
    @ManyToOne
    private Product product;
    private int quantity;
}
```

Code explanation

This entity represents a single item within a shopping cart, linking a Product with a specific quantity.

- **@ManyToOne:** Defines a many-to-one relationship. Many CartItem instances can be associated with one Product.

8. Repeat steps 4-6 to create **Order.java** with the following content:

```
package com.sharanamvaishali.ecommerce.model;
import jakarta.persistence.Entity;
import jakarta.persistence.GeneratedValue;
import jakarta.persistence.GenerationType;
import jakarta.persistence.Id;
import jakarta.persistence.OneToMany;
import jakarta.persistence.CascadeType;
import jakarta.persistence.Table;
import java.time.LocalDateTime;
import java.util.ArrayList;
import java.util.List;
import lombok.Data;
import lombok.NoArgsConstructor;
import lombok.AllArgsConstructor;
@Entity
@Data
@NoArgsConstructor
@AllArgsConstructor
@Table(name = "customer_order")
public class Order {
    @Id
    @GeneratedValue(strategy = GenerationType.IDENTITY)
    private Long id;
```

```
    private String customerName;
    private String shippingAddress;
    private LocalDateTime orderDate;
    @OneToMany(cascade = CascadeType.ALL, orphanRemoval = true)
    private List<CartItem> items = new ArrayList<>();
}
```

Code explanation

This class defines the **Order** entity, which represents a customer's completed purchase.

- **@Table(name = "customer_order"):** This annotation is crucial. It explicitly sets the database table name to customer_order. This is done to avoid a syntax error, as ORDER is a reserved keyword in SQL.
- **@OneToMany:** Defines a one-to-many relationship, indicating that one Order can contain many CartItems.
- **cascade = CascadeType.ALL:** This setting ensures that when an Order is saved or deleted, the associated CartItems are also saved or deleted, simplifying data management.

Data Repository layer

1. Right-click **Source Packages** and select **New → Java Package...**.
2. Enter **repository** as the **Package Name** and click **Finish**.
3. Right-click the **com.sharanamvaishali.ecommerce.repository** package and select **New → Java Interface...**.
4. Enter **ProductRepository** as the **Interface Name** and click **Finish**.
5. Open the ProductRepository.java file and replace its content with the following code:

```
package com.sharanamvaishali.ecommerce.repository;
import com.sharanamvaishali.ecommerce.model.Product;
import org.springframework.data.jpa.repository.JpaRepository;
import org.springframework.stereotype.Repository;
@Repository
public interface ProductRepository extends JpaRepository<Product, Long> {
}
```

Code explanation

This interface defines the repository for the Product entity.

- **@Repository:** Marks this interface as a Spring Data repository, making it eligible for component scanning.
- **extends JpaRepository<Product, Long>:** This is the core of Spring Data JPA's power. By extending JpaRepository, you get a full set of pre-implemented CRUD (Create, Read, Update, Delete) methods like save(), findById(), and findAll() without writing any implementation code yourself.

6. Repeat steps 3-5 to create **CartItemRepository.java** and **OrderRepository.java**, extending **JpaRepository** with their respective model classes.

   a. **CartItemRepository.java**

```
package com.sharanamvaishali.ecommerce.repository;
import com.sharanamvaishali.ecommerce.model.CartItem;
import org.springframework.data.jpa.repository.JpaRepository;
import org.springframework.stereotype.Repository;
@Repository
public interface CartItemRepository extends JpaRepository<CartItem, Long> {
}
```

   b. **OrderRepository.java**

```
package com.sharanamvaishali.ecommerce.repository;
import com.sharanamvaishali.ecommerce.model.Order;
import org.springframework.data.jpa.repository.JpaRepository;
import org.springframework.stereotype.Repository;
@Repository
public interface OrderRepository extends JpaRepository<Order, Long> {
}
```

Code explanation

Similar to ProductRepository, these interfaces provide all necessary database operations for CartItem and Order entities, respectively, thanks to extending JpaRepository.

AI and Business Service layer

1. Right-click **Source Packages** and select **New → Java Package…**.
2. Enter **service** as the **Package Name** and click **Finish**.
3. Right-click the **com.sharanamvaishali.ecommerce.service** package and select **New** a **Java Class…**.
4. Enter **AIRecommendationService** as the **Class Name** and click **Finish**.
5. Open the AIRecommendationService.java file and replace its content with the following code:

```
package com.sharanamvaishali.ecommerce.service;
import com.sharanamvaishali.ecommerce.model.Product;
import org.springframework.beans.factory.annotation.Value;
import org.springframework.stereotype.Service;
import org.springframework.web.client.RestTemplate;
import org.springframework.http.HttpEntity;
import org.springframework.http.HttpHeaders;
import org.springframework.http.MediaType;
import java.util.List;
import java.util.stream.Collectors;
import com.fasterxml.jackson.databind.JsonNode;
```

```
import com.fasterxml.jackson.databind.ObjectMapper;
@Service
public class AIRecommendationService {
    @Value("${gemini.api.key}")
    private String geminiApiKey;
    private final RestTemplate restTemplate = new RestTemplate();
    private final ObjectMapper objectMapper = new ObjectMapper();
    public List<Product> getRecommendations(List<Product> cartProducts,
                                            List<Product> allProducts) {
        if (cartProducts.isEmpty()) {
            return List.of(); // No recommendations if cart is empty
        }
        String prompt = "Given the following products in a shopping cart: " +
                        cartProducts.stream().map(Product::getName)
                        .collect(Collectors.joining(", ")) + ". Recommend 3
                        similar products from the following list (names only
                        , comma-separated): " + allProducts.stream()
                        // Exclude products already in cart
                        .filter(p -> !cartProducts.contains(p))
                        .map(Product::getName).collect(Collectors.joining(", "));
        String geminiApiUrl = "https://generativelanguage.googleapis.com
                              /v1beta/models/gemini-flash:generateContent
                              ?key=" + geminiApiKey;
        HttpHeaders headers = new HttpHeaders();
        headers.setContentType(MediaType.APPLICATION_JSON);
        String requestBody = "{\"contents\":[{\"parts\":[{\"text\":\
                             "" + prompt + "\"}]}]}";
        HttpEntity<String> entity = new HttpEntity<>(requestBody, headers);
        try {
            String response = restTemplate.postForObject(geminiApiUrl,
                              entity, String.class);
            JsonNode root = objectMapper.readTree(response);
            String recommendedText = root.path("candidates").get(0)
                                     .path("content").path("parts").get(0)
                                     .path("text").asText();
            // Parse the recommended text and find matching products
            List<String> recommendedNames = List.of(recommendedText.split(", "))
                                            .stream().map(String::trim)
                                            .collect(Collectors.toList());
            return allProducts.stream()
                    .filter(p -> recommendedNames.contains(p.getName()))
                    .collect(Collectors.toList());
        } catch (Exception e) {
            e.printStackTrace();
            // Fallback: return some popular products or handle gracefully
            return allProducts.stream().limit(3).collect(Collectors.toList());
        }
    }
}
```

Code explanation

This service is responsible for integrating with the Gemini AI.

- **@Service:** Marks this class as a Spring service bean, where business logic resides.
- **@Value("${gemini.api.key}"):** Injects the API key from application.properties into the geminiApiKey variable.
- **getRecommendations():** This method constructs a prompt based on the products in the user's cart, sends it to the Gemini Flash API endpoint using RestTemplate, parses the comma-separated text response, and returns a list of matching Product objects from the database.

> This is a simplified integration. For a production-grade application, consider more robust error handling, rate limiting, and structured response parsing for the Gemini API.

6. Repeat steps 3-5 to create **ProductService.java** with the following content:

```
package com.sharanamvaishali.ecommerce.service;
import com.sharanamvaishali.ecommerce.model.Product;
import com.sharanamvaishali.ecommerce.repository.ProductRepository;
import org.springframework.beans.factory.annotation.Autowired;
import org.springframework.stereotype.Service;
import java.util.List;
import java.util.Optional;
@Service
public class ProductService {
    @Autowired
    private ProductRepository productRepository;
    public List<Product> findAllProducts() {
        return productRepository.findAll();
    }
    public Optional<Product> findProductById(Long id) {
        return productRepository.findById(id);
    }
}
```

Code explanation

A simple service that acts as a facade for ProductRepository. It provides methods to find all products or a single product by its ID. This layer separates the data access logic from the controllers.

- **@Autowired:** This annotation performs dependency injection, providing an instance of ProductRepository to this service at runtime.

7. Repeat steps 3-5 to create **CartService.java** with the following content:

```
package com.sharanamvaishali.ecommerce.service;
import com.sharanamvaishali.ecommerce.model.CartItem;
```

```
import com.sharanamvaishali.ecommerce.model.Product;
import org.springframework.beans.factory.annotation.Autowired;
import org.springframework.stereotype.Service;
import java.util.ArrayList;
import java.util.List;
import java.util.Optional;
import java.util.concurrent.ConcurrentHashMap;
import java.util.Map;
import jakarta.servlet.http.HttpSession;
import java.math.BigDecimal;
@Service
public class CartService {
    @Autowired
    private ProductService productService;
    // Using a map to simulate session-based cart for simplicity in this example
    // In a real application, this would be backed by a database
    // or dedicated session management
    private Map<String, List<CartItem>> userCarts = new ConcurrentHashMap<>();
    public List<CartItem> getCart(HttpSession session) {
        return userCarts.computeIfAbsent(session.getId(),k -> new ArrayList<>());
    }
    public void addToCart(HttpSession session, Long productId,
int quantity) {
        List<CartItem> cart = getCart(session);
        Optional<Product> productOpt = productService.findProductById(productId);
        if (productOpt.isPresent()) {
            Product product = productOpt.get();
            Optional<CartItem> existingItem = cart.stream()
                    .filter(item -> item.getProduct().getId().equals(productId))
                    .findFirst();
            if (existingItem.isPresent()) {
                existingItem.get().setQuantity(existingItem.get().getQuantity()
                            + quantity);
            } else {
                cart.add(new CartItem(null, product, quantity));
            }
        }
    }
    public void updateCartItemQuantity(HttpSession session,
                                       Long productId, int quantity) {
        List<CartItem> cart = getCart(session);
        cart.stream()
            .filter(item -> item.getProduct().getId().equals(productId))
            .findFirst().ifPresent(item -> item.setQuantity(quantity));
    }
    public void removeCartItem(HttpSession session, Long productId) {
        List<CartItem> cart = getCart(session);
        cart.removeIf(item -> item.getProduct().getId().equals(productId));
    }
    public void clearCart(HttpSession session) {
        userCarts.remove(session.getId());
```

```
    }
    public BigDecimal calculateTotal(HttpSession session) {
        return getCart(session).stream().map(item -> item.getProduct().getPrice()
                .multiply(new BigDecimal(item.getQuantity())))
                .reduce(BigDecimal.ZERO, BigDecimal::add);
    }
}
```

Code explanation

This service handles all shopping cart logic.

- For this example, the cart is stored in a Map in server memory, with the user's HttpSession ID as the key. This is a simple approach for demonstration; in a real-world application, you would persist the cart in a database or a distributed cache like Redis.
- The methods addToCart(), updateCartItemQuantity(), removeCartItem(), and calculateTotal() provide the core functionalities for managing a user's shopping cart.

CartService uses HttpSession to manage the cart for demonstration purposes. In a production environment, you would typically persist cart data to a database or use a more robust session management solution.

8. Repeat steps 3-5 to create **OrderService.java** with the following content:

```
package com.sharanamvaishali.ecommerce.service;
import com.sharanamvaishali.ecommerce.model.CartItem;
import com.sharanamvaishali.ecommerce.model.Order;
import com.sharanamvaishali.ecommerce.repository.OrderRepository;
import jakarta.servlet.http.HttpSession;
import org.springframework.beans.factory.annotation.Autowired;
import org.springframework.stereotype.Service;
import org.springframework.transaction.annotation.Transactional;
import java.time.LocalDateTime;
import java.util.List;
@Service
public class OrderService {
    @Autowired
    private OrderRepository orderRepository;
    @Autowired
    private CartService cartService;
    @Transactional
    public Order placeOrder(HttpSession session, String customerName,
                            String shippingAddress) {
        List<CartItem> cartItems = cartService.getCart(session);
        if (cartItems.isEmpty()) {
            throw new IllegalStateException("Cannot place an empty order.");
        }
        Order order = new Order();
        order.setCustomerName(customerName);
        order.setShippingAddress(shippingAddress);
```

```
        order.setOrderDate(LocalDateTime.now());
        order.setItems(cartItems);
        orderRepository.save(order);
        cartService.clearCart(session); // Clear cart after order is placed
        return order;
    }
}
```

Code explanation

This service is responsible for handling the checkout process.

- **@Transactional:** This is a critical annotation that ensures the placeOrder() method is executed within a single database transaction. If any error occurs while saving the order or its items, the entire operation is rolled back, guaranteeing data consistency.
- The placeOrder() method takes the user's cart items, creates a new Order object, saves it to the database via OrderRepository, and then clears the user's cart.

REST API controller

1. Right-click **Source Packages** and select **New → Java Package…**.
2. Enter **api** as the **Package Name** and click **Finish**.
3. Right-click the **com.sharanamvaishali.ecommerce.api** package and select **New → Java Class…**.
4. Enter **ProductApiController** as the **Class Name** and click **Finish**.
5. Open the ProductApiController.java file and replace its content with the following code:

```
package com.sharanamvaishali.ecommerce.api;
import com.sharanamvaishali.ecommerce.model.Product;
import com.sharanamvaishali.ecommerce.service.ProductService;
import org.springframework.beans.factory.annotation.Autowired;
import org.springframework.http.ResponseEntity;
import org.springframework.web.bind.annotation.GetMapping;
import org.springframework.web.bind.annotation.PathVariable;
import org.springframework.web.bind.annotation.RequestMapping;
import org.springframework.web.bind.annotation.RestController;
import java.util.List;
import java.util.Optional;
@RestController
@RequestMapping("/api/v1/products")
public class ProductApiController {
    @Autowired
    private ProductService productService;
    @GetMapping
    public List<Product> getAllProducts() {
        return productService.findAllProducts();
    }
    @GetMapping("/{id}")
```

```
    public ResponseEntity<Product> getProductById(@PathVariable Long id) {
        Optional<Product> product = productService.findProductById(id);
        return product.map(ResponseEntity::ok)
                      .orElse(ResponseEntity.notFound().build());
    }
}
```

Code explanation

This controller exposes product data as a REST API.

- **@RestController:** This annotation combines @Controller and @ResponseBody. It tells Spring that the methods in this class will return data (like JSON) directly in the response body, rather than returning a view name.
- **@RequestMapping("/api/v1/products"):** Sets the base path for all endpoints in this controller, making them accessible under /api/v1/products.
- **@GetMapping("/{id}") and @PathVariable:** The {id} placeholder in the path is captured by the @PathVariable annotation, allowing you to fetch a specific product.
- **ResponseEntity:** Wraps the response object, allowing you to control the HTTP status code (e.g., returning a 404 Not Found if the product doesn't exist).

Spring MVC web controllers

1. Right-click **Source Packages** and select **New → Java Package…**.
2. Enter **controller** as the **Package Name** and click **Finish**.
3. Right-click the **com.sharanamvaishali.ecommerce.controller** package and select **New → Java Class…**.
4. Enter **ProductController** as the **Class Name** and click **Finish**.
5. Open the ProductController.java file and replace its content with the following code:

```
package com.sharanamvaishali.ecommerce.controller;
import com.sharanamvaishali.ecommerce.service.ProductService;
import org.springframework.beans.factory.annotation.Autowired;
import org.springframework.stereotype.Controller;
import org.springframework.ui.Model;
import org.springframework.web.bind.annotation.GetMapping;
import org.springframework.web.bind.annotation.PathVariable;
import org.springframework.web.bind.annotation.RequestMapping;
@Controller
@RequestMapping("/products")
public class ProductController {
    @Autowired
    private ProductService productService;
    @GetMapping("/")
    public String redirectToProducts() {
        return "redirect:/products"; // Redirects any request to "/" to "/products"
```

```
    }
    @GetMapping
    public String listProducts(Model model) {
        model.addAttribute("products", productService.findAllProducts());
        return "products"; // Refers to products.html
    }
    @GetMapping("/{id}")
    public String productDetails(@PathVariable Long id, Model model) {
        productService.findProductById(id).ifPresent(product -> model
                       .addAttribute("product", product));
        return "product-detail"; // Refers to product-detail.html
    }
}
```

Code explanation

This controller handles requests for the user-facing web pages related to products.

- **@Controller:** Marks this as a traditional Spring MVC controller, where methods return a String representing the name of the Thymeleaf template to render.
- **@GetMapping("/"):** This method is added to handle requests to the root URL (http://localhost:8080/). It returns "redirect:/products", which tells the browser to make a new request to the /products URL, ensuring users always land on the product catalogue page.
- **Model:** An object used to pass data from the controller to the view. Here, we add the list of products to the model so Thymeleaf can render it.

6. Repeat steps 3-5 to create **CartController.java** with the following content:

```
package com.sharanamvaishali.ecommerce.controller;
import com.sharanamvaishali.ecommerce.service.AIRecommendationService;
import com.sharanamvaishali.ecommerce.service.CartService;
import com.sharanamvaishali.ecommerce.service.ProductService;
import jakarta.servlet.http.HttpSession;
import org.springframework.beans.factory.annotation.Autowired;
import org.springframework.stereotype.Controller;
import org.springframework.ui.Model;
import org.springframework.web.bind.annotation.GetMapping;
import org.springframework.web.bind.annotation.PostMapping;
import org.springframework.web.bind.annotation.RequestMapping;
import org.springframework.web.bind.annotation.RequestParam;
@Controller
@RequestMapping("/cart")
public class CartController {
    @Autowired
    private CartService cartService;
    @Autowired
    private ProductService productService;
    @Autowired
    private AIRecommendationService aiRecommendationService;
```

```
    @GetMapping
    public String viewCart(HttpSession session, Model model) {
        model.addAttribute("cartItems", cartService.getCart(session));
        model.addAttribute("cartTotal", cartService.calculateTotal(session));
        // Get AI recommendations
        model.addAttribute("recommendedProducts", aiRecommendationService
                             .getRecommendations(cartService.getCart(session)
                             .stream().map(ci -> ci.getProduct()).toList(),
                             productService.findAllProducts()
        ));
        return "cart"; // Refers to cart.html
    }
    @PostMapping("/add")
    public String addToCart(HttpSession session, @RequestParam("productId")
                              Long productId, @RequestParam(value = "quantity",
                              defaultValue = "1") int quantity) {
        cartService.addToCart(session, productId, quantity);
        return "redirect:/cart";
    }
    @PostMapping("/update")
    public String updateCart(@RequestParam("productId") Long productId,
                              @RequestParam("quantity") int quantity,
                              HttpSession session) {
        if (quantity <= 0) {
            cartService.removeCartItem(session, productId);
        } else {
            cartService.updateCartItemQuantity(session, productId, quantity);
        }
        return "redirect:/cart";
    }
    @PostMapping("/remove")
    public String removeCartItem(@RequestParam("productId") Long productId,
                                  HttpSession session) {
        cartService.removeCartItem(session, productId);
        return "redirect:/cart";
    }
}
```

Code explanation

This controller manages all user interactions with the shopping cart.

- **@PostMapping:** This annotation maps HTTP POST requests, which are used for actions that change data, like adding, updating, or removing items from the cart.
- **@RequestParam:** Extracts data from the request parameters (e.g., from form submissions). productId and quantity are retrieved from the forms in the view.
- When viewing the cart (the viewCart() method), it not only fetches the cart items but also calls AIRecommendationService to get recommendations, which are then added to the model to be displayed on the page.

7. Repeat steps 3-5 to create **CheckoutController.java** with the following content:

```
package com.sharanamvaishali.ecommerce.controller;
import com.sharanamvaishali.ecommerce.model.Order;
import com.sharanamvaishali.ecommerce.service.OrderService;
import jakarta.servlet.http.HttpSession;
import jakarta.validation.Valid;
import org.springframework.beans.factory.annotation.Autowired;
import org.springframework.stereotype.Controller;
import org.springframework.ui.Model;
import org.springframework.validation.BindingResult;
import org.springframework.web.bind.annotation.GetMapping;
import org.springframework.web.bind.annotation.ModelAttribute;
import org.springframework.web.bind.annotation.PostMapping;
import org.springframework.web.bind.annotation.RequestMapping;
@Controller
@RequestMapping("/checkout")
public class CheckoutController {
    @Autowired
    private OrderService orderService;
    @GetMapping
    public String showCheckoutForm(Model model) {
        // Add an empty order object for form binding
        model.addAttribute("order", new Order());
        return "checkout"; // Refers to checkout.html
    }
    @PostMapping("/placeOrder")
    public String placeOrder(@Valid @ModelAttribute("order") Order order,
                      BindingResult result, HttpSession session, Model model) {
        if (result.hasErrors()) {
            return "checkout"; // Return to form if validation errors exist
        }
        try {
            Order placedOrder = orderService.placeOrder(session,
                                 order.getCustomerName(), order.getShippingAddress());
            model.addAttribute("order", placedOrder);
            return "order-confirmation"; // Refers to order-confirmation.html
        } catch (IllegalStateException e) {
            model.addAttribute("errorMessage", e.getMessage());
            return "checkout"; // Return to checkout with error
        }
    }
}
```

Code explanation

This controller manages the final step of the purchasing process.

- **@ModelAttribute("order"):** Binds the form data from the checkout page to an Order object.
- **@Valid:** This annotation triggers the validation process on the order object. If any validation rules (like @NotEmpty) defined in the Order entity are violated, the errors are captured.

- **BindingResult:** This object holds the result of the validation. If result.hasErrors() is true, the controller returns the user to the checkout page to display the errors, rather than proceeding with the order.

Seeding sample data

1. Right-click **com.sharanamvaishali.ecommerce** package and select **New → Java Class....**
2. Enter **DataLoader** as the **Class Name** and click **Finish**.
3. Open the DataLoader.java file and replace its content with the following code:

```
package com.sharanamvaishali.ecommerce;
import com.sharanamvaishali.ecommerce.model.Product;
import com.sharanamvaishali.ecommerce.repository.ProductRepository;
import java.math.BigDecimal;
import java.util.ArrayList;
import java.util.List;
import org.springframework.boot.CommandLineRunner;
import org.springframework.stereotype.Component;
@Component
public class DataLoader implements CommandLineRunner {
  private final ProductRepository productRepository;
  public DataLoader(ProductRepository productRepository) {
    this.productRepository = productRepository;
  }
  @Override
  public void run(String... args) throws Exception {
    List<Product> products = new ArrayList<>();
    products.add(new Product(null, "Jakarta EE 10 for Beginners",
        "Start building the future of enterprise Jakarta today!",
        new BigDecimal("799.00"), "/images/dummy.png"));
    products.add(
        new Product(null, "Spring 6 With Hibernate 6 Project For Beginners",
            "A project-based approach to learning Spring 6 and Hibernate 6.",
            new BigDecimal("850.00"), "/images/dummy.png"));
    products.add(new Product(null, "Spring 6 for Beginners",
        "An introductory guide to Spring Framework 6.",
        new BigDecimal("750.00"), "/images/dummy.png"));
    products.add(new Product(null, "Core Java 23 For Beginners",
        "Learn the fundamentals of Java programming, up to JDK 23.",
        new BigDecimal("700.00"), "/images/dummy.png"));
    products.add(new Product(null,
        "Oracle for Beginners - 2nd Edition (Covers Oracle 23ai)",
        "Revised guide to Oracle database for beginners, including Oracle 23ai "
        + "features.",
        new BigDecimal("900.00"), "/images/dummy.png"));
    products.add(new Product(null, "Oracle for Beginners",
        "A fundamental introduction to Oracle database concepts.",
        new BigDecimal("650.00"), "/images/dummy.png"));
    products.add(new Product(null, "Core Java 8 for Beginners",
```

```
            "Master Java programming with features introduced in Java 8.",
            new BigDecimal("600.00"), "/images/dummy.png"));
        products.add(new Product(null, "Oracle for Professionals",
            "Advanced Oracle topics for experienced users (covers 9i, 10g, 11g).",
            new BigDecimal("1100.00"), "/images/dummy.png"));
        products.add(new Product(null, "Core Java for Beginners",
            "Essential Java programming concepts for new developers.",
            new BigDecimal("550.00"), "/images/dummy.png"));
        products.add(
            new Product(null, "Java EE 6 Server Programming for Professionals",
                "In-depth guide to server-side programming with Java EE 6.",
                new BigDecimal("950.00"), "/images/dummy.png"));
        products.add(new Product(null, "PHP Project for Beginners",
            "Build practical web projects using PHP.", new BigDecimal("450.00"),
            "/images/dummy.png"));
        products.add(new Product(null, "Java EE 7 For Beginners",
            "Learn enterprise application development with Java EE 7.",
            new BigDecimal("800.00"), "/images/dummy.png"));
        products.add(new Product(null, "Struts 2 For Beginners",
            "Introduction to the Struts 2 framework for web applications.",
            new BigDecimal("500.00"), "/images/dummy.png"));
        products.add(new Product(null, "Spring 3 for Beginners",
            "A beginner's guide to Spring Framework 3.", new BigDecimal("680.00"),
            "/images/dummy.png"));
        products.add(
            new Product(null, "Spring 3 With Hibernate 4 Project For Beginners",
                "Hands-on project for Spring 3 and Hibernate 4 integration.",
                new BigDecimal("720.00"), "/images/dummy.png"));
        products.add(new Product(null, "Windows 8 With Office 2013 for Beginners",
            "A basic guide to using Windows 8 and Office 2013.",
            new BigDecimal("350.00"), "/images/dummy.png"));
        products.add(
            new Product(null, "Struts 2 With Hibernate 3 Project For Beginners",
                "Integrate Struts 2 and Hibernate 3 in a practical project.",
                new BigDecimal("600.00"), "/images/dummy.png"));
        products.add(new Product(null, "Java Server Programming For Professionals",
            "Advanced topics in Java server-side development (2nd Edition).",
            new BigDecimal("980.00"), "/images/dummy.png"));
        products.add(new Product(null,
            "Application Development with Oracle & PHP on Linux for Beginners",
            "Develop database applications using Oracle and PHP on Linux.",
            new BigDecimal("700.00"), "/images/dummy.png"));
        products.add(new Product(null, "Instant Oracle",
            "Quick guide to getting started with Oracle.", new BigDecimal("400.00"),
            "/images/dummy.png"));
        products.add(new Product(null, "Ajax for Beginners",
            "Learn asynchronous JavaScript and XML for dynamic web pages.",
            new BigDecimal("380.00"), "/images/dummy.png"));
        products.add(new Product(null, "Java EE 6 For Beginners",
            "Get started with Java EE 6 for building enterprise applications.",
            new BigDecimal("700.00"), "/images/dummy.png"));
```

```
    products.add(new Product(null, "Java EE 5 For Beginners",
        "Foundational concepts of Java EE 5 (2nd Edition).",
        new BigDecimal("680.00"), "/images/dummy.png"));
    products.add(new Product(null, "Hibernate 3 for Beginners",
        "Introduction to Hibernate 3 and Java Persistence API.",
        new BigDecimal("620.00"), "/images/dummy.png"));
    products.add(new Product(null, "Visual Basic 2005 for Beginners",
        "A comprehensive guide to Visual Basic 2005.", new BigDecimal("300.00"),
        "/images/dummy.png"));
    products.add(
        new Product(null, "Java Persistence API In EJB 3 For Professionals",
            "Advanced JPA topics in EJB 3.1 using Glassfish.",
            new BigDecimal("880.00"), "/images/dummy.png"));
    products.add(new Product(null, "JavaServer Pages For Beginners",
        "Learn dynamic web page creation with JSP.", new BigDecimal("470.00"),
        "/images/dummy.png"));
    products.add(new Product(null, "LAMP Programming for Professionals",
        "Master Linux, Apache, MySQL, and PHP for web development.",
        new BigDecimal("750.00"), "/images/dummy.png"));
    products.add(new Product(null, "MySQL 5 for Professionals",
        "Advanced MySQL database administration and development.",
        new BigDecimal("820.00"), "/images/dummy.png"));
    products.add(new Product(null,
        "Java EE Project Using EJB 3, JPA And Struts 2 For Beginners",
        "Build a complete Java EE project integrating EJB 3, JPA, and Struts "
        + "2.",
        new BigDecimal("900.00"), "/images/dummy.png"));
    products.add(new Product(null, "JavaServer Pages Project For Beginners",
        "A project-based guide to developing with JSP.",
        new BigDecimal("510.00"), "/images/dummy.png"));
    products.add(new Product(null, "Software Documentation For Professionals",
        "Best practices for creating effective software documentation.",
        new BigDecimal("600.00"), "/images/dummy.png"));
    products.add(new Product(null, "PHP 5.1 for Beginners",
        "An introductory guide to PHP 5.1.", new BigDecimal("420.00"),
        "/images/dummy.png"));
    products.add(new Product(null, "PHP 7 for Beginners",
        "Learn modern PHP 7 for web development.", new BigDecimal("480.00"),
        "/images/dummy.png"));
    products.add(new Product(null, "Mastering Microservices with Spring Boot",
        "Learn to build resilient and scalable microservices architectures "
        + "using Spring Boot.",
        new BigDecimal("899.00"), "/images/dummy.png"));
    products.add(new Product(null, "Pro Spring Security",
        "A comprehensive guide to securing Spring applications with advanced "
        + "techniques.",
        new BigDecimal("999.00"), "/images/dummy.png"));
    products.add(new Product(null, "Spring Boot Cookbook",
        "Practical recipes for building and deploying Spring Boot applications "
        + "rapidly.",
        new BigDecimal("750.00"), "/images/dummy.png"));
```

```
    products.add(new Product(null, "Building Reactive Microservices in Java",
        "Explore reactive programming principles and implement them with "
        + "Spring WebFlux.",
        new BigDecimal("925.00"), "/images/dummy.png"));
    products.add(
        new Product(null, "Enterprise Integration Patterns with Spring",
            "Integrate disparate systems using Spring's powerful integration "
            + "capabilities.",
            new BigDecimal("850.00"), "/images/dummy.png"));
    products.add(new Product(null, "Java Persistence with Hibernate",
        "The definitive guide to Hibernate, covering JPA and advanced "
        + "features.",
        new BigDecimal("1050.00"), "/images/dummy.png"));
    products.add(new Product(null, "Effective Java (3rd Edition)",
        "A must-read for every Java developer, full of best practices and "
        + "design patterns.",
        new BigDecimal("650.00"), "/images/dummy.png"));
    products.add(new Product(null, "Spring in Action (6th Edition)",
        "Updated guide to building modern applications with Spring 6.",
        new BigDecimal("1200.00"), "/images/dummy.png"));
    products.add(new Product(null,
        "Clean Code: A Handbook of Agile Software Craftsmanship",
        "Learn how to write clean, maintainable, and readable code.",
        new BigDecimal("700.00"), "/images/dummy.png"));
    products.add(new Product(null, "Head First Design Patterns",
        "An engaging approach to learning fundamental design patterns.",
        new BigDecimal("780.00"), "/images/dummy.png"));
    products.add(new Product(null, "Designing Data-Intensive Applications",
        "Understand the fundamental concepts behind data systems.",
        new BigDecimal("1150.00"), "/images/dummy.png"));
    products.add(new Product(null, "Kubernetes: Up and Running",
        "Mastering the Portable, Extensible, and Open-Source Platform.",
        new BigDecimal("980.00"), "/images/dummy.png"));
    products.add(new Product(null, "The Pragmatic Programmer",
        "From Journeyman to Master, timeless advice for software development.",
        new BigDecimal("690.00"), "/images/dummy.png"));
    products.add(new Product(null, "Algorithms (4th Edition)",
        "Comprehensive coverage of algorithms and data structures.",
        new BigDecimal("1300.00"), "/images/dummy.png"));
    products.add(
        new Product(null, "Refactoring: Improving the Design of Existing Code",
            "Techniques for restructuring code without changing its external "
            + "behavior.",
            new BigDecimal("720.00"), "/images/dummy.png"));
    products.add(new Product(null, "Microservices Patterns",
        "Practical guide to designing microservice architectures.",
        new BigDecimal("1020.00"), "/images/dummy.png"));
    products.add(new Product(null,
        "Domain-Driven Design: Tackling Complexity in the Heart of Software",
        "A seminal work on building complex software systems.",
        new BigDecimal("1100.00"), "/images/dummy.png"));
```

```
    products.add(new Product(null, "SQL Antipatterns",
        "Avoid common pitfalls and bad practices in SQL development.",
        new BigDecimal("580.00"), "/images/dummy.png"));
    products.add(new Product(null, "The DevOps Handbook",
        "How to Create World-Class Agility, Reliability, and Security.",
        new BigDecimal("950.00"), "/images/dummy.png"));
    products.add(new Product(null,
        "Clean Architecture: A Craftsman's Guide to Software Structure and "
        + "Design",
        "Principles for crafting well-structured software.",
        new BigDecimal("800.00"), "/images/dummy.png"));
    products.add(new Product(null, "Programming Kotlin",
        "A practical guide to the Kotlin programming language.",
        new BigDecimal("730.00"), "/images/dummy.png"));
    products.add(new Product(null,
        "Hands-On Machine Learning with Scikit-Learn, Keras, and TensorFlow",
        "A complete guide to building intelligent systems.",
        new BigDecimal("1400.00"), "/images/dummy.png"));
    products.add(new Product(null, "Concurrency in Practice",
        "Techniques for writing safe and performant concurrent programs in "
        + "Java.",
        new BigDecimal("880.00"), "/images/dummy.png"));
    products.add(new Product(null, "RESTful Web Services",
        "Designing, Building, and Deploying RESTful APIs.",
        new BigDecimal("670.00"), "/images/dummy.png"));
    products.add(new Product(null, "Learning Spring Boot 3.0",
        "Build modern Java applications using the latest Spring Boot features.",
        new BigDecimal("790.00"), "/images/dummy.png"));
    products.add(new Product(null, "Testing Spring Boot Applications",
        "A guide to effective testing strategies for Spring Boot projects.",
        new BigDecimal("810.00"), "/images/dummy.png"));
    products.add(
        new Product(null, "Full Stack Development with Spring Boot and React",
            "Build complete web applications with modern frameworks.",
            new BigDecimal("1250.00"), "/images/dummy.png"));
    products.add(new Product(null, "Getting Started with GraphQL",
        "An introduction to building APIs with GraphQL.",
        new BigDecimal("600.00"), "/images/dummy.png"));
    products.add(new Product(null, "Designing Microservice Security",
        "Secure your distributed systems with robust patterns.",
        new BigDecimal("970.00"), "/images/dummy.png"));
    products.add(new Product(null, "Cloud Native Java",
        "Designing Resilient Systems with Spring Boot, Spring Cloud, and Cloud "
        + "Foundry.",
        new BigDecimal("1180.00"), "/images/dummy.png"));
    products.add(new Product(null, "Functional Programming in Java",
        "Explore functional programming paradigms in Java.",
        new BigDecimal("760.00"), "/images/dummy.png"));
    products.add(new Product(null,
        "The Phoenix Project: A Novel About IT, DevOps, and Helping Your "
        + "Business Win",
```

```
            "A fictional narrative that illustrates DevOps principles.",
            new BigDecimal("550.00"), "/images/dummy.png"));
        products.add(new Product(null, "Automate the Boring Stuff with Python",
            "Practical programming for total beginners.", new BigDecimal("450.00"),
            "/images/dummy.png"));
        products.add(new Product(null, "Cracking the Coding Interview",
            "189 Programming Questions and Solutions.", new BigDecimal("840.00"),
            "/images/dummy.png"));
        products.add(new Product(null, "Beginning Java Programming",
            "Foundational concepts for new Java developers.",
            new BigDecimal("400.00"), "/images/dummy.png"));
        products.add(new Product(null, "Expert Spring Data JPA",
            "Advanced topics and best practices for Spring Data JPA.",
            new BigDecimal("930.00"), "/images/dummy.png"));
        products.add(new Product(null, "Docker: Up and Running",
            "Shipping software faster with Docker.", new BigDecimal("710.00"),
            "/images/dummy.png"));
        products.add(
            new Product(null, "Git Pro", "The most comprehensive guide to Git.",
                new BigDecimal("520.00"), "/images/dummy.png"));
        products.add(new Product(null, "The C++ Programming Language",
            "The definitive text on C++ by its creator.", new BigDecimal("1350.00"),
            "/images/dummy.png"));
        products.add(
            new Product(null, "Compilers: Principles, Techniques, and Tools",
                "The classic 'Dragon Book' for compiler design.",
                new BigDecimal("1500.00"), "/images/dummy.png"));
        products.add(new Product(null, "Introduction to Algorithms (CLRS)",
            "A standard reference for algorithms.", new BigDecimal("1600.00"),
            "/images/dummy.png"));
        products.add(new Product(null, "Computer Networking: A Top-Down Approach",
            "Fundamental concepts of computer networks.", new BigDecimal("1000.00"),
            "/images/dummy.png"));
        products.add(new Product(null, "Operating System Concepts (Dinosaur Book)",
            "Classic textbook on operating systems.", new BigDecimal("1280.00"),
            "/images/dummy.png"));
        products.add(new Product(null, "Database System Concepts",
            "Foundational knowledge of database systems.",
            new BigDecimal("1120.00"), "/images/dummy.png"));
        products.add(new Product(null, "Designing Distributed Systems",
            "Patterns and Paradigms for Scalable, Reliable Services.",
            new BigDecimal("910.00"), "/images/dummy.png"));
        products.add(new Product(null,
            "Agile Software Development, Principles, Patterns, and Practices",
            "Insights from Robert C. Martin on Agile methods.",
            new BigDecimal("740.00"), "/images/dummy.png"));
        products.add(
            new Product(null, "Software Engineering: A Practitioner's Approach",
                "Comprehensive guide to software development lifecycle.",
                new BigDecimal("830.00"), "/images/dummy.png"));
        products.add(new Product(null, "The Mythical Man-Month",
```

```
            "Essays on Software Engineering.", new BigDecimal("500.00"),
            "/images/dummy.png"));
        products.add(new Product(null,
            "Structure and Interpretation of Computer Programs (SICP)",
            "A classic textbook on computer science.", new BigDecimal("900.00"),
            "/images/dummy.png"));
        products.add(new Product(null, "Code Complete (2nd Edition)",
            "A practical handbook of software construction.",
            new BigDecimal("860.00"), "/images/dummy.png"));
        products.add(new Product(null, "The Go Programming Language",
            "An in-depth guide to Go.", new BigDecimal("770.00"),
            "/images/dummy.png"));
        products.add(
            new Product(null, "Programming Rust", "Fast, safe systems development.",
                new BigDecimal("940.00"), "/images/dummy.png"));
        products.add(new Product(null, "Artificial Intelligence: A Modern Approach",
            "Comprehensive AI textbook.", new BigDecimal("1550.00"),
            "/images/dummy.png"));
        products.add(new Product(null, "Deep Learning (Goodfellow)",
            "The foundational textbook on deep learning.",
            new BigDecimal("1700.00"), "/images/dummy.png"));
        products.add(new Product(null, "Grokking Algorithms",
            "An illustrated guide for programmers and other curious people.",
            new BigDecimal("620.00"), "/images/dummy.png"));
        products.add(new Product(null, "Python Crash Course",
            "A Hands-On, Project-Based Introduction to Programming.",
            new BigDecimal("530.00"), "/images/dummy.png"));
        products.add(new Product(null, "Learning Python",
            "Powerful Object-Oriented Programming.", new BigDecimal("820.00"),
            "/images/dummy.png"));
        products.add(new Product(null,
            "Hands-On Microservices with Spring Boot and Spring Cloud",
            "Build and deploy scalable microservices.", new BigDecimal("1080.00"),
            "/images/dummy.png"));
        products.add(new Product(null, "Spring Data JPA in Action",
            "A practical guide to Spring Data JPA.", new BigDecimal("870.00"),
            "/images/dummy.png"));
        products.add(new Product(null, "Hibernate in Action",
            "Practical applications of Hibernate.", new BigDecimal("775.00"),
            "/images/dummy.png"));
        products.add(new Product(null, "Beginning Spring",
            "An introduction to the Spring Framework.", new BigDecimal("640.00"),
            "/images/dummy.png"));
        products.add(new Product(null, "Pro Spring",
            "Advanced Spring topics for experienced developers.",
            new BigDecimal("1090.00"), "/images/dummy.png"));
        products.add(
            new Product(null, "Spring Framework Guru: A Developer's Handbook",
                "Comprehensive guide to the Spring Framework.",
                new BigDecimal("960.00"), "/images/dummy.png"));
        products.add(new Product(null, "Spring Microservices in Action",
```

```
            "Practical guide to building microservices with Spring.",
            new BigDecimal("1110.00"), "/images/dummy.png"));
        products.add(new Product(null, "Enterprise Java with Spring",
            "Building robust enterprise applications.", new BigDecimal("890.00"),
            "/images/dummy.png"));
        products.add(new Product(null, "Cloud Native Spring in Action",
            "Develop and deploy Spring applications in the cloud.",
            new BigDecimal("1030.00"), "/images/dummy.png"));
        products.add(new Product(null, "Spring Boot: Up and Running",
            "A fast-paced guide to building Spring Boot applications.",
            new BigDecimal("795.00"), "/images/dummy.png"));
        products.add(
            new Product(null, "Spring 5 Recipes", "A Problem-Solution Approach.",
                new BigDecimal("915.00"), "/images/dummy.png"));
        products.add(new Product(null, "Modern Java in Action",
            "Develop apps using Java 8, 9, 10, and 11.", new BigDecimal("705.00"),
            "/images/dummy.png"));
        products.add(new Product(null, "Java Concurrency in Practice",
            "Advanced Java concurrency features.", new BigDecimal("875.00"),
            "/images/dummy.png"));
        products.add(new Product(null, "The Well-Grounded Java Developer",
            "Mastering the Java Platform and new features.",
            new BigDecimal("985.00"), "/images/dummy.png"));
        products.add(
            new Product(null, "Gradle in Action", "Build Automation with Gradle.",
                new BigDecimal("680.00"), "/images/dummy.png"));
        products.add(new Product(null, "Maven: The Definitive Guide",
            "Comprehensive guide to Apache Maven.", new BigDecimal("610.00"),
            "/images/dummy.png"));
        products.add(new Product(null, "Developing with Web Components",
            "Build reusable web components.", new BigDecimal("590.00"),
            "/images/dummy.png"));
        products.add(new Product(null, "HTML and CSS: Design and Build Websites",
            "Beginner-friendly guide to web design.", new BigDecimal("490.00"),
            "/images/dummy.png"));
        products.add(new Product(null, "JavaScript: The Good Parts",
            "Focusing on the best features of JavaScript.",
            new BigDecimal("560.00"), "/images/dummy.png"));
        products.add(new Product(null, "React in Action",
            "Building modern web applications with React.",
            new BigDecimal("805.00"), "/images/dummy.png"));
        products.add(new Product(null, "Angular in Action",
            "Building dynamic web applications with Angular.",
            new BigDecimal("815.00"), "/images/dummy.png"));
        products.add(new Product(null, "Vue.js in Action",
            "Practical guide to building reactive web interfaces.",
            new BigDecimal("765.00"), "/images/dummy.png"));
        products.add(new Product(null, "Learning SQL",
            "Master SQL fundamentals for database management.",
            new BigDecimal("540.00"), "/images/dummy.png"));
        products.add(new Product(null, "NoSQL Distilled",
```

```
            "A Brief Guide to the Emerging World of Polyglot Persistence.",
            new BigDecimal("660.00"), "/images/dummy.png"));
        products.add(new Product(null, "Cassandra: The Definitive Guide",
            "Mastering the world's most scalable database.",
            new BigDecimal("905.00"), "/images/dummy.png"));
        products.add(new Product(null, "MongoDB: The Definitive Guide",
            "Powerful and Scalable Data Storage.", new BigDecimal("885.00"),
            "/images/dummy.png"));
        products.add(new Product(null, "Redis in Action",
            "Real-World Applications for Developers.", new BigDecimal("790.00"),
            "/images/dummy.png"));
        products.add(new Product(null, "Elasticsearch: The Definitive Guide",
            "A Distributed Real-time Search and Analytics Engine.",
            new BigDecimal("990.00"), "/images/dummy.png"));
        products.add(new Product(null, "Kafka: The Definitive Guide",
            "Real-time data streaming.", new BigDecimal("1040.00"),
            "/images/dummy.png"));
        products.add(new Product(null, "RabbitMQ in Action",
            "Distributed Messaging for the Real World.", new BigDecimal("755.00"),
            "/images/dummy.png"));
        products.add(new Product(null, "Microservices with Docker on AWS",
            "Deploying microservices in the cloud.", new BigDecimal("1070.00"),
            "/images/dummy.png"));
        products.add(new Product(null, "Beginning Kubernetes",
            "Container orchestration made simple.", new BigDecimal("845.00"),
            "/images/dummy.png"));
        products.add(new Product(null, "Terraform: Up and Running",
            "Writing Infrastructure as Code.", new BigDecimal("855.00"),
            "/images/dummy.png"));
        products.add(new Product(null, "Ansible: Up and Running",
            "Automating Configuration Management and Deployment.",
            new BigDecimal("735.00"), "/images/dummy.png"));
        products.add(new Product(null, "Learning AWS",
            "A beginner's guide to Amazon Web Services.", new BigDecimal("695.00"),
            "/images/dummy.png"));
        products.add(new Product(null, "Learning Azure",
            "A beginner's guide to Microsoft Azure.", new BigDecimal("685.00"),
            "/images/dummy.png"));
        products.add(new Product(null, "Learning Google Cloud Platform",
            "A beginner's guide to GCP.", new BigDecimal("725.00"),
            "/images/dummy.png"));
        products.add(new Product(null, "Cybersecurity Basics",
            "A practical guide to securing your digital life.",
            new BigDecimal("570.00"), "/images/dummy.png"));
        products.add(new Product(null, "Threat Modeling: Designing for Security",
            "Identify and mitigate security risks.", new BigDecimal("825.00"),
            "/images/dummy.png"));
        products.add(new Product(null, "Cryptography Engineering",
            "Design Principles and Practical Applications.",
            new BigDecimal("975.00"), "/images/dummy.png"));
        products.add(new Product(null, "Network Security Essentials",
```

```
        "Applications and Standards.", new BigDecimal("785.00"),
        "/images/dummy.png"));
    products.add(new Product(null, "Hacking: The Art of Exploitation",
        "Understand the mindset and techniques of hackers.",
        new BigDecimal("630.00"), "/images/dummy.png"));
    products.add(new Product(null, "Cloud Security and Privacy",
        "An Enterprise Perspective on Risks and Compliance.",
        new BigDecimal("965.00"), "/images/dummy.png"));
    products.add(new Product(null,
        "AI Superpowers: China, Silicon Valley, and the New World Order",
        "Kai-Fu Lee's insights on AI's global impact.",
        new BigDecimal("655.00"), "/images/dummy.png"));
    products.add(new Product(null,
        "Life 3.0: Being Human in the Age of Artificial Intelligence",
        "Max Tegmark explores humanity's future with AI.",
        new BigDecimal("745.00"), "/images/dummy.png"));
    products.add(new Product(null, "The Master Algorithm",
        "How the Quest for the Ultimate Learning Machine Will Remake Our "
        + "World.",
        new BigDecimal("800.00"), "/images/dummy.png"));
    products.add(new Product(null,
        "Human Compatible: Artificial Intelligence and the Problem of Control",
        "Stuart Russell on controlling superintelligent AI.",
        new BigDecimal("850.00"), "/images/dummy.png"));
    products.add(new Product(null, "Applied Deep Learning with Python",
        "Hands-on guide for practical deep learning.", new BigDecimal("955.00"),
        "/images/dummy.png"));
    products.add(new Product(null, "Practical Machine Learning with Python",
        "Build and deploy machine learning solutions.",
        new BigDecimal("865.00"), "/images/dummy.png"));
    products.add(new Product(null, "Data Science for Business",
        "What you need to know about data mining and data-analytic thinking.",
        new BigDecimal("770.00"), "/images/dummy.png"));
    products.add(new Product(null, "Introduction to Linear Algebra",
        "Gilbert Strang's classic text for engineers and scientists.",
        new BigDecimal("1100.00"), "/images/dummy.png"));
    products.add(new Product(null, "The Hundred-Page Machine Learning Book",
        "Concise and practical machine learning.", new BigDecimal("480.00"),
        "/images/dummy.png"));
    products.add(new Product(null, "Reinforcement Learning: An Introduction",
        "Richard Sutton and Andrew Barto's comprehensive text.",
        new BigDecimal("1200.00"), "/images/dummy.png"));
    products.add(new Product(null, "Bayesian Methods for Hackers",
        "Probabilistic Programming and Bayesian Inference.",
        new BigDecimal("700.00"), "/images/dummy.png"));
    products.add(new Product(null, "Grokking Deep Learning",
        "An illustrated guide to understanding and building deep neural "
        + "networks.",
        new BigDecimal("890.00"), "/images/dummy.png"));
    products.add(new Product(null, "Natural Language Processing with PyTorch",
        "Building applications with deep learning.", new BigDecimal("1010.00"),
```

```
                "/images/dummy.png"));
        products.add(
            new Product(null, "Computer Vision: Algorithms and Applications",
                "A modern introduction to computer vision.",
                new BigDecimal("1320.00"), "/images/dummy.png"));
        products.add(new Product(null, "Data Structures and Algorithms in Java",
            "A practical approach.", new BigDecimal("790.00"),
            "/images/dummy.png"));
        products.add(new Product(null, "Learning Spring Boot: Second Edition",
            "A practical guide to building production-ready applications.",
            new BigDecimal("820.00"), "/images/dummy.png"));
        products.add(new Product(null, "Spring Cloud in Action",
            "Build microservices with Spring Cloud.", new BigDecimal("1050.00"),
            "/images/dummy.png"));
        products.add(new Product(null, "Mastering Apache Kafka",
            "Architecting and building real-time event streaming systems.",
            new BigDecimal("1150.00"), "/images/dummy.png"));
        products.add(new Product(null,
            "Clean Code: A Handbook of Agile Software Craftsmanship",
            "A guide to writing comprehensible and manageable code.",
            new BigDecimal("700.00"), "/images/dummy.png"));
        products.add(new Product(null,
            "The Art of Computer Programming, Vol. 1: Fundamental Algorithms",
            "Donald Knuth's foundational series.", new BigDecimal("1800.00"),
            "/images/dummy.png"));
        products.add(
            new Product(null, "System Design Interview - An Insider's Guide",
                "Master common system design questions.", new BigDecimal("999.00"),
                "/images/dummy.png"));
        products.add(
            new Product(null, "Patterns of Enterprise Application Architecture",
                "Martin Fowler's classic on enterprise software design.",
                new BigDecimal("1200.00"), "/images/dummy.png"));
        products.add(new Product(null, "Site Reliability Engineering",
            "How Google Runs Production Systems.", new BigDecimal("1100.00"),
            "/images/dummy.png"));
        productRepository.saveAll(products);
        System.out.println("Seeded " + products.size() + " products.");
    }
}
```

Code explanation

This component is responsible for populating the database with initial data when the application starts.

- **@Component:** Marks this as a generic Spring-managed bean.
- **implements CommandLineRunner:** This interface has a single method, run(). Spring Boot automatically executes this run() method once after the application context has been loaded, making it the perfect place to perform initial setup tasks like seeding a database.

- The code creates a large, realistic list of Product objects, and saves them all to the database in a single operation using productRepository.saveAll().

Views and Frontend (Thymeleaf)

1. In the **Projects** window, expand your **ECommerceApp** project.
2. Navigate to **Source Packages → src/main/resources → templates**.
3. Right-click the **templates** folder and select **New → HTML File...**.
4. Enter **products** as the **File Name** and click **Finish**.
5. Open the products.html file and replace its content with the following HTML:

```
<!DOCTYPE html>
<html xmlns:th="http://www.thymeleaf.org">
    <head>
        <title>Product Catalog</title>
        <link rel="stylesheet" href="/css/style.css">
    </head>
    <body>
        <div class="container">
            <h1>Sharanam and Vaishali Ecommerce Application</h1>
            <div class="product-grid">
                <div th:each="product : ${products}" class="product-item">
                    <img th:src="${product.imageUrl}" alt="Product Image"
                            class="product-image">
                    <h2 th:text="${product.name}"></h2>
                    <p th:text="${product.description}"></p>
                    <p class="price" th:text="'₹' + ${product.price}"></p>
                    <a th:href="@{/products/{id}(id=${product.id})}" class="btn">
                        View Details</a>
                    <form th:action="@{/cart/add}" method="post">
                        <input type="hidden" name="productId"
                               th:value="${product.id}">
                        <button type="submit" class="btn add-to-cart-btn">
                               Add to Cart</button>
                    </form>
                </div>
            </div>
            <a href="/cart" class="btn view-cart-btn">View Cart</a>
        </div>
    </body>
</html>
```

Code explanation

This is the main product catalogue page.

- **xmlns:th="http://www.thymeleaf.org":** Declares the Thymeleaf namespace, enabling its special attributes.

- **th:each="product : ${products}":** This is a loop. It iterates over the list of products passed from the controller and repeats the div for each product.
- **th:text, th:src, th:href:** These attributes dynamically replace the content of HTML tags with data from the product object (e.g., name, image URL, and a link to the detail page).
- **<form th:action="@{/cart/add}" ...>:** Creates a form that submits a POST request to the /cart/add endpoint when the "Add to Cart" button is clicked, including the productId as a hidden input.

6. Repeat steps 3-5 to create **product-detail.html** with the following content:

```
<!DOCTYPE html>
<html xmlns:th="http://www.thymeleaf.org">
    <head>
        <title>Product Details</title>
        <link rel="stylesheet" href="/css/style.css">
    </head>
    <body>
        <div class="container">
            <h1 th:text="${product.name}"></h1>
            <img th:src="${product.imageUrl}" alt="Product Image"
                 class="product-detail-image">
            <p th:text="${product.description}"></p>
            <p class="price" th:text="'Price: ₹' + ${product.price}"></p>
            <form th:action="@{/cart/add}" method="post">
                <input type="hidden" name="productId" th:value="${product.id}">
                <label for="quantity">Quantity:</label>
                <input type="number" id="quantity" name="quantity" value="1"
                       min="1" class="quantity-input">
                <button type="submit" class="btn add-to-cart-btn">Add to Cart
                </button>
            </form>
            <a href="/products" class="btn back-to-products-btn">Back to
            Products</a>
        </div>
    </body>
</html>
```

Code explanation

This template displays the details for a single product. It uses th:text to show the product's name, description, and price, and includes a form to add the product to the cart with a quantity selector.

7. Repeat steps 3-5 to create **cart.html** with the following content:

```
<!DOCTYPE html>
<html xmlns:th="http://www.thymeleaf.org">
    <head>
        <title>Shopping Cart</title>
```

```
        <link rel="stylesheet" href="/css/style.css">
    </head>
    <body>
        <div class="container">
            <h1>Your Shopping Cart</h1>
            <div th:if="${cartItems.isEmpty()}" class="empty-cart-message">
                Your cart is empty. <a href="/products" class="btn">
                Continue Shopping</a>
            </div>
            <div th:unless="${cartItems.isEmpty()}">
                <table class="cart-table">
                    <thead>
                        <tr>
                            <th>Product</th>
                            <th>Price</th>
                            <th>Quantity</th>
                            <th>Subtotal</th>
                            <th>Actions</th>
                        </tr>
                    </thead>
                    <tbody>
                        <tr th:each="item : ${cartItems}">
                            <td th:text="${item.product.name}"></td>
                            <td th:text="'₹' + ${item.product.price}"></td>
                            <td>
                                <form th:action="@{/cart/update}" method="post"
                                      class="quantity-form">
                                    <input type="hidden" name="productId"
                                           th:value="${item.product.id}">
                                    <input type="number" name="quantity"
                                           th:value="${item.quantity}" min="1"
                                           class="quantity-input">
                                    <button type="submit"
                                            class="btn update-quantity-btn">
                                    Update</button>
                                </form>
                            </td>
                            <td th:text="'₹' + ${item.product.price.multiply(new
                                java.math.BigDecimal(item.quantity))}"></td>
                            <td>
                                <form th:action="@{/cart/remove}" method="post">
                                    <input type="hidden" name="productId"
                                           th:value="${item.product.id}">
                                    <button type="submit" class="btn remove-item-
                                            btn">Remove</button>
                                </form>
                            </td>
                        </tr>
                    </tbody>
                </table>
                <h2 class="cart-total">Total: <span th:text="'₹' + ${cartTotal}">
```

```
                </span></h2>
                <a href="/checkout" class="btn checkout-btn">Proceed to
                Checkout</a>
            </div>
            <div class="recommendations">
                <h3>Similar Products (AI Recommendations)</h3>
                <div class="product-grid">
                    <div th:each="product : ${recommendedProducts}"
                         class="product-item">
                        <img th:src="${product.imageUrl}" alt="Product Image"
                             class="product-image">
                        <h2 th:text="${product.name}"></h2>
                        <p class="price" th:text="'₹' + ${product.price}"></p>
                        <form th:action="@{/cart/add}" method="post">
                            <input type="hidden" name="productId"
                                   th:value="${product.id}">
                            <button type="submit" class="btn add-to-cart-btn">
                            Add to Cart</button>
                        </form>
                    </div>
                </div>
            </div>
            <a href="/products" class="btn back-to-products-btn">Continue
            Shopping</a>
        </div>
    </body>
</html>
```

Code explanation

This template displays the contents of the shopping cart.

- **th:if="${cartItems.isEmpty()}":** This block is displayed only if the cart is empty.
- **th:unless="${cartItems.isEmpty()}":** This block is displayed only if the cart has items. It contains a table that iterates over cartItems.
- The forms for updating quantity and removing items submit POST requests to the /cart/update and /cart/remove endpoints.
- The "Similar Products" section at the bottom iterates over recommendedProducts (from the AI service) and displays them.

8. Repeat steps 3-5 to create **checkout.html** with the following content:

```
<!DOCTYPE html>
<html xmlns:th="http://www.thymeleaf.org">
    <head>
        <title>Checkout</title>
        <link rel="stylesheet" href="/css/style.css">
    </head>
    <body>
        <div class="container">
```

```
            <h1>Checkout</h1>
            <div th:if="${errorMessage}" class="error-message"
                 th:text="${errorMessage}"></div>
            <form th:action="@{/checkout/placeOrder}" th:object="${order}"
                  method="post" class="checkout-form">
                <div class="form-group">
                    <label for="customerName">Your Name:</label>
                    <input type="text" id="customerName"
                           th:field="*{customerName}" required class="form-control">
                    <span th:if="${#fields.hasErrors('customerName')}"
                          th:errors="*{customerName}" class="error-text"></span>
                </div>
                <div class="form-group">
                    <label for="shippingAddress">Shipping Address:</label>
                    <textarea id="shippingAddress" th:field="*{shippingAddress}"
                              rows="4" required class="form-control"></textarea>
                    <span th:if="${#fields.hasErrors('shippingAddress')}"
                          th:errors="*{shippingAddress}" class="error-text">
                    </span>
                </div>
                <button type="submit" class="btn place-order-btn">Place
                Order</button>
            </form>
            <a href="/cart" class="btn back-to-cart-btn">Back to Cart</a>
        </div>
    </body>
</html>
```

Code explanation

This page contains the final checkout form for the user to enter their details.

- **th:object="${order}":** This binds the form to the order object passed from the controller.
- **th:field="*{customerName}":** This is a two-way data binding attribute. It sets the name and value of the input field to match the customerName property of the order object. When the form is submitted, the entered value is set back onto the object.
- **th:if="${#fields.hasErrors('customerName')}":** This checks if there are validation errors for a specific field and displays the error message if so.

9. Repeat steps 3-5 to create **order-confirmation.html** with the following content:

```
<!DOCTYPE html>
<html xmlns:th="http://www.thymeleaf.org">
    <head>
        <title>Order Confirmation</title>
        <link rel="stylesheet" href="/css/style.css">
    </head>
    <body>
        <div class="container">
            <h1>Order Placed Successfully!</h1>
```

```
            <p>Thank you for your order, <span th:text="${order.customerName}">
            </span>!</p>
            <p>Your Order Number is: <strong>
            <span th:text="${order.id}"></span></strong></p>
            <p>Shipping Address: <span th:text="${order.shippingAddress}">
            </span></p>
            <h3>Order Details:</h3>
            <table class="cart-table">
                <thead>
                    <tr>
                        <th>Product</th>
                        <th>Quantity</th>
                        <th>Price</th>
                    </tr>
                </thead>
                <tbody>
                    <tr th:each="item : ${order.items}">
                        <td th:text="${item.product.name}"></td>
                        <td th:text="${item.quantity}"></td>
                        <td th:text="'₹' + ${item.product.price.multiply(new
                            java.math.BigDecimal(item.quantity))}"></td>
                    </tr>
                </tbody>
            </table>
            <a href="/products" class="btn">Continue Shopping</a>
        </div>
    </body>
</html>
```

Code explanation

This is the final page shown to the user after a successful order. It simply displays the details of the order object that was placed, including the order number, shipping details, and a summary of the items purchased.

Create the Styling (CSS)

1. Right-click **src/main/resources → static** and select **New → Folder**.
2. Enter **css** as the **Folder Name** and click **Finish**.
3. Right-click **css** and select **New → Empty File...**.
4. Enter **style.css** as the **File Name** and click **Finish**.
5. Open the style.css file and add the following basic CSS to beautify the application:

```
body {
    font-family: Arial, sans-serif;
    margin: 0;
    padding: 20px;
    background-color: #f4f4f4;
```

```
    color: #333;
}
.container {
    max-width: 1200px;
    margin: 0 auto;
    background-color: #fff;
    padding: 20px;
    border-radius: 8px;
    box-shadow: 0 0 10px rgba(0, 0, 0, 0.1);
}
h1, h2, h3 {
    color: #0056b3;
    text-align: center;
    margin-bottom: 20px;
}
.product-grid {
    display: grid;
    grid-template-columns: repeat(auto-fill, minmax(250px, 1fr));
    gap: 20px;
    margin-top: 20px;
}
.product-item {
    background-color: #f9f9f9;
    border: 1px solid #ddd;
    border-radius: 8px;
    padding: 15px;
    text-align: center;
    box-shadow: 0 2px 5px rgba(0, 0, 0, 0.05);
    display: flex;
    flex-direction: column;
    justify-content: space-between;
}
.product-image {
    max-width: 100%;
    height: 150px;
    object-fit: contain;
    margin-bottom: 10px;
}
.product-item h2 {
    font-size: 1.2em;
    margin-top: 10px;
    margin-bottom: 5px;
    color: #333;
}
.product-item p {
    font-size: 0.9em;
    color: #666;
    flex-grow: 1;
}
.price {
    font-weight: bold;
```

```
    color: #e67e22;
    font-size: 1.1em;
    margin-top: 10px;
    margin-bottom: 15px;
}
.btn {
    display: inline-block;
    background-color: #007bff;
    color: white;
    padding: 10px 15px;
    border-radius: 5px;
    text-decoration: none;
    transition: background-color 0.3s ease;
    border: none;
    cursor: pointer;
    font-size: 1em;
    margin-top: 10px;
}
.btn:hover {
    background-color: #0056b3;
}
.add-to-cart-btn {
    background-color: #28a745;
    margin-top: 15px;
}
.add-to-cart-btn:hover {
    background-color: #218838;
}
.view-cart-btn, .checkout-btn {
    display: block;
    width: fit-content;
    margin: 20px auto;
    background-color: #6c757d;
}
.view-cart-btn:hover, .checkout-btn:hover {
    background-color: #5a6268;
}
.product-detail-image {
    max-width: 400px;
    display: block;
    margin: 20px auto;
    border: 1px solid #ddd;
    border-radius: 8px;
}
.quantity-input {
    width: 60px;
    padding: 5px;
    border: 1px solid #ccc;
    border-radius: 4px;
    text-align: center;
    margin-right: 5px;
```

```
}
.cart-table {
    width: 100%;
    border-collapse: collapse;
    margin-top: 20px;
}
.cart-table th, .cart-table td {
    border: 1px solid #ddd;
    padding: 12px;
    text-align: left;
}
.cart-table th {
    background-color: #f2f2f2;
    font-weight: bold;
}
.cart-total {
    text-align: right;
    font-size: 1.5em;
    margin-top: 20px;
    color: #0056b3;
}
.remove-item-btn, .update-quantity-btn {
    background-color: #dc3545;
    padding: 5px 10px;
    font-size: 0.9em;
}
.remove-item-btn:hover, .update-quantity-btn:hover {
    background-color: #c82333;
}
.empty-cart-message {
    text-align: center;
    padding: 30px;
    border: 1px dashed #ccc;
    border-radius: 8px;
    margin-top: 30px;
    font-size: 1.1em;
    color: #555;
}
.recommendations {
    margin-top: 40px;
    padding-top: 20px;
    border-top: 1px solid #eee;
}
.recommendations h3 {
    text-align: center;
    color: #007bff;
}
.checkout-form {
    max-width: 600px;
    margin: 20px auto;
    padding: 20px;
```

```
    border: 1px solid #eee;
    border-radius: 8px;
    background-color: #f9f9f9;
}
.form-group {
    margin-bottom: 15px;
}
.form-group label {
    display: block;
    margin-bottom: 5px;
    font-weight: bold;
}
.form-control {
    width: calc(100% - 22px); /* Account for padding and border */
    padding: 10px;
    border: 1px solid #ccc;
    border-radius: 4px;
    font-size: 1em;
}
textarea.form-control {
    resize: vertical;
}
.error-message {
    color: #dc3545;
    background-color: #f8d7da;
    border: 1px solid #f5c6cb;
    padding: 10px;
    margin-bottom: 20px;
    border-radius: 5px;
    text-align: center;
}
.error-text {
    color: #dc3545;
    font-size: 0.9em;
    margin-top: 5px;
    display: block;
}
.place-order-btn {
    display: block;
    width: 100%;
    margin-top: 20px;
}
.back-to-products-btn, .back-to-cart-btn {
    display: block;
    width: fit-content;
    margin: 20px auto;
    background-color: #6c757d;
}
.back-to-products-btn:hover, .back-to-cart-btn:hover {
    background-color: #5a6268;
}
```

Code explanation

This CSS file provides all the visual styling for the application. It uses classes to define the layout (like the product grid), colours, fonts, and spacing for all the HTML elements, making the website visually appealing and user-friendly.

Add Book image

Create an **images** folder inside **src/main/resources/static** for the dummy image placeholder.

1. Right-click **src/main/resources/static** and select **New → Folder**.
2. Enter **images** as the **Folder Name** and click **Finish**.
3. Place a generic image file named **dummy.png** inside this **images** folder. You can use any placeholder image you prefer for this purpose.

Running and testing

Run the application

1. In NetBeans, right-click the project (e.g., **ECommerceApp**) and select **Run**.
2. This starts the Spring Boot application, and you see log messages indicating that the embedded Tomcat server has started on port **8080**.

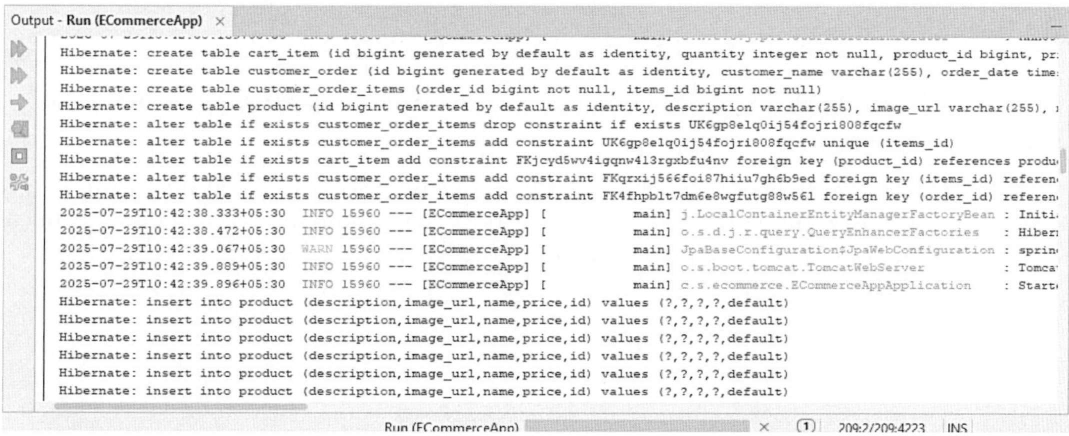

Navigate the website

1. Open your web browser and navigate to **http://localhost:8080/products** to see the product catalogue.

2. You are directed to the list of products, as seeded by the **DataLoader** file.

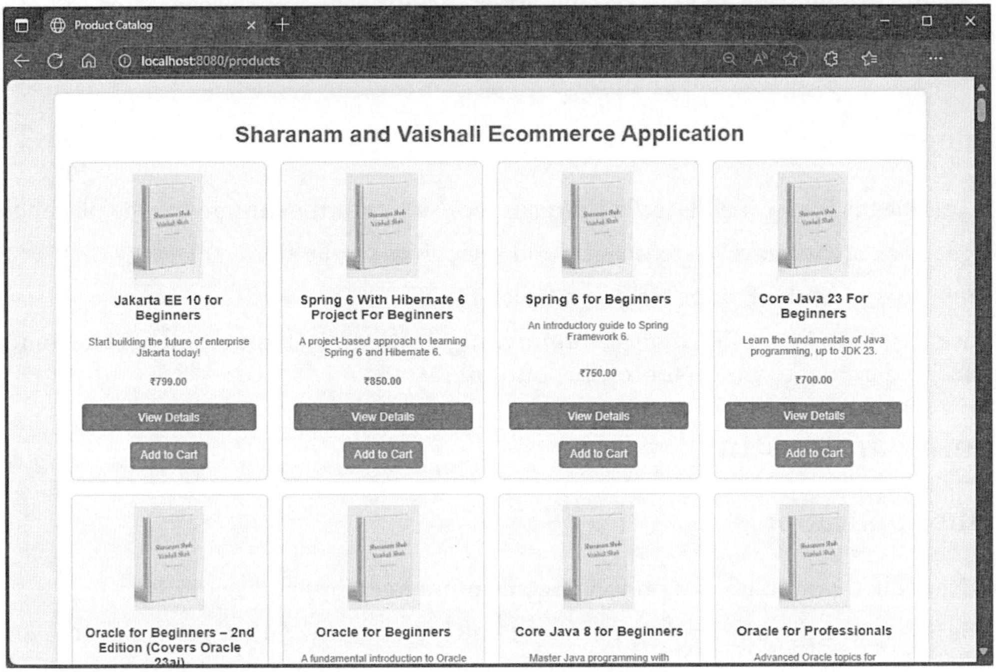

Add items to your cart

1. Click on the **Add to Cart** button for various products on the product catalogue page.
2. This takes you to the cart page.
3. Observe the **Similar Products (AI Recommendations)** section at the bottom of the cart page. As you add different items to your cart, the recommendations should dynamically change based on the logic implemented in the **AIRecommendationService** file.

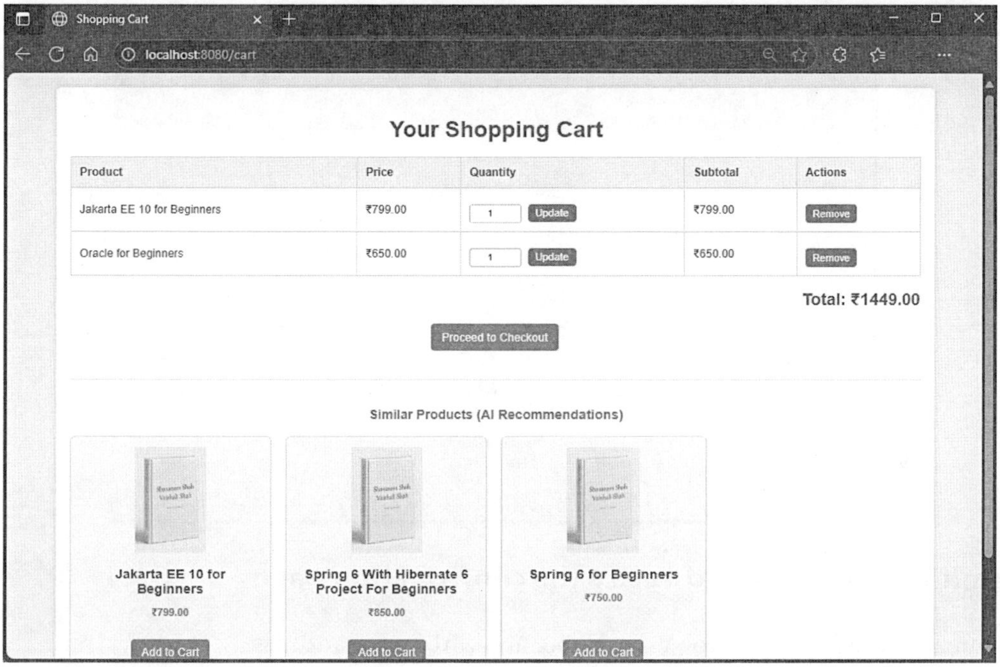

Proceed to checkout

1. From the cart page, click **Proceed to Checkout**. The Checkout page appears.

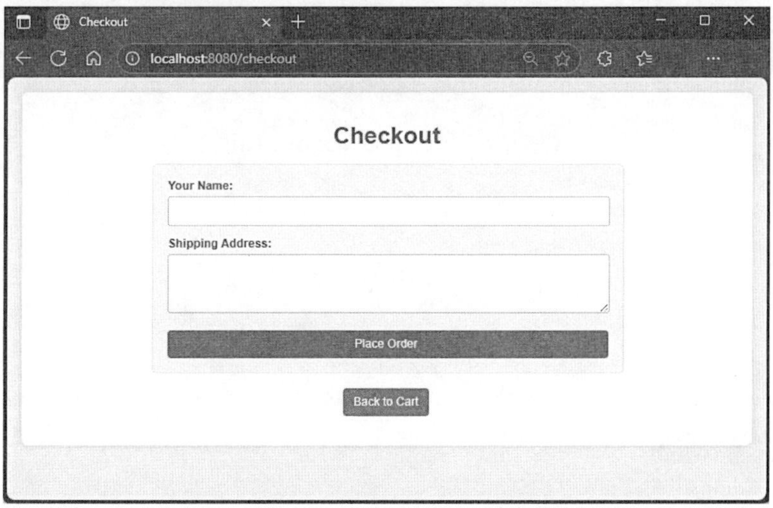

2. On the checkout page, try submitting the form with empty **Your Name** or **Shipping Address** fields.

3. Observe the validation error messages appearing below the respective input fields.

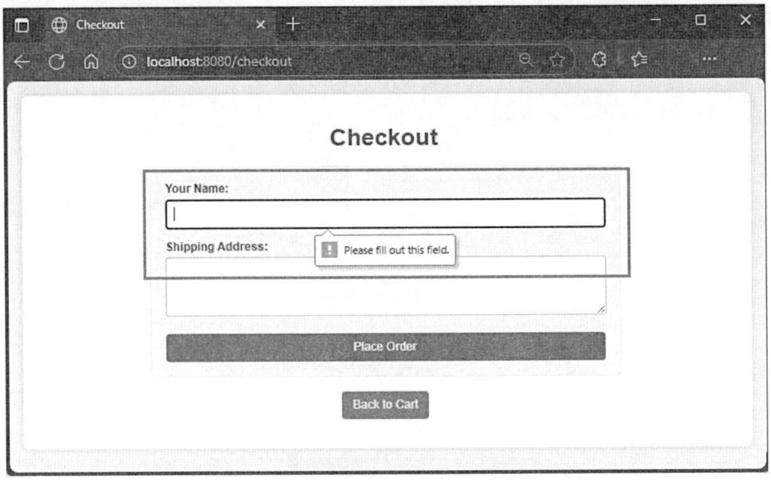

Submit a valid order and verify the confirmation page

1. Enter valid information for **Your Name** and **Shipping Address**.
2. Click **Place Order**.
3. You are directed to the **Order Confirmation** page, displaying your name, your order number, shipping address, and the details of the items in your order.

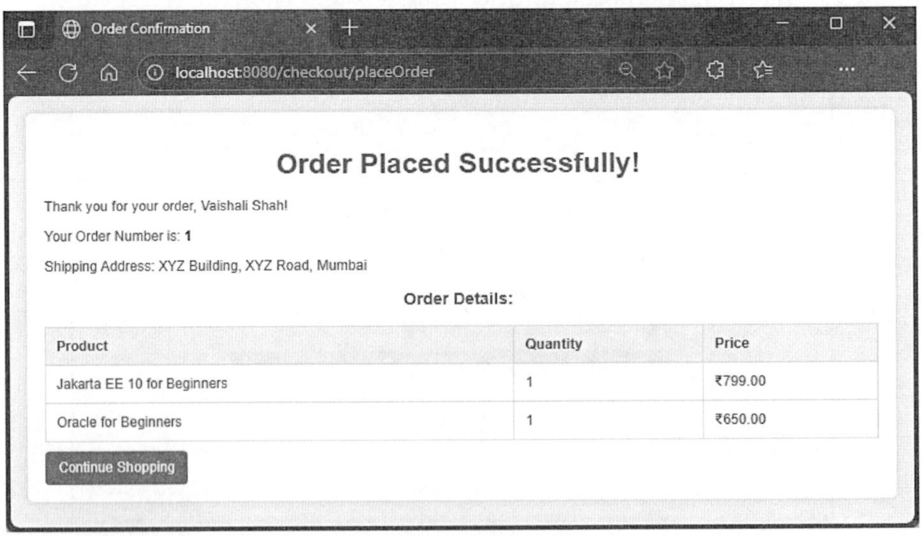

Use REST Client to test the REST API endpoints

1. In NetBeans, select **Tools → REST Client**. **REST Client** tab appears.
2. In the REST Client tab, in the drop-down list select **GET** and the type **http://localhost:8080/api/v1/products** in the adjoining textbox. Click **Send**.
3. You receive a JSON array containing all product details.

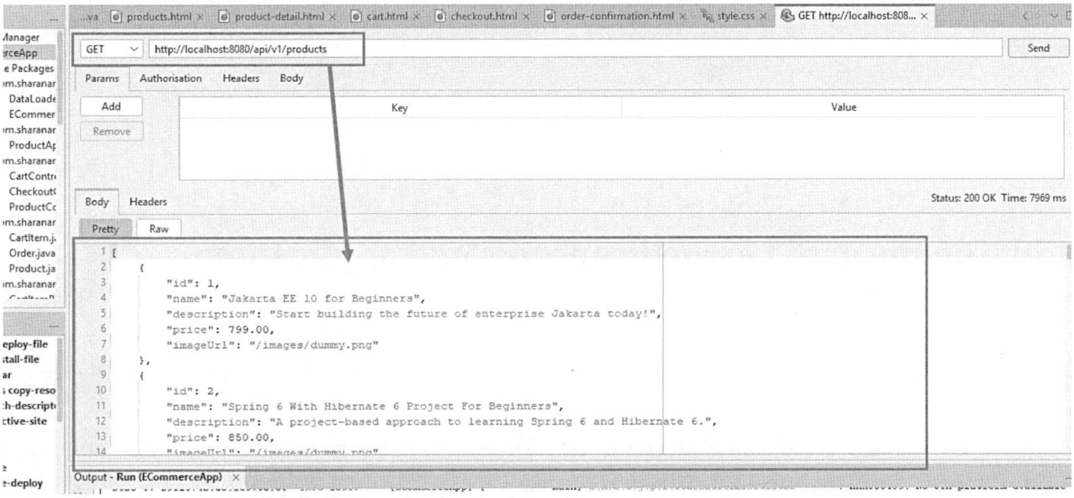

4. Again, in the REST Client tab, in the drop-down list select **GET** and the type **http://localhost:8080/api/v1/products/1** (or replace 1 with any valid product ID) in the adjoining textbox. Click **Send**.
5. You receive a JSON object containing the details of the product with the specified ID.

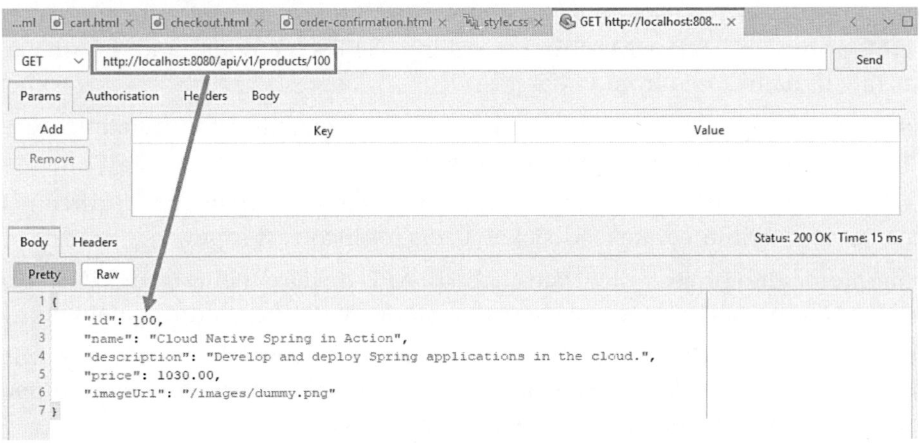

6. If the ID does not exist, no JSON object is shown.

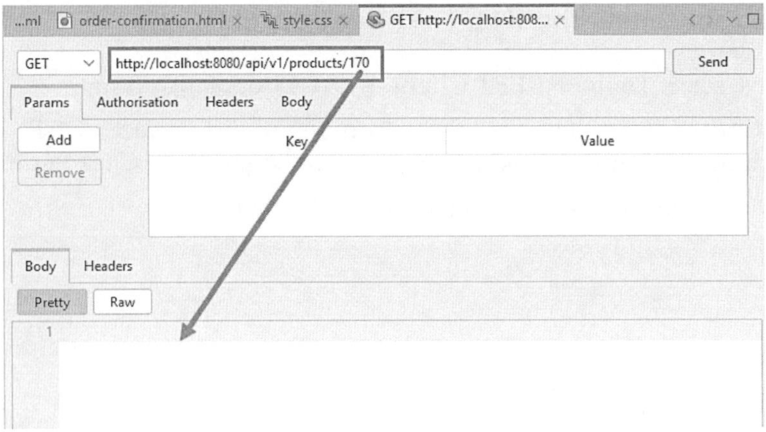

Bridging the gap: Learned concepts and application implementation

This comprehensive project seamlessly integrates many key concepts you have learned throughout this book.

- It demonstrates a complete **Dependency Injection** pattern, where services, repositories, and controllers are automatically wired together by Spring, reducing boilerplate code and enhancing modularity.
- The application showcases a full **JPA/Hibernate** implementation, from defining persistent entities with annotations like **@Entity** and **@GeneratedValue** to leveraging Spring Data JPA's **JpaRepository** for out-of-the-box CRUD operations.
- **Spring MVC** is extensively utilized with **@Controller** annotations managing web requests, **@GetMapping** and **@PostMapping** handling HTTP methods, and **@PathVariable** for extracting dynamic data from URLs.
- **Thymeleaf** is employed for server-side rendering, enabling the dynamic generation of HTML views based on data from the backend.
- **Jakarta Bean Validation** with **@Valid** annotations ensures data quality directly from web forms, providing immediate feedback to users for incorrect input.
- Furthermore, the project illustrates **REST API** development using **@RestController**, providing endpoints for external clients to interact with the product catalogue.
- The integration of **AI** via the Gemini API demonstrates how intelligent, value-added features can be embedded into a standard e-commerce application, offering personalized recommendations and enhancing the user experience.

Exploring application behaviour: A practical run-through

When you run the **ECommerceApp** project:

1. Spring Boot automatically configures and launches an embedded web server (Tomcat by default) on port **8080**.
2. The **DataLoader** component, being a **CommandLineRunner**, executes its **run()** method immediately after the application context is initialized, populating the H2 in-memory database with the initial product data.
3. When you access http://localhost:8080/products, the **ProductController**'s **listProducts()** method is invoked. This method uses **ProductService** to fetch all products from **ProductRepository** (which in turn interacts with Hibernate and the H2 database).
4. The product data is then added to the Thymeleaf model, and the **products.html** template is rendered, dynamically displaying each product.
5. Adding items to the cart or updating quantities triggers **POST** requests to **CartController**.
6. **CartService** manages the cart state (in session memory for this example) and performs calculations.
7. When the cart page is loaded, **CartController** invokes **AIRecommendationService**. This service constructs a prompt based on your cart items and sends it to the Gemini API using an HTTP client.
8. The API's response is then parsed to identify recommended products from your database, which are then displayed on the cart page.
9. The checkout process involves **CheckoutController**, which handles the submission of customer and shipping details.
10. The **@Valid** annotation triggers Bean Validation, ensuring the entered data conforms to the rules defined in the **Order** entity.
11. If validation passes, the **OrderService**'s **placeOrder()** method, annotated with **@Transactional**, ensures that the order creation and cart clearing operations are treated as a single, atomic database transaction.
12. Finally, the REST API endpoints in **ProductApiController** demonstrate how Spring's **@RestController** efficiently exposes data as JSON, useful for single-page applications or mobile clients.

Harnessing basic Java development in real-world contexts

This e-commerce application represents a significant milestone in your development journey, showcasing your ability to build a robust, full-stack web application with intelligent features. This project highlights that modern Java development with Spring Boot extends far beyond simple "Hello World" examples.

- In real-world contexts, such applications serve as the backbone of online retail, subscription services, digital marketplaces, and much more.
- The ability to manage product catalogues, handle user interactions (like shopping carts), process orders, and integrate with external services (like AI for recommendations or payment gateways) is fundamental.
- Your understanding of Spring Data JPA and Data Persistence empowers you to build applications that reliably store and retrieve critical business data.
- Spring MVC and Thymeleaf provide the means to create engaging and intuitive user interfaces.
- Furthermore, the inclusion of a REST API demonstrates your capacity to design and build interoperable systems, crucial for modern microservices architectures or for supporting diverse client applications (web, mobile, desktop).
- The AI integration component underscores the growing importance of embedding intelligence directly into applications to provide personalized experiences and drive business value.

This comprehensive project is a powerful testament to your full-stack development capabilities and your readiness to tackle professional Spring development roles.

Wrapping up

- **Integrated frameworks:** Combined Spring Boot, Data JPA, Hibernate, and Thymeleaf.
- **Built core features:** Implemented product discovery, shopping cart, and order processing.
- **Developed REST APIs:** Created endpoints for product data access.
- **Applied validation:** Used Jakarta Bean Validation for form data integrity.
- **Enhanced with AI:** Integrated Gemini AI for product recommendations.
- **Seeded realistic data:** Included over 100 sample products, including author's books.

Congratulations on successfully completing your final project, the AI-enhanced e-commerce website! You have not only built a complex application from the ground up but also integrated advanced features like AI recommendations, demonstrating a comprehensive understanding of modern Java web development. This project serves as a strong foundation for your portfolio, showcasing your ability to tackle real-world challenges and build scalable, intelligent applications.

Appendix

A

Section 06: Appendix

Taking your Spring Boot & Data Persistence journey further

You have completed a rich, hands-on journey through Spring Boot & Data Persistence, building real-world Java applications with modern techniques and tools. This appendix gives you not just ideas, but **practical, detailed mini-projects and challenges**—like "homework"—based directly on your book's chapters. These will strengthen your skills, expose you to new areas (including AI features), and prepare you for the real world.

Detailed project challenges & next steps

Enhance your to-do list or Shopping Cart app

1. **Add user registration & login**
    a. Use **Spring Security** to set up user registration and login screens.
    b. Implement a user database table (with unique username/email and encrypted password).
    c. Store each to-do list or cart so only the logged-in user can access their own data.
    d. Extend the UI to welcome users by name after login.

   e. Allow password reset by sending an email—use a library like **Spring Boot Starter Mail** for email sending.

2. **Implement task/item completion and filtering**
   a. Add a ***completed*** status to each item.
   b. Display completed vs. pending items with a filter button: use a GET endpoint (e.g., **/items?completed=true**) that returns only completed tasks.
   c. Visually mark completed items in the list (e.g., strikethrough text).

3. **Export and import lists**
   a. Add a feature to ***download*** the entire list in CSV, JSON, and Excel formats.
   b. Allow users to ***upload*** a file to import tasks, using multipart upload endpoints.

REST API extensions

1. **Mobile and web front-ends**
   a. Build a simple mobile app (with Android or React Native) OR a web app (with React, Angular, or plain JavaScript) that connects to your REST API.
   b. Implement features like viewing items and adding/deleting tasks from the mobile or web interface.
   c. Document your REST endpoints with **Swagger/OpenAPI**, and show the docs to others.

2. **Security upgrade: rate limiting and input sanitization**
   a. Limit how quickly users can hit endpoints (for example, **no more than 10 requests per minute**).
   b. Use libraries like Bucket4J or implement simple in-memory counters for rate limiting.

3. **Personalized endpoints**
   a. Add endpoints that greet the user based on time of day or suggest the next task based on task creation.
   b. Use query parameters and path variables dynamically in your URL design.

Data and Validation projects

1. **Complex relationships**
   a. Design "students in classes" or users with multiple roles using @ManyToMany annotation.
   b. Write and test endpoints to enroll/unenroll students or assign roles.

2. **Data validation expansion**
    a. Apply advanced Bean Validation annotations, such as ensuring phone numbers have valid formats or creating custom validators for password confirmation fields.
    b. Write integration tests to verify your validations work correctly.
3. **Switch databases**
    a. Clone your project and change database configuration to PostgreSQL or another database.

Add AI features – Start simple!

1. **Smart suggestions (product or task)**
    a. Create a REST endpoint that takes user history as input.
    b. Call an external AI API such as OpenAI or Hugging Face (free tiers available) to generate personalized suggestions.
    c. Return these suggestions to display in your application UI.
2. **Sentiment analysis**
    a. Allow users to submit comments or reviews.
    b. Use an external sentiment analysis API to classify comments as positive or negative.
    c. Display sentiment results alongside the comments in your UI.
3. **In-app AI chatbot**
    a. Add an endpoint like **/ask-ai** to accept user questions.
    b. Forward these to a chatbot API and return the AI-generated answers.
    c. Show chatbot responses in your web or mobile frontend.
4. **Visual AI ideas**
    a. Implement image upload functionality.
    b. Call public AI image classification APIs to label or categorize images.
    c. Display classification results to users for enhanced interaction.

Build and showcase a project portfolio

1. **Personal website with project gallery**
    a. Use Spring Boot with Thymeleaf or a modern front-end framework (React, Vue) for your portfolio.
    b. List your projects with screenshots, technologies used, and brief descriptions.

   c. Add a "What I learned" section for each project.

2. **Blogging section**
   a. Integrate a simple blog where you share your learning experiences or challenges.
   b. Implement comment functionality with validation and moderation.

3. **Share and get feedback**
   a. Deploy your portfolio on GitHub Pages, Heroku, or other free hosting platforms.
   b. Share your projects with peers or developers in forums for feedback and code review.

How to work through these detailed homework ideas

- **Schedule:** Choose one mini-project or challenge per week or month depending on your learning pace.
- **Document:** For each project, write a README file that explains setup steps, how to run it, and key features.
- **Version control**: Use Git and GitHub to track your changes and manage your codebase.
- **Debug & reflect**: Note what issues you face and how you overcome them; this reflection deepens learning.
- **Collaborate**: Pair up with friends or participate in coding communities to share knowledge and solve problems together.

Conclusion: Turn knowledge into real-world confidence

With these practical, structured project ideas, this book becomes your launchpad. Instead of just learning concepts, you are encouraged to **build real things** that showcase your growing skills in Spring Boot, JPA and Hibernate, and even AI-powered applications.

Every project completed boosts your confidence and portfolio. Keep building, exploring, and experimenting. Your journey from beginner to skilled Java developer continues with every line of code you write.

Your next big application is only one challenge away. Enjoy the adventure!

Index

U

V

W

X

For Books on following Subjects

- Business, Management & Finance
- Career Development, Career Guides
- Catering & Hotel Management / Recipes
- Civil Engineering
- Computers
- Communication
- Dental / Health / Medical
- Economics
- Electrical Engineering
- Electronics & Communication
- English
- Entrepreneurship
- Environmental Engineering
- Event Management
- Fiction
- Forensic Science
- General Titles
- HRD
- International Trade
- Law
- Learning Disability
- Mathematics
- Mechanical Engineering
- Media
- Mobile Computing
- Motivation & Self Help
- Parenting
- Patent
- Physics
- Project Management / Software Engineering
- Real Estate
- Statistics

Publishers We Represent

O'REILLY®
THE X TEAM
BEP BUSINESS EXPERT PRESS Leader in applied, concise business books
FRANKLIN, BEEDLE
The MIT Press
IT REVOLUTION
PyQML
The Pragmatic Engineer
Sandiver Publishing
Make: Community
ROBERTO VITILLO
ByteByteGo
Matt Harrison
Jaewoong
TOWARDS AI
STATQUEST! TRIPLE BAM!!
James Turnbull
Nathan Hunter
sitepoint
JORGE BRASIL
Nigel Poulton
RMC LEARNING™ SOLUTIONS
Rheinwerk Computing
Kt. Academy
Pragmatic Bookshelf